ANTE-NICENE CHRISTIANITY

CHRISTIANITY

THE FIRST THREE CENTURIES

ANTE-NICENE CHRISTIANITY

THE FIRST THREE CENTURIES

J ORR — Professor of Apologetics and Systematic Theology, United Free Church College, Glasgow

THE EARLY CHURCH: ITS HISTORY AND LITERATURE

F J A HORT — Hulsean Professor and Lady Margaret's Reader in Divinity in the University of Cambridge

THE SIX LECTURES ON THE ANTE-NICENE FATHERS

G H BOX — Lecturer in Rabbinical Hebrew, King's College, London; Canon of St. Albans, Hertfordshire

THE JEWISH ENVIRONMENT OF EARLY CHRISTIANITY

WITH AN APPENDIX CONTAINING A TRANSLATION OF
"THE TEACHING OF THE TWELVE APOSTLES"

Edited by

BRENT WALTERS — Curator, The Ante-Nicene Archive
Dean, College of Early Christian Studies

Copyright © 1993 Brent S. Walters

The Ante-Nicene Archive
Post Office Box 26248
San Josè, California 95159

The Ante-Nicene Archive has published this work in cooperation with Bibliographics, Inc.

First Revised Edition

Printed in the United States of America

Walters, Brent S. (editor)
Ante-Nicene Christianity (The First Three Centuries)

Library of Congress Catalog Card Number   93-073023
International Standard Book Number (ISBN)   0-9628369-1-5

DEDICATION

The two of you are only anonymous on earth, and although you requested your names to be withheld, we are certain that they are numbered with those in the heavenly "scroll of life."

ACKNOWLEDGEMENTS

The Ante-Nicene Archive is a research library which specializes in the history, literature, culture, and religion of the first three centuries of the common era. The term "ante-Nicene" refers to that period of Christian history prior to the great councils of the church, specifically the Council of Nicea in 325. Currently, the Archive maintains one of the largest collections of books, periodicals, essays, papers, and facsimiles about these centuries in the United States, and is invaluable to anyone who wishes to investigate Roman, Jewish, or Christian history and literature.

The editor would like to express his gratitude to all those who have contributed to the advancement of the Archive and would like to encourage scholars and students to submit essays for its holdings and publication. The library may be contacted by mail:

The Ante-Nicene Archive
Post Office Box 26248
San Josè, California 95159

My deepest gratitude is extended to Sheila M. Shrum and to Andrew Beaulac—both of whom proofed the text of this book. The three works included in this volume have been altered in format. The character of these slight revisions takes the form of extended footnotes from the main text and of the addition of headings in certain places. The words of the text have not been modified—except where there was a need for the modernizing of a few words in order to make the text more readable. No attempt has been made by the editor to supplement the original works with subsequent discoveries or recent scholarship in the same fields of research. These have been selected for reprint because of their uncompromising contents and for their unsurpassed insights. This book has been published in cooperation with Bibliographics, Inc. While all the holdings of the library are privately sought, purchased, processed, and maintained, their use has been granted to qualified scholars, faculty and students.

INTRODUCTION

The most valuable understanding we can grasp as twentieth century believers is of our origins. In an age such as ours—in which interpretation has replaced apostolic intent for some and the simple message of "the Way" has been substituted for later advances in Christendom—reviewing the faith of our founders should be a strict matter of policy, not a fleeting pastime. Most Christians in our country are content and well assimilated into society, yet this "security" is precisely what the patristic writers disapproved of most vehemently. If we are not distinguished from the world, then we must be the products of its influence. Believers are often reduced to nuts, bolts, and replaceable parts in the institutional machinery of religion, a nefarious invention of the human spirit, a product with differing hues. Many of the differences between Catholics, Orthodox, and Protestants, as well as their varying denominations, are depreciated when the Ante-Nicene church is understood properly. No contemporary church can lay claim to the diversity of these three centuries, nor boast of the unity that bonded its members. Investigation of this period is essential for twentieth century integrity.

There are three areas of research concerning this period: its history, its literature, and its environment. Each of these topics are included in this volume. Its history is discussed by J. Orr, professor of apologetics and theology in Glasgow; its literature is brilliantly introduced by F. J. A. Hort, Hulsean professor in divinity at the University of Cambridge; the Jewish influences upon the early church are presented by G. H. Box, lecturer in Rabbinical Hebrew at King's College, London. Most histories of the church cover the breath of the subject in great detail and should be consulted for advanced study; Orr's work is the finest brief introduction on the Ante-Nicene period. Hort is one of the finest scholars from England. His monumental contributions to patristic and biblical research have never been superseded. His lectures in this volume acquaint readers with the eleven most prominent writers from the first three centuries of the church. Box provides an insightful essay on the influences of Rabbinic thought on early Christianity. These are superb contributions and excellent additions to any home library.

The most commonly asked questions of the Archive are about Ante-Nicene Christianity. It seems as though there is a revival of interest in church origins. Hundreds of inquiries are received each month, and the only way we know to answer each of them is to publish a series of books about the early church. The first in this series is an introduction to the history and literature of this era. We hope that it will provide the first of several steps toward a library of proven works in this field. As the library develops so will an understanding of our Jewish roots, historic past, and Christian origins. Each contribution in this series will be taken from the holdings of the Ante-Nicene Archive. As a knowledge of our past is rediscovered, beliefs and practices of the church will inevitably be redefined. This process will bring with it the enticement of further separation between those who yearn for apostolic intention and those who wish to assimilate the church beyond those intentions. Be careful to read this book with a mind that leans toward application, and not with a soul that leads to deconstruction and division.

One further warning must be given: The first three centuries of the church are represented by men who, while maintaining the central teachings of the faith, often differed with regard to interpretation of the more "secondary" issues. If you desire to find a consensus of thought or a unified dogma from this early period, then you will be profoundly disappointed. The early fathers did not always agree, nor did they maintain identical interpretations, yet out of their differences harmony was well established and unity was carefully fostered. Here is a helpful reminder: While our early founders may not have known the later developments of the faith, they did know how to discern between heresy and apostolic tradition. Much of what is being taught in churches today is the by-product of post-Reformation thought, most of which was codified fifteen centuries after the apostles passed from memory. The influence of the reformers is at times more prominent than that of the apostles; so do not be surprised if a few modern doctrines are absent in the thoughts of that time. A study of this era reveals a gradual development in thought from Jesus to the apostles and from the apostles to their disciples; then arrive the noble defenders of the faith, followed by the interpreters of scripture and tradition, and the founders of institutional Christendom.

CONTENTS

FJA HORT, SIX LECTURES ON THE ANTE-NICENE FATHERS

GH BOX, THE JEWISH ENVIRONMENT OF EARLY CHRISTIANITY

THE EARLY CHURCH
ITS HISTORY AND LITERATURE

WRITTEN BY

JAMES ORR

Professor of Apologetics and Systematic Theology
United Free Church College, Glasgow

EDITED BY

BRENT WALTERS

Curator, Ante-Nicene Archive
Dean, College of Early Christian Studies

London: Hodder and Stoughton
1901

San Jose: The Ante-Nicene Archive
Bibliographics Incorporated
1993

CONTENTS

THE JEWISH AND GENTILE PREPARATIONS

THE OLD TESTAMENT PREPARATION

The history of the church may be said in strictness to begin with the Day of Pentecost. The Day of Pentecost, however—the conception of the church altogether—had its antecedents. The New Jerusalem did not come down from heaven quite as it is pictured in the Apocalypse, without manifold links of connection with the past. Paul has this in view when he says that it was in "the fullness of time" that God sent forth his Son.[1] Manifestly, the Christian church has a peculiar and genetic relation to the Old Testament. For the Old Testament community was also in its way a theocracy—a church.[2] The word "ecclesia," used in the New Testament to designate the Christian society, is that chiefly used in the Septuagint as the equivalent of the Hebrew word "qahal," assembly or congregation.[3]

Though bound up with national forms, that theocracy ever cherished in its bosom the consciousness of a universalistic destiny. Older than the national form in its existence was the patriarchal—the covenants with the fathers—and here already we have the clear enunciation of the idea that Israel was a people called with a view to the ultimate blessing of the race.[4] That idea reaches its fullest expression in the glowing predictions of the prophets and the Psalms.[5] With the prophets, too, we see the rise of a new era—the thought of a church within a church, a true and spiritual Israel within the natural Israel—which is the birth of the church idea proper.[6] A further important step in the natural formation of the church consciousness was taken in the Babylonian exile, when the people, driven from their land, and deprived of holy city, temple and sacrifices, became a church in the full meaning of the word. Their return to Palestine did not annul this feature of their religious life. On the contrary,

---

[1] Galatians 4:4.

[2] Compare Acts 7:38; Hebrews 2:12.

[3] On terms, compare Hort's Christian Ecclesia, Lecture One.

[4] Genesis 12:3, 18:18, and so on.

[5] For example, Isaiah 60; Psalms 87.

[6] Compare Isaiah 8:16-18.

their return was marked by a new development of religious institutions—priestly government, the formation of a canon of scripture, the rise of scribism, the reading and teaching of the law—all which prepared the way for the liberation of the church idea from its national and political form.

THE POST-EXILIAN PREPARATION

Of special importance in this connection are the four following series of facts:

(1) *The rise and spread of synagogue worship.*

The synagogue may go back to the days of Ezra; in any case it was a prominent institution after the return, both in Judea and in the lands of the dispersion.[1] We note about it, in contrast with the temple, its local character, giving it practical universality; its simple and spiritual worship—reading of law and prophets, reciting of prayers, singing or rather chanting of psalms, a discourse or exhortation, in which the passage read was expounded and applied, a concluding blessing; and the absence of all priestly or sacerdotal offices. The officials were the "elders" (probably identical in towns with the civic elders), the "archisynagogos" or "ruler" (one or more), who had the charge of the public worship, the "minister" or servant.[2] There was considerable freedom in the service. The scriptures were read, the prayers recited, the exhortations given, not by officials, but by persons selected from the congregation.[3] The resemblance to a simple Christian service is obvious.

(2) *The rise of the Jewish sects.*

The greater part of the period after the exile is an absolute blank in our knowledge. The one thing certain is that from the time of Ezra the nation set before it as its ideal the strict observance of the law of Moses. Hence the rise of an order of men whose special business it was to guard, develop and expound the law—the order of the scribes. When the curtain lifts again

---

[1] Acts 15:21.

[2] Luke 4:20, corresponding to the modern sacristan or beadle, "collectors of alms," with an "interpreter" (Targumist) to give the sense of the lessons in the current Aramaic. The "ten men of leisure," said to be retained to form a quorum, are subject of controversy.

[3] Luke 4:16-20; Acts 13:15.

in the time of Antiochus Epiphanes (175 BC), we find ourselves in a different atmosphere, and the three parties of historical note among the Jews are already in existence. The Pharisees first appear as a party of protest against the lax Hellenizing tendencies of the period. The name they bore—"Assidaeans"[1]— denotes them as the strictly "pious" or "Puritans" of their day. Parties of this kind, however, are peculiarly liable to degeneration, and in their exaggerated scrupulosity and excessive literalism, the "Assidaeans" soon sunk into the "Pharisees" (separated) as we know them in the gospels. The Sadducees (from Zadok), on the other hand, were not a religious party at all, but simply a political or aristocratic clique, into whose possession the honors of the high priesthood and other influential offices hereditarily passed. They represent the worldly-wise, diplomatic, time-serving party in the state, men of skeptical, rationalistic temper, and epicurean in their view of life.

Of much greater importance for the history of the church, though not mentioned in the gospels, is the third of these parties—the Essenes. These had their chief settlement in the desert of Engedi, on the northwest shore of the Dead Sea, but were found also in the towns and villages throughout Palestine. Their total number was about 4,000. At Engedi they lived as a sort of brotherhood with customs of their own. They offered no animal sacrifices, contenting themselves with sending to the temple gifts of incense. They abounded in lustrations, and wore white garments. They rejected marriage, and practiced community of goods. Their employments were chiefly agricultural, but in the towns they exercised trades. They had the peculiar custom (perhaps Oriental) of greeting the sunrise with prayers. They forbade slavery, war, and oaths, were given to occult studies, had secret doctrines and books, and so on. The superficial resemblances have led some to trace Christianity itself to Essene sources, but in fundamental ideas no systems could be more opposed. We shall see that Essenism probably became ultimately merged in a form of Christianity.

(3) *The Judaism of the dispersion.*

The dispersion had its origin in the captivities, but was more due to voluntary settlements for trade. The Greek rulers did

---

[1] Hebrew "Chasidim."

everything they could to attract settlers to their newly-founded cities, and the troubles in Palestine made multitudes willing to leave their native country. Thus it came about that there was hardly a land or city where Jews were not to be found. They sometimes had rights of citizenship, and in many places, as in Alexandria, enjoyed special privileges. The effect on the Jew himself was profoundly and insensibly to modify his whole manner of thought. A freer spirit was necessarily introduced. From being a citizen of Zion, he became a citizen of the world. The dispersion provided points of contact for Christianity through the spread of the synagogues, the circulation of the Jewish scriptures in the Greek tongue, above all through the creation of a large body of proselytes. But outside the circle of proselytes proper there was in most communities a following of converts—the devout persons of the New Testament[1]—who, while attending the synagogues, only observed the Mosaic law in certain leading points. Many of the first converts of the gospel were drawn from this class. It is noteworthy that the admission of proselytes was not only by circumcision and sacrifice, but by baptism, and, if Talmudic statements are to be trusted, the children of proselytes were baptized with their parents.

(4) *The contact of Jewish thought, particularly at Alexandria, with Hellenic culture and philosophy.*

The classical name here is Philo, though elements of Philo's doctrine are already met with in the apocryphal Book of Wisdom. Philo was born about 20 BC, and lived till near the middle of the first century. He was therefore a contemporary of both Christ and Paul. Profoundly versed in Greek philosophy and literature, he sought to bring about an amalgamation of Jewish and Greek modes of thought. His characteristic doctrine is that of the Logos or "Word" of God, whom he conceives of partly in Platonic and Stoical fashion, but whom, at the same time, following hints of the Old Testament and of the Jewish schools, he tends to hypostatise, or interpose as a distinct personality between God and his creation. His doctrine has often been compared with that of the Apostle John. There are, however, radical contrasts.[2]

---

[1] Acts 10:2, 22, 13:16, 26, and so on.
[2] The apostle has his feet on historic facts (John 1:14; 1 John 1:1-3).

PROVINCIAL MISSION OF GREECE AND ROME

The splendor of Athens in the age of Pericles should not blind us to the fact that for Greece as a whole the fifth century BC was an age of decline.[1] The great colonizing energy of Greece was in the previous century. The mission of the Greeks was not to be the rulers, but the intellectual educators of mankind. The rule passed to Macedonia, and for a brief moment it seemed as if Alexander's dream of a Greek empire of the world was to be realized. His empire fell to pieces at his death, but his great design was fulfilled of diffusing Greek letters and culture wherever his arms had gone. Rome gradually gathered up fragments of the Macedonian empire, but Rome herself yielded to the intellectual supremacy of Greece. It cannot be too firmly grasped how profoundly Greek influences had taken possession of the Roman empire at the beginning of the Christian era. Greek language, Greek philosophy, Greek literature, Greek culture were everywhere. Rome itself was at this time in great measure, what Juvenal calls it, a Greek city. It is a fact which may not always strike us that the epistle to the Romans was written in Greek.

While, however, profoundly influenced by Greece, Rome's providential mission was different from hers. It was the task of Greece to show what the human mind can do at its highest and best in the way of natural development; to teach the world the elements of her own culture and civilization; to give it a language fitted for every noble purpose of thought and life. It was the function of Rome to bind the nations together into a great political unity—to weld them by strong bonds of law and government into a vast, universal commonwealth. The practical instinct of the Roman people and their genius for government enabled them to accomplish this as no other people of the world could have done. It is no chance coincidence that the hour of completion of this great political fabric was also that of the birth of Christianity—that the two events almost completely synchronized. The world empire and the world religion came into being together.

Philo's theory would have repelled an incarnation.

[1] Compare Freeman.

THE GREEK PREPARATION

The very intensity of the intellectual development in Athens tended to hasten a moral dissolution. The Greek religion was not one which would bear looking at critically. The popular theology in Greece was simply that of the poems of Homer. When this is said, it is easy to see that its foundations must have been swept away the moment men began to inquire rationally into the causes of things, and to entertain more elevated moral conceptions. Morality in the older period had rested largely on tradition—on custom. Now a spirit of inquiry had set in which would allow nothing to custom. A class of popular educators had arisen who had no difficulty in dissolving the most cherished beliefs in the play of their skeptical dialect. Other causes aided the collapse. Even the enervation of morals by the refinement and luxury of the prosperous period was not so fatal to moral life as the long-continued and exhausting wars of states, with their woeful lack of principle in public men, the constant breach of faith in treaties, the strife of factions, and like evils.

But Greece had a more important service to do for Christianity than simply to reveal the depths of her own moral impotence. The preparation had a positive side as well. With the overthrow of the old religion there was going on, on the part of the nobler spirits, a search for a more rational and abiding foundation for religion; with the overthrow of the old morality there began with Socrates the search for a deeper ground of morality in man's own nature; with the breaking up of the old states there was seen in Stoicism the rise of the conception of a state or commonwealth based on reason, wide as the world, and embracing man in a new brotherhood. In these three directions therefore, (1) a more inward view of morality, (2) the recognition of a common nature in man, and the reaching out to a universal form of society, and (3) a tendency to Monotheism, clearly discernable in all the nobler minds, we are to look for the positive preparation for Christianity in the ancient world. But all these advances of the human spirit could not avert the dissolution of belief and morals.[1]

---

[1] The note of uncertainty in later Greek philosophy is very marked (Skeptical schools). The most earnest minds were those who felt it most deeply. Dissatisfied with human opinion they felt, as Plato phrases it,

THE ROMAN PREPARATION

If the philosophy of Greece could not save Greece itself, it was not to be expected that it would be able to save Rome. The Romans were a people of graver, more serious disposition than the Greeks. They had not the quick, versatile imagination of the Greeks. Their gods were mostly personifications of abstract ideas (justice, pity, clemency, pleasure, and the like). Religion was to them a very serious part of the business of life, to be engaged in with strict formality, and punctilious observance of prescribed rites. Their gods were viewed, too, as more really the guardians of fidelity and virtue in household and state than among the Greeks. All testimonies accordingly bear witness to the severe virtue and simple manners of the early Romans.

This simplicity did not endure. With the growth of power—especially after the fall of Carthage and Corinth—there was a great inrush of foreign customs. The Greek gods came with the Greek culture, and a change took place in Roman religion for the worse. Altered conditions in the state cooperated to bring about deterioration of morals. The old distinction of patrician and plebeian was supplanted by that of rich and poor. The wars destroyed agricultural industry, and threw the land into the hands of wealthy men, who farmed their estates by gangs of slaves. Slavery became the basis of the social structure, and labor was despised as beneath the dignity of citizens. The populace were supported by doles from the state, or largesses from nobles, and lived only to be fed and amused.[1] The sanguinary spectacles of the amphitheater fostered in them a cruel and bloodthirsty spirit. Marriage lost its sacredness, and licentiousness flooded society.

What all this meant for religion it is not difficult to foresee. The chief features, in a religious respect, are: (1) The wide prevalence of skepticism, or total unbelief among the cultured or educated classes; and (2), the vast growth of superstition and a great influx of foreign cults among the people in general. The cults chiefly in favour were the Oriental, and this again shows that the religious consciousness had entered on a deeper phase.

---

the need of some "word of God," which would more surely carry them (Phaedo).

[1] Juvenal, "bread and games."

For, whatever the defects of the Oriental religion, there was expressed in most of them a deeper feeling of the discord, the pain, the mystery of life, and many of their rites showed a longing for redemption.

Special importance attaches to the rise of an entirely new cult—the worship of the emperor. In Caesar worship the religion of paganism may be said to have culminated. The Roman people had long been familiar with the idea of a genius of the Republic. Now, when all the powers and offices were gathered up in the emperor, be became to ordinary eyes an almost godlike being. From this the step was easy to formal apotheosis. The Senate took this step when they decreed divine honors to the emperors—many of them the basest and vilest of mankind. Yet this worship of the emperor took root, and, in the provinces especially, gained amazing popularity. A special class of guilds ("augustales") sprang up to attend to it. The peculiarity of it was that it was the one worship which was common to the whole empire. In it also the Roman Empire expressed its inmost spirit. As the deification of brute power, it was the strongest possible antithesis to the worship of Christ. It was the worship of the beast.

Luxurious, frivolous, skeptical and corrupt as the age was, however, there is not to be overlooked in it the presence of certain better elements. As in Greece, so here, the preparation was not wholly negative. Stoicism and Platonism had received a religious tinge (Seneca, Plutarch), and an elevating influence on the purer minds. There were, doubtless, numerous individual examples of virtue. The collegia (organized associations or guilds) of the empire, and the mysteries have intimate and curious relations with the history of the church in the first centuries.[1] The burial societies were legal, and the Christians took advantage of this for their protection. When all is said, the verdict of history on that old world must be that it was as corrupt as it could well be to exist at all, and what was worse, had not within itself any principle of regeneration.

---

[1] Dr. Hatch would explain from the former several of the offices of the early church (compare Hort, pages 128-210). The mysteries of Mithras, Professor Harnack says, were in the third century the strongest rival of Christianity. Their strange caricatures of Christian rites were a source of perplexity to the fathers.

CHRISTIANITY AND ROMAN LAW

What is sometimes said of the tolerance of the Romans requires to be taken with considerable modification. The Romans had laws enough against foreign rites; even where the practice of a foreign religion was permitted, this permission did not extend to Romans. Christianity, therefore, fell under the ban of the laws in a double respect. It was unsanctioned ("religio illicita"), and it drew away Romans from the established religion. Even with this disadvantage, however, it might have escaped, for the authorities found it impracticable rigidly to enforce the laws. But there were special features about Christianity which, from a Roman standpoint, made tolerance impossible. Christianity was not a national religion.

The sentiment of antiquity respected the gods of other nations; but Christianity appeared rather in the light of a revolt against the ancient faith from which it sprang, and had no national character of its own. It had no visible deity or temple, and to the popular mind seemed a species of atheism. Specially, it could not fail to be seen that, with its exclusive claims, it struck at the very existence of the Roman state religion. If its precepts were admitted, the state religion would be overthrown. The more earnest men were, therefore, to maintain or revive the prestige of the established system, the more determinedly must they oppose this new superstition. The irreconcilability of Christianity with the established religion came naturally to its sharpest point in the refusal of Christians to offer at the shrine of the emperor. This was an act of disobedience in a vital point, which could not be passed over.

Add to this the manner in which Christianity came into conflict with the laws prohibiting secret and nocturnal gatherings; the powerful material interests affected by its spread;[1] the odium in which Christians were held on account of the crimes imputed to them by their enemies; the outbursts of popular fury to which they were opposed in times of public calamity; and it will readily be understood how, even when there was no general persecution, they lived in a constant state of insecurity, and how the very "name" of Christian should be sufficient to condemn them.

---

[1] Compare Acts 19:24-27.

THE APOSTOLIC AGE AND LATER JEWISH CHRISTIANITY

Into the pagan world such as we have described it Christ's religion came as the breath of a new life. "The time is fulfilled," said Jesus, "and the kingdom of God is at hand."[1] In Christ's life, deeds, preaching of the gospel of the kingdom, death and resurrection, the moveless foundations of the church were laid. Christ's last injunction to his apostles was to abide at Jerusalem till they should receive "the promise of the Father."[2] In the outpouring of the Spirit at Pentecost the New Testament church was born.[3]

THE CHURCH OF THE APOSTLES

Obvious reasons compel a glance at the phenomena of the Apostolic age. Three main stages in the development may be distinguished:

(1) The first takes us to the martyrdom of Stephen, and may be called the period of unbroken unity with Jewish institutions. The church in this stage was composed wholly of Jewish believers, and was presided over by the apostles as a body. The first disciples stood in unbroken unity with the temple and synagogue.[4] Their specifically Christian fellowship expressed itself in domestic gatherings.[5] Even the apostles did not dream of parting with their national usages,[6] but probably thought of the gentile mission to which they knew themselves called,[7] as an incorporation into the Jewish privilege. How long this naive stage lasted is uncertain, but the need must early have been felt for the more independent assemblies. This became imperative when, under the new impulse of love, the so-called "community of goods" was introduced.[8]

---

[1] Mark 1:15.

[2] Luke 24:49; Acts 1:4-5.

[3] Acts 2.

[4] Acts 2:46, 3:1. Much later Saul sought the Christians in the synagogues (Acts 9:2).

[5] Acts 2:46.

[6] Compare Peter's scruples, Acts 10.

[7] Matthew 28:19; Acts 1:8, 2:21, 39.

[8] Acts 2:44-45. It is in this connection with the judgment on Annias

The oldest definite step in organization we read of was the appointment of the seven,[1] called for by the disputes between Hebrews and Hellenists (Greek-speaking Jews) about daily distribution. It is customary to see in these "seven" the prototypes of the "deacons"; but it may be questioned whether the design went farther than to meet a particular emergency. Naturally, as believers multiplied, similar associations tended to spring up in the surrounding districts.[2] These appear to have stood in a certain relation of dependence on the mother church in Jerusalem.[3] But the distinction of the Hellenist and Hebrew has a further influence, and one of greater importance. It lay in the nature of the case that the Hellenistic Jews were men of a freer, more cosmopolitan spirit than their Hebrew compatriots. From their circle came Stephen, the forerunner of Paul. It seems plain that Stephen had clearly grasped the principle of salvation by faith, and the spirituality and inwardness of Christ's religion generally, rendered obsolete the prescriptions of the law.[4]

(2) The second stage extends from the martyrdom of Stephen to the Council of Jerusalem, and may be termed the period of the founding of the gentile churches. The birth of gentile Christianity was not an event which took place all at once, or without being prepared for within the church itself. The first barrier broken down was that between Jews and Samaritans;[5] a second was broken down when Philip sought and baptized

---

and Sapphira that the word "church" first occurs (5:11, not in Acts 2:47). Even yet we must beware of attributing to these gatherings of the disciples too formal an organization. Everything is as yet fluent, growing, unconstrained. The first mention of elders is in Acts 11:30, and, doubtless, the analogy followed there was that of the Jewish synagogue.

[1] Acts 6.

[2] Acts 9:31; Galatians 1:22.

[3] Even when so important a church as that of Antioch was formed, it seemed the natural thing to send delegates to it from Jerusalem to look after its welfare (Acts 11:22).

[4] Acts 6:13-14. His address in his defence turns throughout on this idea, that God's revelations are not tied to times and places, and that his worship is not necessarily bound up with these (Acts 7). It was this that led to his martyrdom for blasphemy. It did not occur to anyone that he had left a successor in the young man at whose feet the cloths were laid, and who was the most clamorous for his destruction.

[5] Acts 8:5-8.

the Ethiopian eunuch;[1] a third and greater one was removed when Peter was sent to Cornelius;[2] the last was broken down when some men of Cyprus and Cyrene, likewise Hellenes, boldly struck into a new line, and began to preach the gospel to the Greeks at Antioch.[3] This was quite a new departure. Previously, it is said, the word had been preached to none but Jews only;[4] now it was preached to the gentiles, and a purely gentile church was founded. The special thing to notice is how the church at Jerusalem received the tidings of these advances. It did so in a way worthy of it. It saw itself being led into new paths, but it was not disobedient to the heavenly vision.[5]

Meanwhile God had been preparing his own instrument for this work. The conversion of Saul is one of the most remarkable facts in history; one also the most far-reaching in its effects.[6] It is not an unlikely conjecture that the reason why Saul opposed the Christians with so unrelenting a hostility was that, with his powerful, consistent intellect, he saw more clearly than others that the logical consequence of this system was the utter overthrow of Judaism. When, therefore, it pleased God to reveal his Son in him,[7] this was to him one and the same thing as the call to preach the gospel to the gentiles. A prolonged retirement to Arabia was followed by a fifteen days' visit to Peter at Jerusalem; the next few years were spent in his native district.[8] Thence he was brought by Barnabas to help him at Antioch, where a powerful church had been established, and the disciples had received the name by which they have since been known— "Christians."[9]

From this point begins a new development. Paul and Barnabas are separated for a mission to the gentiles.[10] We need not

---

[1] Acts 8:26-40.

[2] Acts 10.

[3] Acts 11:20-21.

[4] Acts 11:19.

[5] Compare 8:14, 11:18, 22-23.

[6] "Pharisaism has fulfilled its historical mission when it has brought forth this man" (Harnack).

[7] Galatians 1:15.

[8] Galatians 1:17-21.

[9] Acts 11:26.

[10] Acts 13:2.

follow the apostle in his missionary journeys. His progress is marked by light points, for it was a principle with him, neglecting outposts, to aim at the great centers. This enables us to trace him as he goes along—at Antioch in Pisidia, at Philippi, at Thessalonica, at Athens, at Corinth, at Ephesus—till finally his desire was gratified in a way he had not looked for, and he saw Rome also.[1] The conditions under which these churches planted by Paul had their origin caused them to present certain peculiarities. (a) They were free to a greater extent than the Palestinian churches from the law and the synagogue; (b) they were mostly mixed churches—composed in varying proportions of Jews and gentiles; and (c) they were more completely independent than the Palestinian and Syrian churches. The latter, it was noted, stood in a certain relation of dependence on the mother church at Jerusalem. The only bond of union among the Pauline churches was their consciousness of a common faith, and the personality of their great apostle, whose letters and travels from church to church kept them in touch with him and with one another.

(3) The third stage extends from the Council of Jerusalem (inclusive) to the end of the Apostolic age, and is marked as the period of the great controversy between Jew and gentile. The church in Jerusalem appears to have been considerably reinforced by the more conservative section.[2] These had been content to be silent when it was only the case of one individual (the eunuch), or one family (Cornelius), or one church (Antioch), directly under the eyes of their own delegates. Now (close of the first missionary journey), the gentile mission had been pushed far and wide, and there seemed a danger that their distinctive Jewish privilege would be altogether swamped. A reactionary party accordingly emerged, whose watchword was "Except you be circumcised, you cannot be saved."[3] Their machinations at Antioch led to Paul and Barnabas being sent up to the apostles and elders at Jerusalem for a settlement of this question, and to the calling of the great council.[4] The chief points to be noted are

---

[1] Romans 1:15, 15:32.
[2] Acts 6:7, 15:5, 21:20.
[3] Acts 15:1, 5, 24.
[4] Acts 15.

the entire agreement of the Jerusalem leaders with Paul on the main issue,[1] and the broad basis on which the decision was arrived at—"The apostles and elders, with the whole church."[2]

The decision itself was of the nature of a compromise, but it left untouched a point of great importance for the future peace of the church. The Jews were not to insist on circumcision; the gentiles were to observe precepts.[3] But it was not settled whether Jews were at liberty to dispense with the customs of their nation. On this point real difference of opinion still existed. Paul was probably the only one perfectly clear in principle; the majority of the Jewish believers took the other view. The difference was one which was bound to emerge in mixed churches—especially in eating.[4] The question of principle, however, once raised, could only be settled in one way in the interests of the liberty and unity of the church.[5] Still, as a matter of usage, the Jewish Christians continued to walk faithfully in the customs of their fathers.[6] It will be seen from this that the Judaizing party which opposed Paul with so much bitterness in the churches did not consist entirely of those who insisted on circumcision.[7]

---

[1] Thus also Galatians 2. Some do not identify these visits.

[2] Acts 15:23.

[3] Acts 15:28-29.

[4] Hence the collision of Peter and Paul at Antioch (Galatians 2:11-14), which turned on this point.

[5] Compare the epistles of Peter and James, which lay not the slightest stress on the observance of the law of Moses—this though both are directly writing to the Diaspora.

[6] Thus even Paul, Acts 21:24, 28:17 (compare the description of James (from Hegesippus) in Eusebius, History 2.23).

[7] This was the nature of the opposition in Galatia (Galatians 5:1-4, 6:13-14). But it would include also those who, without insisting on the circumcision of the gentiles, resented the abrogation of the law for the Jews. This was probably the nature of the opposition at Corinth, where we do not read of any attempt to raise the question of circumcision, but of attacks on Paul's apostleship, and the attempt to form a Petrine in opposition to the Pauline party (1 Corinthians 1:12, 9:1). After this the controversy seems to have died down (a last trace in Philippians 3:2). From this time Paul had to contend with mixed forms of error, in which legality had a place, but in association with Essenian and other heretical elements (compare Colossians). By the time we reach the gospel and

CONSTITUTION AND WORSHIP OF THE APOSTOLIC CHURCHES

Fresh light has been thrown on these subjects by the recently
discovered Didachè—probably a work of the end of the first
century. With respect to constitution, the chief gain in our
knowledge is the distinction we are enabled to make between
ordinary and extraordinary office-bearers. The ordinary office-
bearers are the elders (or bishops) and deacons. The facts may
be thus exhibited: (1) Each congregation was presided over by a
number of elders or bishops.[1] With these were joined the deacons, who seem to have served or assisted the elders in temporal
matters. (2) Elders and bishops were identical. The names are
interchangeable.[2] (3) The elders had spiritual, and not merely
administrative, functions.[3] They have oversight of the flock,
watch for souls, speak the word, pray with the sick, and so on.[4]
(4) As in the case of the "seven," election was popular (thus also
Didachè), with subsequent ordination.[5]

While this was so, there was a class of extraordinary office-
bearers, to whom the work of teaching and exhorting more
especially belonged. These were the apostles and evangelists,
prophets and teachers.[6] They differed from the others in that
their ministry was itinerant. The Didachè gives minute directions regarding the apostles, prophets and teachers.[7] Their
support is to be voluntary. The apostle is not to tarry more
than two days in one place. If any asks for money, he is a false
prophet. The prophet may settle in a congregation and become

---

epistles of John we are moving in an atmosphere far above these oppositions, and find all antitheses resolved in the calm assurance of the
possession of "eternal life."

[1] Acts 11:30, 14:23; Titus 1:5, and so on.

[2] Acts 20:17, 28; Philippians 1:1; 1 Timothy 3:1, 8; Titus 1:5, 7. There
is no reason for supposing that the persons described more generally in
1 Corinthians 12:28; 1 Thessalonians 5:12; Hebrews 13:8, and so on, are
other than the elders.

[3] This against Hatch. His conjecture that the designation "bishops"
in gentile churches was suggested by the guilds connects itself with his
idea that their functions were mainly financial or administrative.

[4] Acts 20:28; Hebrews 13:17; 1 Peter 5:2; James 5:15.

[5] Acts 6:5; 1 Timothy 4:14, 5:22; Titus 1:5.

[6] Acts 13:1; 1 Corinthians 12:28; Ephesians 4:11.

[7] Chapters 11-13.

what we would call its pastor. If prophets or teachers are absent, the bishops and deacons perform their service. Besides this special and general ministry in the church, there were cases in which the ordering of the affairs of the church was put into the hands of specially appointed apostolic delegates—men like Timothy and Titus. Their position is probably to be looked on as deputed and exceptional, and adapted to the circumstances of a transition period.[1]

The above was the general constitution of the gentile churches, and the Jewish churches in the main agreed with it. In one important respect, however, a different type was presented by the church at Jerusalem. This church, we saw, was presided over by the apostles, and took an oversight of the Jewish churches in its neighborhood. Afterwards its presidency was in the hands of James, the Lord's brother, who, from his personal preeminence and relationship to Christ, held practically apostolic rank. From this circumstance the idea seems to have grown up that the head of the church at Jerusalem should be a blood relation to Christ; and, after James' martyrdom (c. AD 70), a cousin of the Lord, Symeon, was elected.[2] He held this position till his own martyrdom (c. AD 107). Soon after, in the reign of Hadrian, the Jewish church in Jerusalem came to an end.

In its worship, as in its constitution, the church was modelled partly on the usage of the synagogue. In Jewish-Christian, and even wider circles the name "synagogues" was long in use for Christian assemblies.[3] What was new came from the freer spirit which Christianity introduced, and from the entrance of specific Christian ideas and observances. Chief among these new elements may be noted: (1) The new day of Christian service—the first day of the week, or Lord's Day.[4] (2) The exercise of the spiritual gifts—tongues, prophesyings, and so on.[5] (3) The singing of Christian hymns.[6] (4) The reading of the apostolic

---

[1] Compare 1 Timothy 1:3; Titus 1:5.

[2] Hegesippus in Eusebius, History 3.11.

[3] Compare James 2:2.

[4] Acts 20:7; 1 Corinthians 16:2; Revelation 1:10: thus also Didachè.

[5] 1 Corinthians 12.

[6] Compare Ephesians 5:19. Fragments of these hymns are believed to be found in such passages as Ephesians 5:14; 1 Timothy 3:16.

letters.[1] (5) The observance of baptism and the Lord's Supper (breaking of bread, eucharist).[2] The crowning act of the New Testament religious service was the Lord's Supper, with which in this age was always combined the Agape, or "love-feast." The two formed, indeed, one sacred meal, in the course of which, after blessing, bread was broken and wine drunk after the example of the Lord.[3] Different types of observance may, however, be distinguished. In gentile churches the service tended to be adapted to the freer model of the Greek feast;[4] in Jewish churches there was closer adherence to the ritual of Passover.[5]

TRANSITION TO LATER JEWISH CHRISTIANITY

We have found two parties in Jewish Christianity—one our extreme Pharisaic party, who not only observed the law themselves, but would have imposed it on the gentiles; the other, more tolerant and liberal, and friendly to the mission of Paul. A series of events now took place which had the twofold effect of (1) finally separating the Jewish Christian church from the older Judaism; (2) finally separating the two Jewish parties— the stricter and more tolerant—from each other. Such events were: (a) The catastrophe of the destruction of Jerusalem (AD 70). Warned, it is said, by a divine revelation (more probably mindful of the predictions of the Lord), the Christians had

---

[1] Colossians 4:16; 1 Thessalonians 5:27.

[2] Baptism, after Oriental custom, was administered generally, though not exclusively, by immersion. Another method was pouring, for which directions are given in the Didachè (chapter 7, illustrated also in catacomb pictures. Compare the baptism of the Spirit by outpouring, Acts 2:33, 10:46, and so on). The rite was administered on profession of faith—hence primarily to adults—and was frequently accompanied with spiritual gifts (for example, Acts 19:16). Opinions differ as to the baptism of the children of believers. A class of cases may indicate that the Jewish analogy was followed of receiving the household with its head (Acts 16:15, 33; 1 Corinthians 1:16; compare 1 Corinthians 7:14).

[3] 1 Corinthians 11:23-34.

[4] Hence the abuses at Corinth, 1 Corinthians 11.

[5] The eucharistic prayers in the Didachè are on the latter model (chapters 9-10). The directions do not include the words of institution; but these may be presumed to be presupposed.

withdrawn to Pella, in the Decapolis, and there beheld the storm sweep over their doomed nation which wrought its overthrow. So awful a providence could not but lead them to ponder anew their relation to a system which had thus perished, as it were, under the visible curse of God. (b) The revival of Rabbinism, and increasing hostility of the Jews. The political fall, far from destroying Rabbinism, became the occasion of a great increase in its power (new center at Jamnia, schools opened, court of justice established, and so on). This stiffening and concentration of Judaism was accompanied by a bitterly intensified hostility to the Christians, who, repelled, cursed, persecuted by their brethren according to the flesh, were naturally influenced to ally themselves more closely with gentile believers. (c) Matters were brought to a crisis by the great rebellion under Barcochba ("son of a star"), in the reign of Hadrian (AD 132), when the refusal of Christians to enlist under the banner of the false Messiah exposed them to the worst cruelties. The revolt was followed by the erection on the site of Jerusalem (AD 135) of a new heathen city, Aelia Capitolina, from which by express decree all circumcised persons were excluded. The old Jerusalem church was thus finally dispossessed, and a gentile church took its place, which served itself heir to its traditions and prestige.

NAZARENES AND EBIONITES

The same causes which led to the separation of Jewish Christianity from Judaism proper led also to the separation of its two sections from each other. It is evident that the narrower of these sections, the old opponents of Paul, had never really grasped the essential nature of Christianity, and were bound to become more reactionary as time went on. Even the more liberal section, who recognized the legitimacy of the gentile mission, were necessarily hindered by their environment from attaining any large and worthy conception of the religion they professed; and, cut off from the great developing body of gentile Christianity, tended likewise to become a historical anachronism. This is what actually happened. Justin Martyr (c. AD 150) describes two kinds of Jewish Christians, one of whom did not wish, while the other did, to impose the law upon the gentiles. The latter he already treats as heretical.

Jerome (beginning of fifth century) knows of the two classes distinguished by like peculiarities, whom he names respectively Nazarenes and Ebionites. Supplementing his statements by those of the others, we gain the following points. The Nazarenes (oldest Jewish name for Christians[1]) were a sect small in numbers. Their chief seats were in Syria, about Pella, in Bashan, and so on, where they lived among the Jews quite apart from the gentile community. They held themselves, as Jews, under obligation to observe the law, but did not extend this obligation to the gentiles, and recognized the mission of Paul. They used an Aramaic gospel called the "Gospel of the Hebrews," corresponding, with considerable changes and interpolations, to our Gospel of Matthew. They regarded Jesus as born of the Virgin Mary, and in a special way filled with the divine Spirit, who came upon him at his baptism.

The Ebionites ("poor"), on the contrary, held the law to be binding to all, and refused to have any fellowship with uncircumcised gentiles. They bitterly calumniated Paul. Jesus they regarded as a mere man, chosen to be the Messiah for his legal piety. Their version of the gospel omitted the story of the supernatural birth. The identity of the two parties with those formerly described seems as clear as it can be, and is not set aside by the fact that other fathers (for example, Irenaeus, Origen, Eusebius), to whom the Nazarenes were not well known,[2] group all under the common designation of Ebionites, attributing to them the views of the law proper only to the narrower section, while aware of the distinction in their views of Christ. Neither party had a future. The Ebionites were still numerous in the fourth century, but, as a sect formally rejected, seem to have melted away in the first half of the fifth century. The Nazarenes are not heard of after the time of Jerome.

ESSENE EBIONITISM—THE "CLEMENTINES"

The Ebionites above described are of the ordinary Pharisaic type. But Epiphanius (end of the fourth century) is our authority for another type of Ebionitism, whose peculiarities are best

---

[1] Acts 24:5.

[2] Epiphanius and Jerome had firsthand knowledge of them. Augustine, like Jerome, looks kindly on the Nazarenes.

explained by supposing a fusion, some time after the fall of Jerusalem, of Jewish Christianity with Essenism.[1]   An interesting
monument of this party appears to remain in the so-called Cle-
mentine writings ("Recognitions" and "Homilies"), originating
in the latter part of the second century (possibly in the beginning
of the third).[2]   The titles do not designate distinct works, but
denote divergent recensions or forms of the same work, which
again embody older documents.   In character the Clementines
are a story or romance—an early instance of the religious
novel—one, too, wrought out with no slight literary art.

Clement, to whom the writings are attributed, is represented
as the son of a noble Roman, whose wife and twin children had
become lost, and who himself disappeared in seeking for them.
The youthful Clement's mind is consumed with an ardent passion for truth.   He meets with Barnabas at Rome ("Homilies,"
Alexandria), and ultimately attaches himself to Peter at Caesarea. Peter's great mission appears to be to follow Simon Magus
(a supposed mask for Paul) about from place to place and
counteract his influence.   Clement is instructed by Peter, acts as
his amanuensis, and sends accounts of his discourses, debates
with the Magus, and so on, to James at Jerusalem. In the course
of their travels reunions are effected of all the members of
Clement's family (mother, twin brothers, father)—hence "Recognitions." This romance is the framework in which theological
ideas are skilfully set.   The Ebionitism of the "Homilies" is the
more pronounced, but the type of doctrine in both forms is
similar.

The key thought is that of the one "true prophet," who,
changing form and name, goes down through the ages, appear-
ing now as Adam, now as Moses, now as Christ.   Christianity
is thus the repromulgation of the eternal law.   Over against
Adam, as the true prophet, stands Eve as the bringer in of false
or "female" prophesy, to which is attributed everything in the
Old Testament false or unworthy of God. Sacrifice is rejected
(in the "Recognitions" viewed as a provisional expedient; in the

---

[1] Thus Neander, Ritschl, and so on.

[2] The first to mention them is Origen. The "Recognitions" exist only
in a Latin translation; the complete Greek text of the "Homilies" was
first published in 1853. There is also an "Epitomè" of the "Homilies."

"Homilies" as a work of false prophesy). A remarkable feature in these works is that the point of circumcision is conceded (only baptism), and the gentile mission itself is taken over from Paul, and claimed for Peter. The ecclesiastical system is that of the second century episcopacy.[1]

GENTILE CHRISTIANITY: NERO TO DOMITIAN (AD 64-96)

The indications in the New Testament of a rapid progress of the gospel are filled out by traditions of the labors of the apostles after their dispersion from Jerusalem (Thomas in Parthia, Thaddaeus in Edessa, Andrew in Scythia, and so on), often untrustworthy, but in their main features bearing out an early extensive diffusion of Christianity throughout the countries of the known world. Corroboration will be found in the fact now to be recited.

FIRST CONTACT WITH THE EMPIRE

The world has rarely seen more perfect specimens of human wickedness than in the series of emperors who succeeded Augustus. "The dark, unrelenting Tiberius"[2] was followed by the mad Caligula, and he by the dull, sottish Claudius (AD 41), to whose reign belongs the first distinct notice we have of the presence of Christianity in the empire. The historian Suetonius relates that Claudius "banished from Rome all Jews, who were continually making disturbances at the instigation of one Chrestus."[3] There

---

[1] In these circles the Lord's Supper was observed with water (Epiphanius). Intimately connected with the Ebionites of the Clementines were the Elkesaites, who take their name from a supposed leader, Elkesai, in the reign of Trajan. It has been plausibly conjectured, however, that "Elkesai" ("hidden power") is rather the name of a revelation book, with which this sect is always associated. It was actively circulated in the third century. This book, of whose origin mythical accounts are given, aimed at an amelioration of discipline by teaching a second forgiveness of sins through baptism. Unlike the Clementines, it insisted on circumcision. The whole movement appears to show a bold attempt to popularize a type of Ebionitism on gentile soil, and within the catholic episcopate. It is met, however, with no permanent success.

[2] Gibbon.

[3] This is the banishment referred to in Acts 18:2 (AD 52).

is little doubt that "Chrestus" is the misspelt name of "Christ," and that what Suetonius alludes to is tumults in the Jewish quarters which had arisen through the preaching of Christ. This is six years before the epistle to the Romans (AD 58), and shows how remarkably Christianity had already spread in the capital.[1] In AD 54 Claudius was poisoned to make way for his step-son Nero, in whom every vice that tongue can name seemed concentrated. Under Nero happened what is usually reckoned as the first persecution, though this mode of enumerating persecutions is in many ways misleading.

THE PERSECUTION UNDER NERO

One night (AD 64) Rome was discovered to have been set on fire by an unseen hand. The fire spread with terrible rapidity till ten out of fourteen quarters of the city were destroyed. Popular suspicion fastened this crime on Nero, and he, to avert odium from himself, turned it on the Christians. A frightful persecution ensued. An "immense multitude" were convicted, not so much, as Tacitus confesses, on evidence of having set the city on fire, as on account of their "hatred of the human race." To the most exquisite tortures were added mockery and derision. Some were covered with the skins of wild beasts, and thrown to be devoured by dogs; others were crucified; numbers were burnt alive; and many, covered with pitch, were lighted up when the day declined, to serve as torches during the night.[2] The emperor lent his own gardens for the spectacle, and heightened the gaity of the occasion by games. The persecution was local, but so terrible an event occurring in the capital could not but have the most serious consequences affecting the status and treatment of Christians in the provinces.[3]

Apart from its inherent pathos, the persecution yields instructive light on the rapidly growing numbers of the new sect, and on the estimate in which they were held by the pagans. When even an intelligent writer like Tacitus can speak of them as universally detested, and deservedly punished for their crimes,

---

[1] Compare Romans 1:8, and Tacitus below.

[2] "At the stake they shine, Who stand with throat transfixed, and smoke and burn" (Juvenal).

[3] Compare 1 Peter and Apocalypse.

and of their religion as a "pernicious superstition," it is easy to imagine how the ignorant and unreasoning crowd must have thought and felt regarding them! It was not only into the lower strata of society, however, that Christianity had penetrated. We have at least one interesting case in this reign to show that it had found its way into higher circles as well. Tacitus relates that in AD 57 a very distinguished lady, Pomponia Graecina, wife of Aulus Plautius, commander of the army in Britain, was accused before her relatives of having adopted a "foreign superstition," which led her into habits of seclusion and melancholy. This "foreign superstition" has been generally understood to be Christianity; and the discovery of a crypt in the catacombs connected with the Pomponian "gens" (one descendant bearing this very name, Pomponius Graecinus), puts the matter beyond doubt.

MARTYRDOM OF PAUL AND PETER

To this reign of Nero, according to the concurrent testimony of antiquity, belong the martyrdoms of the two great apostles—Paul and Peter. That Paul suffered at Rome, having carried the gospel "to the extreme limit of the west," is attested by Clement (AD 96); and is indeed evidenced by his own latest epistle,[1] which anticipates a speedy death by the sword of the executioner.[2] His second imprisonment is probably to be regarded as an after effect of the terrible persecution already described. His trial seems to have had two stages. He himself writes pathetically that at his first answer or defence he could get no one to act as his patron or advocate[3]—a testimony to the general terror Nero's recent acts had inspired. He suffered, tradition says, on the Ostian Road, probably AD 67 or 68.

To the same period must be assigned the martyrdom of his brother apostle—Peter. The fiction of Peter's seven years' episcopate at Antioch and twenty-five years' episcopate at Rome

---

[1] 2 Timothy.

[2] Clement's language favors the supposition that he did not meet this fate at the end of the imprisonment recorded in Acts 28:30-31, but had a new period of activity, journeying perhaps as far as Spain (compare Romans 15:28).

[3] 2 Timothy 4:16.

(source in the Clementines[1] and in apocryphal Acts) may be disregarded. On the other hand there is a consensus of testimony to the fact that Peter came to Rome in the end of his life, and suffered martyrdom about the same time as Paul. This we may accept as the historical nucleus round which embellishments of legend subsequently gathered. The story of Peter desiring to be crucified with his head downwards is first found in Origen (beginning of third century).[2]

THE EMPIRE TILL DOMITIAN

From Nero to Domitian, the next emperor who concerns us, is thirteen years (AD 68-81). In this short interval no fewer than five emperors were raised to the purple. The reigns of three of them (Galba, Otho, Vitellius) were compressed in the brief space of eighteen months. Vespasian and Titus were good rulers. Their names are connected with the Jewish war and the destruction of Jerusalem. On the death of Titus (AD 81), not without suspicion of poison, the empire was taken by Domitian, Vespasian's younger son. Historians say he took Tiberius for his model. His moroseness, dissimulation, cruelty of disposition, are dwelt on by all who speak of him. Under him took place what it is customary to call the second persecution.

THE PERSECUTION UNDER DOMITIAN

Domitian began as a precisian, but ere long developed qualities which made him what Pliny calls "the enemy of all good men." His rapacity and lust of blood found a fitting prey in the Christians. Clement (AD 96) speaks of "a vast multitude of the elect" who suffered for Christ, and gives vivid glimpses of the indignities they endured.[3] An interesting story is told by Hegesippus, of two grandchildren of Jude, the brother of the Lord, whom

---

[1] In an epistle prefixed to the "Homilies" Peter is represented as transferring his episcopate to Clement.

[2] Most beautiful of the legends about Peter is the well-known "Quo Vadis" story (fourth or fifth century). Peter was fleeing from the city when he met the Lord carrying his cross. "Lord," he asked, "to where are you going?" "I go to Rome," said Jesus, "to be crucified again." Smitten with the rebuke, Peter turned back to prison and to death.

[3] 1 Clement 4.

Domitian caused to be brought before him, but dismissed as simpletons on finding that they had no money, and expected only a celestial kingdom.[1] A more remarkable instance in every way is that of Flavius Clemens, the consul, and his wife, Domitilla, who, the heathen historian Dion Cassius informs us, were in this reign (AD 96) accused of "atheism," and "going after the customs of the Jews." These two persons were of the highest rank. Clemens was the cousin, Domitilla the niece, of the emperor, and their two sons had been adopted by Domitian as his heirs. Yet Clemens was put to death, and his wife was banished to an island in the Aegean. The peculiarity of the charge implies Christianity, and this is now confirmed by the discovery of the cemetery of Domitilla in the catacombs.[2] Other discoveries show that Christianity had penetrated into the family of the Flavians.

LAST DAYS OF JOHN

To this reign also, if the oldest witnesses are to be trusted, is to be referred the banishment of the apostle John to Patmos,[3] and the composition of the Apocalypse. It is in any case to the period after Nero we must assign John's removal to Asia Minor, and his labors and teaching in Ephesus, of which there is ample attestation. Here, surrounded by a circle of friends and disciples, he continued to an extreme old age, his residence broken only by the banishment above mentioned. Among those about him in his later days we have notices of the apostles Philip and Andrew, of Polycarp, of a second John (the "elder"), and of other "elders," who continued his tradition. Ephesus, in short, in the closing years of the century, became the new center of the church, as Jerusalem had been earlier, and Rome was to be

---

[1] In Eusebius, History 3.20.

[2] So near even in that early age had Christianity come to the throne of the Caesars! Dion further related that "many others" were put to death or had their goods confiscated on the same charge, and instances Acilius Glabrio, who had been consul with Trajan, and whose family was one of the most illustrious in the state. In 1888 the crypt of the Glabriones, in the catacombs, was likewise laid bare by De Rossi.

[3] Tacitus tells us, with evident reference to this reign, that the islands were filled with exiles, and the rocks stained with murder (History 1.2).

later. As John grew old, tradition relates, his friends gathered
round and besought him to write down what he had taught
about Christ. Thus his gospel originated.[1] Many beautiful stories remain to us of John's later days, how, for instance, when
too weak to repair to church, he caused the young men to carry
him thither, and, being unable to speak much, contented himself
with saying "Little children, love one another";[2] or the fine story
told by Clement of Alexandria of his reclaiming the young man
who had become a robber. John's life is said to have extended
into the reign of Trajan, that is, beyond AD 98. His tomb was
shown in Ephesus.

THE CATACOMBS

Reference has been made to the catacombs. These singular excavations are immense subterranean burial places of the early
Christians, in the fields around Rome, near the great roads,
within a circle of three miles from the city. They began in the
first century, probably as private burial places in the vineyards
or gardens of the wealthier converts. The older cemeteries,
which formed the nucleus of the catacombs, can in this way in
several instances be distinguished. These smaller burial places,
as the excavations proceeded, ran into each other, and formed
larger areas. The extent of the catacombs is enormous. They
consist of a vast maze or labyrinth of passages, often in de-
scending levels, intersecting each other in all directions, with
little rooms or vaults on either side. The total length of the
passages is reckoned at some 587 geographical miles. These
corridors with the accompanying chambers are literally packed
with graves. The number of the dead interred in them has been
variously estimated, but can hardly be less than 2,000,000. This
fact speaks volumes for the extent to which Christianity had
spread in and around Rome during the three centuries or there-
abouts that the catacombs were in use.[3]

---

[1] There seem to have been two editions of it, if we may judge from
the supplementary chapter 21, itself attested by a note from the elders
(21:24-25).

[2] Jerome.

[3] The oldest cemeteries, as those of Lucina (Pomponian), of Domitilla, of Priscilla, and the like, are distinguished by their architectural

Special interest attaches to the art-features, symbols and inscriptions of the catacombs. They make large use of painting. The oldest tombs exhibit this art in the highest perfection.[1] The symbols of the catacombs bear striking testimony to the circle of ideas in which the Christian mind moved, and to the hopes by which it was sustained. They are of all kinds, from the rudest scrawls to carefully executed designs. Most were biblical, a few pagan.[2] Favorite symbols were the anchor, the dove, the ship, the palm, the crown. The cross is not early. Chief among emblems, on account of its mystical significance, was the fish. It finds its explanation in the fact that the letters of the Greek name "ichthus" stand for the first letters of the names of Christ—"Jesus Christ, the Son of God, Savior." Like the symbols, the inscriptions are often rude in style, but show also how differently death, and everything connected with it, was looked upon in Christian, as compared with pagan circles. The inscriptions are marked by a rare simplicity—often no more than "in peace"—but breathe always the spirit of hope, trust, and charity toward others.[3]

THE AGE OF THE APOSTOLIC FATHERS (AD 96-117)

With the mild Nerva, after the murder of Domitian (AD 96), begins the series of what are sometimes known as "the five good emperors." Nerva was succeeded (AD 98) by the frank and soldier-like Trajan, under whom we reach, as ordinarily reckoned, the third persecution.

---

elegance and classical style of decoration.

[1] Afterwards painting becomes conventional, and often, as in the pictures which stand for Noah in the Ark, Jonah and the fish, and so on, sinks well-nigh to the ridiculous. The biblical representations embrace scenes from both Old and New Testaments. The figure of the Good Shepherd appears from the very first, and there are early representations of baptism and the Lord's Supper.

[2] Orpheus, and so on.

[3] There is about them nothing horrible or revengeful. The tools of labor are portrayed, but not the instruments of torture. They speak to the power that overcomes death. The catacombs were long ago lost to knowledge, were rediscovered by Bosio in 1578, and have been carefully explored in the present century by De Rossi and his coadjutors.

THE PERSECUTION IN BITHYNIA—PLINY AND TRAJAN

A correspondence preserved to us between Pliny and the emperor serves as a flashlight to reveal the extraordinary progress made by Christianity in certain parts of Asia Minor in the beginning of the second century. Pliny at the time (AD 112) was proconsul of the extensive province of Bithynia-Pontus. So widely spread was Christianity in this province that the temples were almost deserted, the sacred rites had long been suspended, and sacrificial victims could scarcely find purchasers. Persons of all ages and ranks, and of both sexes, had embraced the new "superstition." Information had been laid before the proconsul, and numbers of Christians had already been put to death. The test applied was to offer wine and incense before the images of the gods and emperor, and to revile Christ. The multitude of the persecutions involved Pliny in doubt as to how he should act, and he referred to the emperor for direction. Trajan's reply in effect was that he was not to look for cases, or receive anonymous information, but if Christians were brought before him and proved obstinate, he was to punish them.

If this letter of Trajan afforded Christians a measure of protection, in other respects it was a distinct worsening of their position. Hitherto Christians had fallen only under the general laws of the empire; now they were, so to speak, singled out as a party definitely proscribed. Their illegal standing was directly affirmed. Henceforth the very name of Christian sufficed to condemn them. On the other hand, Pliny's letter is a powerful vindication of the Christians. Investigation, even under torture, had demonstrated that their proceedings were perfectly innocent, and that all that could be charged against them was (as Pliny judged of it) an absurd and extravagant superstition. The letter throws valuable light also on the worship of the time. The Christians met, it is told, on a "stated day" (Sunday) before daybreak, sang a hymn to Christ as God, and bound themselves by an oath (the pledge of the supper?) to abstain from every kind of crime; in the evening they reassembled to eat a harmless meal (the Agape, now separated from the supper). This latter meeting they discontinued after Pliny's prohibition. Not without reason has this remarkable epistle been called "the first apology for Christianity."

MARTYRDOM OF IGNATIUS—THE IGNATIAN EPISTLES

Ignatius, bishop of Antioch, is the first martyr-hero of whom we have a definite account. The often told story of his condemnation by Trajan, his dialogue with the emperor, his play upon the word "Theophoros" ("God-bearer"), and so on, is derived from old "Acts," and is imaginary. All we really know of the martyr is drawn from his own much controverted epistles. The Middle Ages were familiar with an enlarged and interpolated edition of twelve epistles.[1] From these we glean that Ignatius was tried and condemned at Antioch (c. AD 110), not by the emperor but by the governor, and was sent across Asia Minor under the care of ten guards ("leopards," he calls them) to Rome, to be thrown to wild beasts. The road to Smyrna, where a halt was made, divides into two, a northern and a southern. The martyr was taken by the upper route, but the churches along the lower route were asked to send delegates to meet him at that city. The church of Smyrna at the time was presided over by the holy Polycarp.

This brings us to the origin of the epistles. Before leaving, Ignatius wrote letters to the churches along the lower road (Ephesians, Magnesians, Trallians); one also to the Romans, breathing an ardent desire for martyrdom. The remaining three letters (Philadelphians, Smyrnaeans, and a personal one to Polycarp) were written from Troas, the next important halting place. He passes thence to Philippi, and this is the last glimpse we get of him. The call at Philippi, however, was the occasion of obtaining for us another valuable relic of the period in the Epistle of Polycarp, to whom the Philippians had written, asking for copies of the martyr's letters.[2] In due time Ignatius would arrive at Rome, would be delivered into the proper custody, then when the fete-day came would be led into the blood-stained arena, to meet his death at the jaws of the beasts, amidst the

---

[1] In 1644 Ussher brought to light a shorter Latin edition of seven epistles, and the Greek text of these was discovered soon after (six by Vossius). This corresponds with the number known to Eusebius. In 1845 a yet shorter Syriac edition of three epistles, much abbreviated, was discovered by Cureton; but opinion has now fairly well settled down in favor of the seven Vossian epistles as the genuine Ignatius.

[2] To this is probably due the collection of these letters.

roar of thousands of delighted spectators. His epistles are his legacy—and his photograph. Of warm Syrian temperament, eager and impetuous, a born "impeller of men," yet consumed with a passionate devotion to Christ, which made him not count his life dear to him if, at any cost, he could "attain" to union with his Lord, he is to all ages the typical "martyr."

THE LITERATURE OF THE PERIOD—THE "APOSTOLIC FATHERS"

The name "Apostolic Fathers" is given to a number of writings whose authors were believed to be, in the strict sense, apostolic men, that is, either contemporaries (for example, Clement, Barnabas, Hermas) or disciples (Polycarp, Ignatius) of the apostles. This use of the designation is now abandoned. No one pretends to find in each of the authors of these writings direct personal relationship with the apostles. In another respect, however, these writings are fitly grouped together. They all emanate from the Sub-apostolic age, and represent the thought and feeling of a period in regard to which they are nearly the only Christian monuments we possess. Incomparably inferior to the writings of the New Testament (a fact which the authors themselves were fully aware of), they have yet many beauties and a distinct interest. Leaves and scraps of a lost literature— for such they really are—they are far from lacking in variety of subject and style.

At the head of the list stands the Epistle of Clement to the Corinthians (AD 96).[1] The author, formerly, but mistakenly, identified with the Clement of Philippians 4:3, is the same who appears in the early lists as the third of the Roman bishops (Linus and Anacletus being the first and second), whose fabulous history is given in the Clementines.[2] The occasion was a revolt of the Corinthian church against certain of its elders, which had issued in their forcible expulsion from office. Clement writes in name of the Roman church to urge concord and

---

[1] The dates are approximate only. The complete Greek text of Clement, and of the so-called second Clement, was discovered by Bryennios at Constantinople (1873) in the same volume from which the Didachè was afterwards published (1883).

[2] Some scholars would identify him with Flavius Clemens, but on insufficient grounds.

submission to authority. The tone is one of "sweet reasonableness," yet in parts there is a note of imperiousness.[1] The epistle is an early witness to Paul's (first) letter to the Corinthians, in which the apostle also dissuades from contentions. Its closing chapters (59-60) are a prayer of a distinctly liturgical character. The so-called second epistle of Clement is really an ancient homily or sermon—the first of the kind we possess. It seems to be a read exhortation. Its date may be about AD 130-140. It is a simple edifying production, with here and there a touch of ultra-spiritualizing. A peculiarity in it is the quotation of several sayings of our Lord from an apocryphal source.[2]

A third writing, the so-called Epistle of Barnabas, derives its name from the belief that it was the production of the companion of Paul. Internal evidence entirely negates this supposition. The epistle was written after the destruction of Jerusalem (to which event it alludes), and bears a strongly anti-Judaic character. Yet it is of very early date (AD 70-100). Its literary peculiarities suggest that it emanated from Alexandria. It is marked by excessive fondness for allegorizing, and by a far-fetched, fanciful style of treatment generally. It aims at imparting a higher "knowledge" ("gnosis") in the mystical interpretation of types.[3] Both Barnabas and, in a slighter degree, Hermas incorporate matter found in the earlier chapters of the Didachè—thus raising an interesting literary problem.

The Shepherd of Hermas is our oldest allegory. It has been fitly called the "Pilgrims' Progress" of the early church. It was held in the highest repute in the church; is spoken of even as "scripture."[4] The author was at one time identified with the Hermas of Romans 16:14; but this is now abandoned. An early notice makes him the brother of Pius I, bishop of Rome (AD 140-155). He speaks of himself, however, as a contemporary of Clement of Rome,[5] and the simplicity of the church order in the book agrees with this earlier date (AD 100). Hermas, according

---

[1] Which Dr. Lightfoot not unfairly regards as prophetic of future claims to domination.

[2] Chapters 4, 5, 12; possibly the Gospel of the Egyptians.

[3] For example, Abraham's 318 servants, chapter 9; clean and unclean beasts, chapter 10.

[4] Irenaeus and Origen.

[5] Chapter 4.

to his own account, was the slave of a Roman lady, named Rhoda, who set him free and showed him many kindnesses. His book consists of three parts—Visions, Mandates, and Similitudes. The chief figure in the Visions is the church, represented by a venerable lady, who appears younger in each new vision. In the last Vision the savior appears as a shepherd (hence the name), and bids him write down the commandments and parables he would give him. The Mandates show acquaintance with the Didachè. The Similitudes contain ten parables, and give their interpretations.[1]

The epistles of Ignatius (AD 110) have already been described. Their chief interest is in their bearings on the origin of episcopacy. Allusion has also been made to the origin of the Epistle of Polycarp to the Philippians (AD 110), a beautiful letter, remarkable in a critical respect for the use it makes of 1 Peter and 1 John, and for the authentication it gives to Paul's epistle to the same church. One of the finest of all the post-apostolic writings is the Epistle of Diognetus, which, though it really belongs to the next period (c. AD 150), is best taken here. It found its way into our list from the belief that its author was a disciple of the apostles; then was long attributed to Justin Martyr. The Diognetus to whom it is addressed may not improbably have been the tutor of Marcus Aurelius of that name. It combats idolatry, defends theism, and gives a strong and clear presentation of evangelical truths. One thought dwelt on is the cosmopolitan character of Christianity. "What the soul is in the body, that Christians are in the world."

The "Didachè," or "Teaching of the Apostles" (one of the most valuable "finds" of recent years) has been before us in an earlier connection. It is in part a book of moral instruction, in part our oldest work on church order (baptism, eucharist, offices). The literary relations with Barnabas and Hermas can best be explained by supposing that both the Didachè and Barnabas work up material from an older source—a moral treatise on "the two ways" ("there are two ways, one of life and one of death, and there is a great difference between the two ways"), which, in that case, must go back to apostolic times. The book in its present form may be dated about AD 100.

---

[1] They remind one of Bunyan's Interpreter's House.

There remain certain fragments of Papias, bishop of Hierapolis. Papias was a man of weak judgment, but a diligent collector of traditions about the sayings of our Lord. He wrote a work in five books entitled "An Exposition of Oracles of the Lord," which is alleged to have been still in existence in 1218 at Nismes. It may yet possibly be recovered. Eusebius gives from it well known extracts on the authorship of two of the gospels (Matthew and Mark). Papias was martyred about the same time as Polycarp (c. AD 155).

THE THEOLOGY OF "THE APOSTOLIC FATHERS"

The writings above named have little independent theological worth, but are valuable as reflecting the state of mind in the early church ere theological reflection had yet well begun. The descent from the full and vigorous presentation of doctrine in the apostolic epistles is very marked. There is plentiful use of scriptural language, but often little real insight into its meaning. As if to efface past differences, and emphasize catholicity, there is a studious linking together of the names of Peter and Paul as of equal honor and authority. But the sharp edges are taken off the thoughts of both, with the result that we have what has been called an average type of doctrine,[1] in which common features are retained, and distinctive features tend to be lost.

The christology of these writings is in the main strong and clear. It follows the lines of New Testament teaching on the preexistence, deity, incarnation, and true humanity as well as true divinity of the Son. Hermas has been thought to be an exception, but his ninth Similitude, in which he compares Christ to a "rock" and a "gate"—a "rock" because it is old (so the Son of God is older than all creation, and was the Father's adviser in creation), and a "gate" because it is new (so he was made manifest in the last days that we may enter the kingdom of God through him), should clear him from this imputation.[2] On the doctrine of salvation there is greater vagueness. In some of the

---

[1] See Ritschl.

[2] Professor Harnack makes Hermas a representative of an "adoptionist," in contrast with a "pneumatic," type of christology. There is a tendency in Hermas to confuse "Son" and "Spirit."

writings the evangelical note is feeble and hardly discernible (Hermas and Didachè), in others it is remarkably pronounced (Polycarp and Epistle to Diognetus). By most stress is laid on the bloodshedding, the sufferings, the death of Christ, as the medium of cleansing and redemption, but there is no attempt at explanation.

Pauline phraseology is used, but the Pauline thought is generally blunted, and, under the conception of Christianity as a "new law" (Barnabas, Hermas, Didachè), there is a tendency to obscure the relation of faith and works, and to lay a one-sided emphasis on obedience as the condition of salvation. Forgiveness is connected with baptism; the rule after that is obedience, and good works[1] aid repentance in the covering of sin. "Almsgiving removes the burden of sin."[2] In eschatology, besides retaining the ordinary elements of apostolic doctrine (resurrection, return of Christ to judgment), most of the fathers seem to have been millenarians.[3] This doctrine, especially when bound up with material and sensuous elements, as in Papias, is named chiliasm. The punishment of the wicked is viewed as eternal ("For after we have departed out of the world, we can no more make confession there, or repent any more."[4]

THE IGNATIAN EPISCOPACY

We are brought at this stage face to face with the question of the origin of episcopacy. Two sets of facts meet us: (1) A large body of evidence exists to show that, in the sub-apostolic age, in the churches of the West at least, the constitution was not essentially different from that which earlier prevailed. The churches are ruled by elders or bishops and deacons, and there is no hint of any higher office. Thus, in Clement's epistle, elders and bishops are still the same persons, and these, with deacons, are the only office bearers recognized. This is evidence for both Rome and Corinth. The writer, afterwards called bishop of Rome, makes no claim of the kind for himself. The testimony of

---

[1] For example, almsgiving.

[2] 2 Clement 16.

[3] That is, hold the doctrine of 1000 years' reign of Christ upon the earth (Barnabas, Papias; Didachè speaks of first resurrection).

[4] 2 Clement 8.

Hermas, likewise emanating from Rome, is to the same effect. Hermas knows only of bishops who are also elders. The names are interchangeable. The Didachè bears the same witness, "Choose for yourselves bishops and deacons." A higher order is unknown. Ignatius, in his Epistle to the Romans, fails in any reference to a bishop existing in that city similar to the bishops in Antioch, Smyrna, Ephesus, and so on.[1] This, in so strenuous an upholder of episcopacy, shows that even in his time there was still no monarchical bishop in Rome. Polycarp's Epistle to the Philippians bears testimony of the same kind for Philippi. There was still in that church no office higher than the apostolic bishops and deacons.

(2) When we turn to the remaining epistles of Ignatius different conditions confront us. It will be observed that the evidence under this head relates to the churches of a defined area—Syria and Asia Minor. We find not only a bishop for each church distinct from the presbyters (elders), but the most extravagant exaltation of the office of the bishop. The bishop is as God, and the presbyters as the council of God. Or the bishop is as Christ, and the presbyters are as the council of the apostles. The presbyters are to be attuned to the bishop, as the strings of a lyre to the lyre. The great thing is to be united with the bishop. Without the bishop it is not lawful to baptize or celebrate the eucharist. There is here, therefore, as clearly three grades of office bearers—bishops, presbyters and deacons—as formerly there were two. Other evidence confirms the testimony of these epistles.[2]

How, now, is this state of things to be accounted for, by apostolic authority, or by the operation of natural causes, elevating the episcopate from the presbyterate? It is important, in answering this question, to look precisely at the nature of the Ignatian episcopate. Distinction must be made between the facts to which Ignatius witnesses and the theory he holds. Ignatius was firmly persuaded that in exalting the power of bishops he was taking the best means of securing the peace and unity of

[1] Mr. Gore, therefore, oversteps the evidence when he says, on the strength of a rhetorical expression of Ignatius, that Ignatius knows of "no non-episcopal area."

[2] We have Polycarp, for example, at Smyrna, Papias at Hierapolis.

the church. But it does not follow that bishops had yet all the power he claimed for them. The very vehemence of his advocacy implies that they had not. When facts are calmly considered, it is surprising to discover how little affinity, after all, the Ignatian bishop has to the bishop of the developed episcopal system. (1) He is a purely congregational, not a diocesan bishop.[1] (2) He makes no claim to apostolical succession.[2] (3) He has no sacerdotal functions.[3] Such are the facts—a government by presbyters in the churches of the West; a form of congregational episcopacy in Asia Minor and Syria. By the middle of the second century all the churches would seem to have advanced to the Ignatian stage.

How did the change come about? The theory of a direct appointment of bishops, as a third higher order, by the original apostles is no longer tenable in view of the above.[4] Apart, however, from the objection that the functions of prophets and bishops were distinct, this, even if admitted, would cover only a fragment of the facts. We have seen that even at the beginning of the second century leading apostolic churches had no one man bishop, and it is pure assumption that the bishops of all other churches owed their origin to the "settling down" of travelling prophets. There is not a word of this in Ignatius. There remains the possibility that the system, however introduced, had the sanction of apostles—at least of the Apostle John.[5] Clement of Alexandria has a statement that John went about from place to place establishing bishops and organizing churches. The fact can neither be proved nor disproved, for Clement may

---

[1] Each several church—Antioch, Smyrna, Ephesus, Tralles, and so on—had its own bishop, who, in this respect, differs little from the modern "pastor."

[2] There is no hint of this in Ignatius. Had the idea existed, so keen a defender of episcopacy could not have passed it over.

[3] "There is not throughout these letters the slightest tinge of sacerdotal language with reference to the Christian ministry" (Lightfoot). This should be decisive as to the ideas of the age in question.

[4] Canon Gore, accordingly, would supplement the action of the original apostles by that of "apostolic men"—such apostles and prophets as we read of in the Didachè. We cannot doubt, he thinks, that one of these prophets settling down in a church would become its bishop (pastor?).

[5] Lightfoot.

well be reading back into John's action a meaning from his own times,[1] and we have no clue to the nature of the bishops (a plurality or single). In any case this is hardly an account of the origin of the system.[2]

THE AGE OF THE APOLOGISTS (AD 117-180)

The period of the Apologists is covered by the three remaining names in our list of the "good emperors." They are Hadrian (AD 117-138), Antoninus Pius (AD 138-161), and Marcus Aurelius (AD 161-180). The period is marked externally by intermittent, but severe persecution of the Christians, and by the commencement of written attacks on Christianity; internally by the rise of apology, and the development of Gnosticism and Montanism. Despite persecution, the remarkable progress of the church is continued.

HADRIAN AND ANTONINUS PIUS

The attitude of the versatile emperor Hadrian, in whose reign written apology began, was on the whole not unfavorable to Christianity. There is, however, evidence that both in his reign and that of his successor, though no formal persecution is reckoned, the Christians were continually exposed to harassment

---

[1] Mr. Gore says about Tertullian that we have to acknowledge "a little idealizing" in his statements about the apostolic institution of the episcopates at Corinth and Philippi (page 336).

[2] Of that the simplest explanation is probably the truest. The president of the Council of Elders ("primus inter pares"), as the official representative of the church, having the ordinary direction of business, the conduct of public worship (a sort of archisynagogos), and generally an outstanding man, would naturally acquire a position of prominence in distinction from the other elders. (The "angel" of the Book of Revelation, 2:1, 8, 12, and so on, might find his analogue here. But it is doubtful if an individual is meant at all.) Times of stress and trial, such as came to the church after the death of the apostles, when tendencies to disintegration and schism were rife, would powerfully strengthen his authority. The need of the time was good leaders, strong and stable government, wise direction. Under these circumstances, episcopacy, such as we know it in Ignatius' day, may well have arisen without the assumption of any apostolic interposition.

and outbreaks of violence. A rescript of the emperor to Fundanus, the proconsul of Asia, whose predecessor had written, much as Pliny did, to ask direction, forbids him to receive irregular accusations, or to yield to popular outcry. If Christians are proved to break the laws, they are to be punished, but libellers are to be punished still more severely.[1]

Hadrian nominated to succeed him Antoninus, better known (from his dutifulness in insisting on the deification of Hadrian) as Antoninus Pius. With him was associated during his reign of twenty-three years his nephew, Marcus Aurelius. Antoninus was, however, the acting and responsible emperor. His clemency, uprightness, and affableness of disposition are the praise of all historians. His reign has commonly been regarded as free from the stain of persecution. This is a mistake, though probably the emperor himself was not to blame. It is doubtful whether he is the Antoninus who, when proconsul of Asia, after some Christians had been condemned, and when the rest in great numbers presented themselves at his tribunal, said: "Miserable men, if you desire to die, have you not ropes and precipices?"[2] But the two "Apologies" of Justin Martyr, and his "Dialogue with Trypho"—all of this reign—are indubitable evidence that Christians were everywhere objects of hatred and persecution, and had to endure losses, tortures, and death for their religion.[3]

THE MARTYRDOM OF POLYCARP

We have, however, one undoubted instance of martyrdom in this reign, the details of which, preserved in a contemporary narrative, throw light upon the whole. Polycarp of Smyrna has already been before us in connection with Ignatius. Of his earlier life we know little. He was eighty-six years old at the time

---

[1] It is a moot point whether breaking the laws here means more than the mere proof that one was a Christian.

[2] Tertullian.

[3] For example, Dialogue 110; specific cases in 2 Apology 1.2. Melito of Sardis, another apologist, speaks of numerous edicts issued by Antoninus (for example, to the Larissaeans, Thessalonians, Athenians, forbidding the cities to take new measures against the Christians. This shows that the emperor both knew of these persecutions, and, in accordance with his humane character, took steps to check their violence.

of his martyrdom (AD 155): so may have been born AD 69 or 70. He was a disciple of John, in Asia Minor, and often repeated to the youthful Irenaeus (who was his disciple) the things he had heard from the apostle.[1] The account of his martyrdom is given in a beautiful and affecting letter of the church of which he was bishop. The great festival of Asia was being held at Smyrna. Some cause had aroused the fury of the populace against the Christians. The Jews are specially mentioned as active in the persecution. Several Christians had already perished amidst dreadful torments, when the cry went up, "Let search be made for Polycarp."

Polycarp at first concealed himself, then, on his retreat being discovered, surrendered himself to the will of God. On the way to the city he was taken up into the chariot of the captain of police, who, with his father, urged him to recant. Failing in their object, they thrust him out with violence. Arrived at the stadium, he was interrogated by the proconsul, "Swear by the genius of Caesar; say, Away with the Atheists!" Polycarp, looking to heaven, said, "Away with the atheists!" "Revile Christ," urged the proconsul. "Fourscore and six years have I served him," was the memorable reply, "and he has done me no wrong. How can I blaspheme my King who saved me?" The herald proclaimed, "Polycarp has confessed himself a Christian," and the cry rose to have a lion let loose on him. But the games were ended. The shout then was that he should be burned alive. Polycarp, at his own request, was only bound, not nailed to the stake. It seemed for a time to the wondering bystanders as though the fire refused to touch him. To end the scene, an executioner was ordered to stab him.[2] The poor malice of the Jews frustrated even the desire of the brethren for possession of his body, which was consumed. The bishop's death stopped the persecution, and probably sent many home to think, with the consequence that they became Christians too. Such, at least, we know to have been a frequent outcome of these martyrdoms.[3]

---

[1] On his visit to Anicetus, the Roman bishop, see chapter 8.

[2] The legendary feature of a "dove" issuing from his side is not in the oldest version (Eusebius), and is probably a corruption or interpolation.

[3] Justin, Dialogue 110; 2 Apology 2.12.

THE AGE OF THE ANTONINES—MARCUS AURELIUS

Marcus Aurelius is the classic representative of his age. Vespasian, in the previous century, had instituted a salaried hierarchy of teachers (rhetoricians, grammarians, philosophers) by whom the Romans were to be lectured into wisdom and virtue. The result was a species of ethical, philosophical, and even religious revival in the empire. Paganism had its itinerant preachers,[1] whose orations or harangues were the counterparts of the Christian sermons. These tendencies came to a head in the reign of Marcus Aurelius. For once in the world's history, Plato's dream of a state which had a philosopher for its ruler, and was governed by philosophic maxims, seemed about to be realized. Personally, Marcus is justly reckoned one of the noblest characters of heathenism. His "Meditations" embody the highest ideal of stoical morality, in union with a firm confidence in a rational ordering of the world, characteristic of the later Stoicism.

Yet it is the Stoical, not the Christian ideal. It lacks the tenderness, humility, dependence, benignity, hopefulness of the Christian temper. Between Christianity, with its confession of sin and moral weakness, and Aurelius, with his philosophic self-sufficiency, passive resignation, stern suppression of passion, and cheerless fatalism, there could be nothing but antagonism. There is but one allusion to Christianity in the "Meditations," and it breathes the iciest contempt.[2] Marcus, too, if a Stoic, was a devoted Roman, fixed in his determination to maintain the established institutions. His character was not without its strain of superstition,[3] and it is noted of him that in his latter years his melancholy disposition grew upon him, and he became peculiarly zealous in heathen rites. It is scarcely wonderful, therefore, that, even under this paragon of emperors, "Christian blood flowed more freely than it had flowed any time during the previous half century"—that "in fact the wound was never staunched during his reign."[4] To him is ascribed what we are accustomed to reckon the fourth persecution.

---

[1] For example, Dion Chrysostom, Maximus of Tyre.
[2] Meditations 11:3.
[3] See Froude, Renan, Uhlhorn, and so on.
[4] Lightfoot.

PERSECUTIONS UNDER MARCUS—THE MARTYRS OF VIENNE AND LYONS

There is one story told of Marcus which, if it could be believed, would clear his memory in part of the stain of persecution. It is the story of the thundering legion. Tertullian and others relate that in one of his campaigns the army was in extreme distress from thirst. The Christian soldiers of the twelfth legion prayed, and, in answer to their prayers, copious showers of rain fell, and a violent storm drove away the enemy. Appended to Justin's first Apology is an alleged epistle from the emperor to the senate, ascribing his deliverance to the prayers of the Christians, and commanding that they be no more molested. Unhappily the epistle is not genuine. It seems certain that the deliverance took place, only the heathen attributed it, not to the prayers of the Christians, but to the interposition of their own gods. In the pagan account Marcus is represented as stretching his hands to heaven, and invoking Jupiter.

The positive evidences of persecution in this reign, and of the emperor's implication in it, are not few. At Rome itself there is the case of Justin Martyr and his six companions, who suffered under the prefect Rusticus (a tutor of Aurelius) about AD 163-166. The emperor could hardly have been ignorant of this case. There is the testimony of Melito of Sardis (c. AD 170) to a very severe persecution in Asia Minor. He speaks of God's servants being persecuted as they never were before by "new edicts" which gave the property of Christians to their accusers. Melito professes to doubt whether these edicts emanated from the emperor, but the doubt can only be assumed for the purposes of his appeal. A proconsul would not issue such "edicts" on his own responsibility. Even the heathen Celsus, who wrote in this reign, speaks of Christ as banished from every land and sea, and of his servants as bound and led to punishment, and put upon the stake.[1]

But the chief persecution we know of, which stands out with the distinctness of a limelight picture in its blending of the horrible and the sublime, is that of the churches of Vienne and Lyons in Gaul. It was a case in which Marcus Aurelius was expressly consulted, and gave his sanction to what was done. The account

---

[1] Origen 8.39.

of it is contained in a circular epistle addressed by the churches to their brethren in Asia and Phrygia[1]—"the pearl of the Christian literature of the second century."[2] Lyons and Vienne were two cities of Gaul where the Rhone and the Saone join. Lyons was a great seat of Caesar worship, and the place of the annual meeting of the Gallic deputies in council. The persecution was in AD 177, in the midst of the closing troubles of Marcus' reign. It began with acts of mob-violence; then the prominent persons of the two churches were arrested, and dragged with clamor and insult before the tribunals. Tortures beyond description were applied to the Christians to make them confess to secret crimes, but without effect.

Four names stand out conspicuous for heroism and constancy—Sanctus, a deacon from Vienne; Maturus, a recent convert; Attalus, from Pergamos; above all, Blandina, a slave girl, whose mistress was also one of the martyrs. Blandina was torn and mangled almost beyond recognition without extorting from her more than the words, "I am a Christian; there is nothing vile done among us." The aged bishop Pothinus (ninety years old) was dragged before the judgment seat, and there so cruelly maltreated that, when cast into prison, he lingered only two days. Irenaeus succeeded him. A new round of torments was devised for the others—mangling by wild beasts, roasting in an iron chair, and so on. Blandina was suspended on a stake and exposed to the attacks of wild animals. But they refused at this time to touch her. Attalus, a Roman citizen, was reserved till Caesar's pleasure should be known.

The final scene of the martyrdom was on the day of the great festival. The emperor's reply had come, ordering that such as confessed themselves Christians should be put to death. All who proved steadfast were brought forth to punishment. The Romans were beheaded; the rest were taken to the amphitheater. Again the round of frightful torture was gone through. Attalus, as a specially notable Christian, was, despite his Roman citizenship, roasted in the chair. Blandina herself, after renewed manglings and burnings, was enclosed in a net and given to be tossed by a bull. Thus, last of all her company, she perished.

---

[1] Possibly written by Irenaeus.
[2] Renan calls it.

The knell of slavery was surely rung when scenes like these could be enacted! The rage of the people wreaked itself even on the lifeless remains of the victims. To prevent resurrection they burned them, and scattered the ashes in the Rhone. What strikes one in the pathetic narrative of these sufferings is its tone of calm sobriety—its utter absence of boasting, or spiritual pride, or over-eager desire for martyrdom. Other religions have their martyrs—but have they martyrs like these?

THE RISE OF APOLOGY

The rise of a written apology for Christianity in this age is a fact of great significance. It shows that Christianity had entered literary circles; shows also the growing boldness of the Christians, and their confidence in their ability to refute calumny and vanquish prejudice by an openly reasoned statement of their case. They had the world against them; but their invincible reliance was on the power of truth. They were ready to lay down their lives as heretofore; but they would not let the world remain in blindness as to the nature of the religion it assailed. They set themselves to vindicate Christianity; to expose also the folly and immorality of the pagan idolatry by which it was opposed. The apologetic literature of the second century, therefore, is both voluminous and rich. It covers a wide area in space. Its authors are men of culture and learning, skilled reasoners, many of them philosophers by profession, who, at the cost of their worldly prospects, put their talent and eloquence at the service of the religion they had espoused.

It breathes throughout a tone of dignity and lofty conviction, and must have been a powerful factor in aiding the progress of Christianity it so strikingly describes. Such an apology was demanded, if by nothing else, by the slanders in circulation about the Christians, and almost universally believed (cannibalism, promiscuous immorality, worship of ass' head, and so on). The refutation of these charges is complete. Scarcely less effective is the reply to the charges of impiety and disloyalty; while the exhibition of the truth and reasonableness of Christian doctrine, and of the purity and simplicity of Christian worship and morality, is heightened by the dark background of heathen irreligion and vice against which it is cast. The apologists may be grouped as those belonging to the reign of Hadrian (Quadratus and Aristides), those of the reign of Antoninus (Justin and Tatian), and those of the time of Marcus Aurelius (Athenagoras, Theophilus, Melito, Minucius Felix, and the rest). Tertullian and Origen belong to the next period.

THE EARLIER APOLOGISTS—JUSTIN MARTYR

The oldest apologist, Quadratus, is little more than a name to us.[1] He addressed an apology to the Emperor Hadrian (Athens, AD 125-126?), of which only a single extract is preserved. He lays stress upon the Savior's miracles. The other apologist of this reign, Aristides, was, till lately, even more completely unknown. It was only known that he was a philosopher of Athens, and had also presented an apology to Hadrian (AD 125-126). In 1889, however, a complete Syriac version of this apology was brought to light[2] (two Armenian fragments earlier). Then the remarkable discovery was made that scholars had this apology all the while, and were not aware of the fact. In a famous mediaeval romance, "Barlaam and Josaphat," an apology for Christianity is put into the mouth of one of the characters. This turns out to be substantially the apology of Aristides, of which the Greek text has thus been obtained. The apology is mainly a defence of theism against the errors of paganism, and a powerful vindication of Christian morality. It testifies to the existence of a written gospel. A third writer, Aristo of Pella, reputed author of a lost dialogue between a Christian (Jason) and a Jew (Papiscus), may belong to the end of this reign. The work is before or about the middle of the century.

Greatest of all the apologists of this period whose works have come down to us is Justin the Martyr. From him we have two Apologies, addressed to Antoninus Pius and the Roman Senate (c. AD 150), and a "Dialogue with Trypho," a Jew, a little later in date. Other writings attributed to him are of doubtful

---

[1] Possibly he is identical with Quadratus, an evangelist mentioned by Eusebius (3.37).

[2] The discovery was made by Dr. Rendel Harris, in the Convent of St. Catherine, Mount Sinai. An inscription in the Syriac version puts the apology under Antoninus, but the ordinary date seems preferable. The author knows the Didachè, or the work on which it is based.

genuineness or spurious. Justin was a native of Flavia Neapolis (Sychem) in Samaria. In the introduction to his "Dialogue" he narrates the manner of his conversion. He had gone from one philosophical school to another in search of truth. A conversation with an old man whom he met on the seashore directed him to the scriptures and to Christ. He became persuaded that here was the only sure and worthy philosophy, and, still wearing his philosopher's cloak, thenceforth set himself to impart to others the light he had obtained. We find him at Ephesus and Rome teaching and disputing in his double capacity of philosopher and Christian. His disputes brought him into collision with one Crescens, a cynic, who plotted his death and that of his disciples. Through the machinations of this man, or in some other way, he and his six companions were apprehended. Brought before the prefect Rusticus, they were condemned to death by decapitation (AD 163-166).[1]

Justin's first Apology is in the main a nobly conceived and admirably sustained piece of argument. It consists of three parts— the first refuting the charges against the Christians, the second proving the truth of the Christian religion, chiefly from prophecy,[2] the third explaining the nature of the Christian worship. The second Apology was evoked by a specially shameful instance of persecution under Urbicus the prefect. The "Dialogue with Trypho" is the account of a long disputation at Ephesus with a liberal minded Jew, and meets his objections to Christianity. Incidentally, Justin's writings throw valuable light on many matters of importance, as, for example, on the existence and use of the canonical gospels, called by him the "Memoirs of the Apostles,"[3] on the victorious spread of Christianity,[4] and on the details of the Christian weekly service.[5] The picture of the

---

[1] The "Acts" of this martyrdom are accepted as reliable.

[2] The apologetic argument from prophecy would need to be wholly recast in the light of modern knowledge; yet the scriptures chiefly relied on are those which the church has always accepted as in a true sense Messianic.

[3] 1 Apology 66-67; Dialogue 10, 100, 103.

[4] Dialogue 117. The catacombs too attest this, and show that Christianity had entered the highest ranks (for example, cemeteries of Praetextatus and Caecilia). See Neglected Factors, pages 132 ff.

[5] 1 Apology 65-67.

last is singularly lifelike and minute. The day of worship, as in Pliny, is Sunday, the service is under the direction of a "president" (not even yet by Justin called a bishop), the reading of the prophets and the gospels is an established part of the service, the president delivers a "homily" or discourse, the congregation rise at prayer, and respond to the prayer of the president with an "Amen," the eucharist is celebrated at the close of the prayer after sermon (the Agape probably in the evening), the distribution is made by the deacons, who take portions to the absent, after the eucharist offerings are made for the poor, the sick, prisoners, and so on.

The other apologist of the reign of Antoninus is Tatian, an Assyrian by birth, and disciple of Justin's. He afterwards fell into gnostic heresy. Tatian's apologetic work is an "Address to the Greeks" (AD 150), learned, but bitter, biting, and contemptuous in spirit. He is better known through his famous "Diatessaron," or "Harmony of the Four Gospels," the discovery of which in its complete form in an Arabic translation is one of the sensations of recent years.[1] This finally establishes the character of the "gospels" described by Justin as in use in the churches.

LATER APOLOGISTS

The apologists of the reign of Marcus Aurelius can be more rapidly enumerated. The first, Athenagoras, was, like Aristides, a philosopher of Athens. He is the most polished and classical in style of all the apologists. His apology, entitled "An Intercession for the Christians" (AD 177), is chiefly devoted to the refutation of the charges against the Christians (atheism, eating human flesh, immorality), and is a piece of calm, reasonable, effective pleading. He wrote also a work on the "Resurrection." Theophilus, bishop of Antioch, belongs to the severe school of apologists. He wrote an apology in three books addressed to his friend "Autolychus" (c. AD 180). He can see no good in the philosophers and poets, whose errors and contradictions he shows up in detail. The few grains of truth he finds in them were stolen, he thinks, from the Hebrew prophets. He has some

---

[1] Published in 1888. Latin of an Armenian translation of a Syriac commentary on the Harmony was published in 1876.

forcible chapters on the purity and beauty of the Christian morality. Theophilus is the first to mention the gospel of John by name. The gospel itself, of course, was in use long before.[1] Melito, bishop of Sardis (c. AD 170), has been quoted on the edicts of emperors. His apology to Marcus Aurelius is known only from extracts. It is characteristic of the age that, in addressing the emperor, he speaks of the new religion as "our philosophy." Melito wrote numerous other works. To him we owe also the first Christian list of the Hebrew scriptures, that is, of the Old Testament canon. Hermias, date uncertain, wrote "A Mockery of Heathen Philosophers," still extant. The title explains the character of the work.

Other writers, whose apologetic works are lost, were Apolinarius, bishop of Hierapolis (c. AD 174), and Miltiades, the former the author of "Five Books against the Greeks," addressed to the emperor, the latter of an apology addressed "To the Rulers of this World," with other treatises. Finally, there is the beautiful and able book of the Latin apologist Minucius Felix. There is a doubt, indeed, whether this work should be placed here, or later, after Tertullian; but the presumption is strong in favor of the earlier date.[2] The piece itself is in the form of a dialogue between Octavius and a heathen Caecilius (friends of Minucius, a Roman advocate)—hence its title Octavius. Caecilius states the case for the old faith and Octavius replies. The intrinsic worth of the book is enhanced by its high artistic and literary merit.

OTHER WRITERS

A passing allusion should be made to two other writers of note in this age—Hegesippus, who wrote five books of "Memoirs" some time between AD 175 and AD 189; and Dionysius, bishop of Corinth (c. AD 170), whose fame rests chiefly on his pastoral epistles, of which he wrote a great many. The works of both are lost, but Eusebius has preserved valuable extracts. The "Memoirs" of Hegesippus were not history in the strict sense, but

---

[1] It was included, for example, in the "Diatessaron" of Tatian.

[2] Fronto, for example, who wrote against the Christians in this reign, is spoken of as a contemporary.

appear to have been a collection of reminiscences of the apostolic and post-apostolic ages, drawn partly from written, partly
from oral sources, in part also from the writer's own observation. The author was extensively travelled, and the information
he had to convey would, if we possessed it, be extremely useful.

THE LITERARY ATTACK ON CHRISTIANITY

No sketch of the literature of this period would be complete
which, besides a survey of the apologists, did not include some
reference to the literary opposition to Christianity. It is another
testimony to the growing importance of Christianity that the
age which saw the rise of a formal Christian apology saw also
the beginnings of a formal literary attack of exceptional skill
and keenness. The earliest of the literary assailants we know
of was Fronto, tutor of Marcus Aurelius, who published an
oration in which he reiterated the scandalous charges brought
against the Christians.[1]

A more formidable assailant was Celsus, whose "True Discourse" (c. AD 180) was the subject of Origen's later classical
refutation in his "Eight Books against Celsus" (AD 249). Celsus
is probably to be identified with an (alleged) Epicurean of that
name, an able literary man, and friend of Lucian, who wrote
also against magic. Of wide reading and undeniable acuteness,
he spares no pains to damage and discredit the Christians,
while acquitting them of the graver calumnies that were current. He first introduces a Jew to gather up the slanders of the
synagogue; then in his own name subjects the gospel history
and beliefs of the Christians to criticism and ridicule from the
standpoint of the true philosophy. Everything in Christianity—
particularly its doctrine of redemption—is an offence to him. It
is not too much to say of his work that, relatively to its age, it
was as trenchant an assault as any that has since come from
the artillery of unbelief. Yet, as far as can be seen, its influence
was nil in stopping the triumphant march of Christianity. Its
obvious unfairness and utter insensibility to the holy love and
power of the Christian religion, deprived it of all effect on minds
that knew from experience what Christianity was.

---

[1] His argument is conjectured by Renan to be nearly textually embodied in the discourse of Caecilius in the "Octavius" of Minucius Felix.

Another typical opponent of Christianity in this age was the skeptical and witty Lucian of Samosata, a born hater of shams, but withal cynical and heartless in his judgments on men and things. In his "Peregrinus Proteus" he describes how a cynic charlatan succeeded in imposing on the Christians, and was made the object of their lavish kindness when in prison for his faith. Yet the picture he draws of the attentions of Christians to their unfortunate brethren, intended to cover them with ridicule, in reality redounds to their highest honor. Only Lucian was not the man to see this!

GNOSTICISM AND MONTANISM (AD 117-180)

The external conflict of the church in this period was with paganism. Its internal conflicts were with Gnosticism and Montanism. The conflict with Gnosticism reacted powerfully on the development of theology; the conflict with Montanism did much to strengthen the bands of ecclesiastical authority. But the apologists also, from the nature of their task, had to state and defend Christian doctrines, that is, to theologize. They are our first theologians. They form the link between the Apostolic Fathers, whose theology is as yet naive and unreflective, and the later church teachers, with whom the construction of a system of Christian truth has become a distinct and conscious aim.[1]

THE APOLOGISTS AS THEOLOGIANS

It is usual in recent years to speak of the apologists as teachers of a rational theology (a doctrine of God, virtue, immortality), which misses the distinctive essence of Christianity—to which Christianity is related only as revelation and supernatural attestation. There is color for this judgment, but it is one-sided and defective. From the necessity of their position, the apologists dealt chiefly with the truths of what we may call "natural religion"—the unity and moral government of God, the creation of the world, judgment to come, a future state of rewards and punishments, and the like—and sought to emphasize these in opposition to pagan idolatry, stoical pantheism, epicurean

---

[1] For example, Origen.

indifferentism, and belief in fate. If they gave these doctrines a rational dress, this is explained by their training and habits as philosophers, and by accommodation to the spirit of the age. It would have been out of place in reasoning with pagans to have discussed the interior doctrines of the Christian religion about which the pagans knew and cared nothing.[1]

But the doctrines taught are Christian doctrines (in contrast with Greek and other speculations), and are treated in their Christian aspects and relations. The morality also is the spiritual morality of the gospel. The apologists, one and all, held strongly to the doctrine of the Trinity, and in this connection gave prominence to the doctrine of the Logos ("Word"), the Father's instrument in the creation of the world, who became incarnate in Jesus Christ. This too is scriptural doctrine.[2] The Logos ("Word") was held to be the source of all rational intelligence and wisdom in men, and what portions of truth heathen sages possessed were due to his presence in their minds.[3] In Christ the whole Word was incarnate; hence in him Christians have the full truth.[4] The apologists are witnesses to gospel facts and hopes—Justin especially. From the writings of Justin a great part of the gospel history can be reproduced.

Further, while most of the apologists confine themselves to the general ("rational") truths indicated above, Justin has something to say of the specific Christian doctrines. Man through disobedience has become the child of necessity and ignorance, and has fallen under the tyranny of the demons.[5] Jesus by his sufferings and death has redeemed us from the curse, and obtained remission of sins for those who repent, believe, and keep

---

[1] Compare Paul, Acts 17:23-31, 24:25.

[2] It is to be noted, however, that, while holding Son and Spirit to be truly of the nature of God, they fell short in one important respect of the doctrine of the later creeds. Assuming in some sense an eternal distinction between the Logos and the Father, they yet seem to have believed that the coming forth of the Son (Spirit also) into distinct personal existence (as second "person" of the trinity) was not eternal, but was immediately prior to creation, and with a view to it.

[3] Compare John 1:4, 9.

[4] Justin.

[5] 1 Apology 10.54-61, and following. The heathen world generally is viewed as ruled by the demons.

his commandments.[1] Forgiveness is bestowed in baptism, which is spoken of as "regeneration."[2] A mystical virtue, in like manner, attaches to the bread and wine of the eucharist, which are no longer "common food and drink," but the flesh and blood of Jesus Christ, through which our own flesh and blood are nourished.[3]

GNOSTICISM—ITS GENERAL CHARACTER

Gnosticism is the peculiar heresy of the second century. It is one of the most remarkable appearances of any age. It may be described generally as the fantastic product of the blending of certain Christian ideas—particularly that of redemption through Christ—with speculations and imaginings derived from a medley of sources in a period when the human mind was in a kind of ferment,[4] and when opinions of every sort were jumbled together in an unimaginable welter. It involved, as the name denotes, a claim to "knowledge"—knowledge of a kind of which the ordinary believer was incapable, and in the possession of which "salvation" in the full sense consisted. This knowledge of which the Gnostic boasted related to the subjects ordinarily treated of in religious philosophy; Gnosticism was a species of religious philosophy. Such questions were the relation of infinite and finite, the origin of the world and of evil, the cause, meaning, purpose and destiny of things, the reason of the difference in men's capacities and lots, the way of salvation, and the like. Imagination ran riot in inventing solutions of these problems, and as the answers which would satisfy the Gnostic had no real relation to Christianity, and could not by any rational process of interpretation be educed from scripture, they had to be drawn from it by applying to the sacred text the method of allegory.

---

[1] For example, Dialogue 94-96.

[2] 1 Apology 61, 66, and following. The sacramentarian idea is thus already well established.

[3] 1 Apology 66. Still it is true that Justin regards Christianity, in accordance with the temper of the time, too much as "a new philosophy" and "a new law."

[4] Greek, Jewish, Parsic, Oriental; philosophies, religions, theosophies, mysteries.

It is difficult to give an intelligible account of systems so multiform and continually changing; and hardly any features can be named common to all systems. The following may serve as a general indication. At the head is the ultimate, nameless, unknowable Being, spoken of as the "abyss." Forming a connecting chain between him and the finite creation are the "aeons"[1] proceeding from the highest Being by "emanation." These "aeons," taken together, form the "pleroma," or fulness of the divine (his self-unfoldings). The origin of the world is generally explained by a fall or rupture in the "pleroma," or the descent of some lower or inferior "aeon." Matter is conceived of as inherently evil—sometimes as independently existing. In all Gnostic systems a distinction is made between the Supreme God and the "demiurge" or author of this lower world.[2] The latter is regarded as an inferior, limited, imperfect Being, and is identified with the God of the Old Testament and of the Jews.

The God of the gospel revealed by Jesus Christ is thus invariably contrasted with the God of creation and of the Old Testament. This might almost be said to be the hinge on which Gnosticism turns. Jesus himself is conceived of either as a heavenly "aeon" who descends to earth, clothed with the appearance of a body—a phantasmal body,[3] or as an earthly Messiah, on whom the heavenly "aeon" descends at the baptism, but leaves him again at the crucifixion. Redemption is through knowledge, and is possible in the full sense only to the "spiritual" part of mankind (the "Gnostics"). The rest are either "carnal," wholly incapable of salvation, or belong to an intermediate class[4] who have a modified benefit. In practical operation Gnosticism was sometimes ascetic (mortifying the body, forbidding marriage, and so on); sometimes, as an assertion of the superiority of the spirit to the flesh, it passed over into unrestrained licentiousness.

---

[1] Or "powers," "angels," and so on.

[2] An exception such as that of Bardesenes (Syria) is hardly worth noting.

[3] The Docetists.

[4] "Psychical," soulish.

THE GNOSTIC SYSTEMS

The beginnings of Gnosticism are already manifest in the New Testament.[1] As known in church history, we may distinguish the early gnostic systems, the semi-developed systems (Ophite, and so on), and finally the developed systems (Basilides, Valentinus, Marcion). At the head of gnostic teachers the fathers always place Simon Magus. Claiming to be "the power of God which is called great" (first and chief of the emanations),[2] Simon had associated with him a female companion of low character (Helena), represented as the "power" next in rank to himself, from whom proceeded the makers of the world. The angels detained this "aeon" in the lower world, and Simon descended to redeem her. His disciple was Menander. A sect of Simonians lingered on till the third century. Among early "Christian" Gnostics a prominent place is given to Cerinthus, the contemporary of John.[3] He distinguishes between the lower, earthly Christ born of Joseph and Mary, and the higher, heavenly Christ who descended on Jesus at the baptism, but left him again before his death.[4]

The semi-developed Gnosis is chiefly represented by the remarkable group of systems known as Ophite (from "ophis," serpent). They derive this name from the honor paid to the "serpent" as the symbol of intelligence. The Creator of this world is an ignorant, imperfect Being (Ialdabaoth, "Son of Chaos"), who thinks himself the Supreme God. It is therefore a merit when the serpent persuades the first pair into disobedience of him.[5]

---

[1] Colossian heresy; 1 Timothy 6:20, "gnosis falsely so called"; Revelation 2:24; John's epistles.

[2] Acts 8:10.

[3] It is he of whom the story is told that John, seeing him one day in a bath at Ephesus, exclaimed: "Let us fly, lest the bath should fall while Cerinthus, the enemy of the truth, is in it."

[4] Carpocrates is the first of the openly licentious Gnostics. Christ in his system has no essential preeminence over others. Hence, in the Carpocratian worship, the image of Christ was placed alongside those of other philosophers (first notice of images). The duty of the Gnostic is to show his contempt for the rulers of the world by unbridled indulgence of the passions. The sect was continued by Epiphanes (son of Carpocrates) and Prodicus.

[5] Genesis 3.

The most characteristic of the multitude of sects bearing this name[1] is the Cainites, who reversed all the ordinary standards of moral judgment, choosing as their heroes the persons whom the Bible condemned.[2] The Syrian Gnosis was represented by Saturninus, said to be a disciple of Menander, whose system is marked by strong dualism and gloomy asceticism. He is reputed one of the founders of the Encratite heresy.[3] To this party Tatian fell away after the death of Justin, holding, it is said, with the other Gnostics, a series of "aeons," and a distinction between the Supreme God and the Demiurge.

It is, however, in the developed Gnostic systems that we naturally see the movement in its perfection. The first great name here is Basilides of Alexandria (reign of Hadrian, AD 117-138), who, with his son Isadore taught a system,[4] afterwards considerably modified in a popular direction. Basilides was a man of powerful speculative intellect. His first principle is a Being so abstract that thought cannot give him a name. The world is continuously evolved from a "pansperma" or "seed of the world," in which all things were originally potentially contained. It is ruled by two great Archons, who yet subserve the designs of the Supreme. There are no "aeons," but the highest "light" descends through the successive spheres till it rests in Jesus of Nazareth. The process is complete when the divine element ("sonship") is all drawn out and restored to God; oblivion then falls on lower intelligences. Many fine sayings are attributed to Basilides.[5]

Valentinus, likewise an Alexandrian, taught in Rome (reign of Antoninus, AD 138-161). His system is as imaginative and poetical as that of Basilides is speculative. It is a sort of poem of the exile of the soul. Sophia, the lowest of the "aeons," burns with desire for the knowledge of the Father, and nearly loses her existence in seeking to obtain it. Harmony is only restored in the pleroma through the creation of two new "aeons" (Christ

---

[1] Naasenes, Peratae, Sethites, and the like.

[2] Cain, men of Sodom, Esau, Korah, and the like.

[3] Condemning marriage, and so on.

[4] Compare Hippolytus.

[5] For example, "I will say anything rather than doubt the goodness of providence."

and the Holy Spirit). The expulsion of the product of this disturbance ("achamoth") leads to a repetition of the tragedy in a lower world; and this, in turn, to the formation of our own world, in which, a third time, the drama of fall and redemption is enacted. The redeemer here is "Jesus the Savior"—an "aeon" produced by the pleroma as a thank-offering to the Father for the restoration of their own harmony. He descends on the earthly Jesus, whose own body, however, is wrought of higher substance.[1]

Lastly we have the system of Marcion of Pontus (disciple of Cerdo), who taught in Rome (c. AD 140-155).[2] Marcion is properly classed among Gnostics, inasmuch as he makes an absolute distinction between the God of the Old Testament and the God of the New Testament, is dualistic, and ascribes to Christ only a seeming body. Otherwise his system is wholly unlike those of other Gnostics. He lays, like Paul, the stress, not on knowledge, but on faith. His system may be described as an overstrained Paulinism. The Pauline contrasts of law and gospel, sin and grace, works and faith, are strained till they break asunder, and become irreconcilable antagonisms. The God of the Old Testament (and of creation) is opposed to the God of the New Testament as the "just" God (ignorant, harsh, rigorous) to the "good" God, whose nature is wholly love. Marcion wrote a book on the "Antitheses" between the Old Testament and the New Testament, and drew up also a canon of scripture,[3] which had but one gospel, that is, a mutilated Luke, and ten epistles of Paul. In practice he was rigorously ascetic.[4] Marcion founded a "church," which endured for some centuries. Of gnostic literature[5] the only complete work that remains to us is the book "Pistis Sophia."[6] Some Ophite manuscripts have recently been discovered. For the rest we are dependent on the descriptions and quotations in the fathers.

---

[1] The disciples of Valentinus (refuted by Irenaeus) are Ptolemaeus, Marcus, (a charlatan), Heracleon, who wrote a commentary on John, and so on.

[2] He was later vigorously refuted by Tertullian.

[3] Marcion's "Canon."

[4] Only water, for example, was used in the Lord's Supper.

[5] Apart from apocryphal gospels, and so on.

[6] Ophite or Valentinian gnosis.

MONTANISM

Montanism is another influence that wrought powerfully in the church from the middle of the second century. It is best explained as a reaction against the growing rigidity of church forms, the increasing laxity in church morals and discipline, and the dying out of the spontaneous element in church life and worship. It had its origin in Phrygia, the population of which had naturally a strong tendency to excitement and extravagance (hence the name "Kataphrygians"). The essence of the movement lay in its claim to be a New Prophecy. Montanus gave himself out as a new organ of the Spirit. The Paraclete promised by the Savior had come in him. He was the founder of the new age or dispensation of the Spirit. With Montanus were associated two prophetesses—Prisca, or Priscilla, and Maximilla. It is characteristic of the Montanist prophecy that it was delivered in trance or ecstasy. One of the oracles of Montanus says: "Behold, the man is as a lyre, and I (the Spirit) sweep over him like a plectrum. The man sleeps and I wake."

The content of the prophecy did not affect doctrine, but chiefly practice. The tendency of the sect was severely ascetic, and its view of church discipline was of the strictest (no forgiveness of mortal sin, and so on). Like most movements of the kind, it was strongly millenarian. The place was even named where the New Jerusalem was to descend—the small village of Pepuza, in Phrygia. In its later form Montanism aimed more at being a simple movement of reform in the direction of stricter life and discipline. The antagonism between the Montanists and the church party grew naturally very bitter. The Montanists called themselves "spirituals," and spoke of the catholics as "psychicals"; the latter denounced the new prophecy as Satanic delusion. Local synods were held which condemned the movement and excommunicated its adherents. Notwithstanding the opposition of the church authorities, however, Montanism spread, and attracted a good deal of sympathy from earnest minds.[1]

---

[1] In North Africa it must have obtained a strong hold. Tertullian of Carthage was its most distinguished convert (AD 202)—indeed, its only great man. When, at a council in Iconium (c. AD 233), it was decided not to recognize Montanist baptism, the separation from the church was complete. By Cyprian's time (AD 250) Montanism must have nearly

APOCRYPHAL WRITINGS

The second century was marked by the production, chiefly in Ebionitic and Gnostic circles, of a profusion of apocryphal gospels, apocalypses, and similar works.[1] Such were the Gospel of the Hebrews, the Gospel of the Egyptians, the first form of the Protevangelium of James, the Gospel of Thomas, the Apocalypse, Preaching, and Gospel of Peter, and so on.[2] The Gnostics had gospels of their own.[3] Of the above named, the Gospel of the Egyptians and Gospel of Thomas originated and were in wide use in Gnostic circles. A special interest attaches to the Gospel of Peter, the use of which was forbidden in church in the end of the second century by Serapion, bishop of Antioch, on account of its docetic character.[4] It begins in the middle of the history of the passion and breaks off in the narrative of the resurrection. The gospel implies the canonical accounts, but greatly alters and adds to them. It bears out the charge of docetism. Jesus when crucified "held his peace as though having no pain." His exclamation on the cross was, "My Power, My Power, You have forsaken me," and so on. The Gnostic trail is apparent.

THE AGE OF THE OLD CATHOLIC FATHERS (AD 180-250)

The death of Marcus Aurelius proved how superficial was the ethical revival associated with his reign. The accession of his son, Commodus (AD 180), reopened the floodgates to the worst evils and vices. The period that followed was one of frequent changes of emperors, of rampant military license, of much disorder and disorganization in the state. This was to the advantage of the Christians, in so far as it drew away attention from them, and left the emperors no time to concert measures to their hurt. But it told also to their disadvantage, in placing them

---

died out in Carthage—at least he never refers to it.

[1] "Acts of Apostles" generally later.

[2] A fragment of the Apocalypse of Peter, which stood in high repute in the early church, was discovered in 1892.

[3] For example, the Cainites had a "Gospel of Jude."

[4] An important fragment of this gospel was discovered in 1886 (at Akhmin, Upper Egypt).

more at the mercy of popular tumult and of governors unfavorably disposed. The very calamities of the empire were made a ground of accusation against them. "If the Tiber overflows the walls," says Tertullian, "if the Nile does not irrigate the fields, if the skies are shut, if the earth quakes, if there is a famine or a pestilence, immediately the cry is raised, 'The Christians to the lion.'"[1] Nevertheless, the church during this period made unprecedented progress, and, under the guidance of the great antignostic fathers (Irenaeus, Tertullian, Clement, Origen, and the like), assumed definitely the character of a church catholic and apostolic.

FROM COMMODUS TO SEVERUS—THE SEVERIAN PERSECUTION

During the evil reign of Commodus no systematic attempt was made to molest the Christians. Marcia, the emperor's mistress, was even friendly to the church, and interested herself on its behalf.[2] Yet, as illustrating the general insecurity above referred to, Clement, writing shortly after the close of this reign, could say, "Many martyrs are daily burned, crucified or beheaded before our eyes."[3] Apollonius, a distinguished senator, suffered in this reign.[4] The murder of Commodus was succeeded by a season of confusion, calamity, and bloodshed. Pertinax was killed after a reign of a few months. Then followed a scene of degradation such as the empire had never yet witnessed. The imperial office was put up to public auction on the ramparts of Rome, and unblushingly sold to the highest bidder. The purchaser, Julianus, did not keep his dearly bought honors long. The legions rejected him, and out of the anarchy that ensued Septimus Severus, the Pannonian general, emerged as the strongest man.

The eighteen years' reign of this emperor (AD 193-211) proved him to be an able and vigorous, if also a stern ruler. He was at first favorably affected to the Christians; his Syrian wife, Julia

---

[1] Apology 40.

[2] For example, in procuring the release of certain confessors from the Sardinian mines.

[3] Stromata 2.20.

[4] His "Acts" have recently been recovered. The Scillitan martyrs in North Africa are now also referred to the reign of Commodus.

Domna, a lady of literary and eclectic disposition, was also friendly. It is not clear what led to his change of policy. He may have been influenced by his growing dislike of illegal associations, or by cases of insubordination like that related by Tertullian ("On the Soldier's Crown"), where a soldier refused to wear the ordinary laurel garland in going up to receive his donative from the emperor. In any case, in AD 202, he issued an edict forbidding under severe penalties conversion to either Judaism or Christianity. Thus was initiated what is reckoned as the fifth persecution, though we have interesting proof from a tract of Tertullian, "To the Martyrs" (before AD 202), that even prior to the publication of this edict martyrdom was far from unknown.

The severity of this persecution seems to have fallen chiefly on Egypt and North Africa, and some noble martyr incidents are recorded from these regions. A chief seat of the persecution was Alexandria. Leonidas, the father of Origen, was put to death at this time by beheading; Origen himself, then a youth of seventeen, would have perished also had not his mother forcibly prevented him from giving himself up. Another conspicuous instance was that of the maiden Potamiaena, who, with her mother, Marcella, was, after many tortures, burned to death with boiling pitch. Her constancy was the occasion of the conversion of others, among them of Basilides, the officer in charge. To North Africa—Carthage or Tuburbium—belong the famous martyrdoms of Perpetua and her companions, of which an account is preserved written partly by Perpetua herself. Perpetua was a young married lady, of noble rank, recently a mother, who, for her faith, was thrown into a loathsome prison with four companions. One was a slave girl, Felicitas; the three others were youths—Revocatus, Saturninus, and Secundulus. All were catechumens, and were baptized in prison.

Perpetua's father was a pagan, and sought by the most heartrending entreaties to induce her to recant. She and her companions stood firm, and were condemned to die at an approaching festival. In prison Felicitas was overtaken by the pangs of maternity. When asked how she would bear the keener pain of being torn by the wild beasts, she answered, "It is I who bear my present sufferings, but then there will be One within me to suffer for me, because I too shall suffer for him." The men were torn to pieces in the amphitheater by wild beasts; the women were exposed in a net to be tossed by a cow, and ultimately killed by the swords of the gladiators. The document which tells the pathetic story has in it a tinge of Montanistic enthusiasm, and contains the first traces of prayers for the dead.[1]

SUCCEEDING EMPERORS—THE PERSECUTION UNDER MAXIMIN

The persecution went on through the whole reign of Severus; in the later stages of it some of Origen's disciples suffered. That it continued into the reign of his son, Caracalla (AD 211-217), is evident from Tertullian's address "To Scapula," in which Severus is spoken of as already dead. But that "common enemy of mankind" was too much absorbed in his vices to trouble about the Christians, and persecution gradually stopped. Under the wicked and effeminate Syrian emperor Elagabalus, nephew of Severus (AD 218-222), the Christians were also allowed peace. Elagabalus had been high priest of the Sun at Emesa, in Syria, and now imported into Rome the lewdest excesses of the Syrian Sun and Astarte worship. He had a settled design of blending all worships with his own, and, as a step to this, every foreign religion, including Christianity, was tolerated.[2] Elagabalus was cut off before the full effect of his plans could be seen, and the church for the first time enjoyed a season of real favor and protection under his gentle and virtuous cousin, Alexander Severus (AD 222-235).

Alexander profitably divided the hours of his day between private devotion, assiduous attention to public business, the cultivation of his mind through literature and philosophy, manly exercises and rational and refined intercourse in the evenings. In religion he was an eclectic. The bust of Christ was placed in his private chapel alongside of those of other persons held in special reverence—Abraham, Orpheus, Apollonius, and so on; and he had inscribed on the walls of his palace and public

---

[1] There is a trace as early as Hermas of purgatorial suffering.

[2] Other influences may have been at work, for we find Hippolytus addressing a treatise to Julia Aquila, the second wife of the emperor. She may therefore be presumed not to have been unfriendly to Christianity.

monuments the maxim, "What you would not have others do to you, do you not to them." This maxim, it is said, he was constantly repeating. Under the reign of such an emperor the position of Christianity was practically that of a "religio licita." The mother of Alexander, Julia Mammaea, who exercised a considerable influence on the government, was also deeply interested in Christianity, and invited Origen to confer with her at Antioch. A reign like Alexander's, however, was naturally displeasing to the rude military, and an unfortunate Persian war led to his murder, and to the accession of the Thracian savage, Maximin (AD 235-238). Under this tyrant occurred what is known as the sixth persecution.

Maximin seems to have been moved in his rage against the church chiefly by hatred of his predecessor. His acts were directed at first only against the heads of the churches. Origen, as a friend of Julia Mammaea, was marked as a victim, and had to flee from Caesarea. Anti-Christian fury, however, once let loose, did not readily confine itself within limits, and the church suffered severely in different places, especially in Cappadocia and Pontus, where destructive earthquakes had awakened the passions of the populace.[1] The times of confusion that followed (the reigns of the two Gordians, of Balbinus and Maximus of Gordian III, AD 238-244), yield nothing for our purpose. During this period the Christians enjoyed a respite, which was continued and even confirmed by the next emperor, Philip the Arabian (AD 244-249). Philip was the son of a Bedouin robber chief—called, therefore, "Philip the Robber"—but he has the distinction of figuring with some ecclesiastical writers as the first Christian emperor. Both he and his wife Severa had correspondence with Origen. It is certain that he looked with very favorable eyes on Christianity, without, however, showing any trace of its influence in his public conduct. At the great secular games (for example, in celebration of the completion of the thousandth year of Rome's existence—which was the great feature of his reign) the ceremonies were entirely pagan. Philip was slain in conflict with Decius (AD 249).

---

[1] A beautiful work of Origen on Martyrdom relates to this persecution.

PROGRESS OF CHRISTIANITY IN THIS PERIOD

The astonishingly rapid spread of Christianity in this age is one of the most remarkable facts about it. The apologetic writers (Tertullian and Origen) give the strongest expression to their consciousness of coming victory. "Men cry out," says Tertullian, "that the state is besieged; the Christians are in the fields, in the ports, in the islands. They mourn, as for a loss, that every sex, age, condition and even rank is going over to this sect."[1] Origen, in the reign of Philip, writes, "Every form of religion will be destroyed except the religion of Christ, which will alone prevail. And indeed it will one day triumph, as its principles take possession of the minds of men more and more every day."[2] With every allowance for rhetorical exaggeration, it is impossible to doubt that Christianity was taking root throughout the empire with a rapidity and vigor that astonished both friends and foes.[3] It included not only great numbers of the population, but persons of all ranks in society. There were Christians of high standing in the households of the emperors.[4]

The very suddenness with which the existence of large and influential churches like those of Carthage, Alexandria and Lyons bursts upon us in this period is evidence of the marvelous energy of propagation Christianity was displaying. It is not, therefore, to be wondered at that the writers of the period point exultantly to this astonishing progress and draw from it an argument for the divineness of their faith. The boast of Tertullian in his "Apology" is, it should be remembered, that of a contemporary: "We are but of yesterday, and yet we have filled every place belonging to you—cities, islands, castles, towns, assemblies, your very camps, your tribes, companies, palace,

---

[1] Apology 1.

[2] Against Celsus 8.68.

[3] The church had spread, in greater or less measure, from Britain in the west to the Tigris in the east, from the Rhine in the north to the Libyan desert in the south. It had extended itself in Gaul and Spain and North Africa, in Asia Minor, in Mesopotamia, in Arabia. It had penetrated across the Danube into the tribes of the barbarians.

[4] The rebukes administered by Tertullian and Clement to the wealthy and luxurious in the churches prove, what other testimonies bear out, that many in these classes had received the gospel.

senate, forum; we leave you your temples only. . . . All your ingenious cruelties can accomplish nothing. Our number increases the more you destroy us. The blood of the martyrs is their seed."[1] However rhetorically colored, there must have been a strong basis of truth in such representations to procure for them any acceptance.

DEVELOPMENT OF THE IDEA OF THE OLD CATHOLIC CHURCH

In its conflicts with Gnosticism and Montanism—especially the former—the church was meanwhile undergoing an internal development which more than paralleled its marvelous outward extension. In combating Gnosticism the fathers were not waging war with an ordinary foe. They had, as we have already seen, to deal with a system which spurned the literal acceptance of the gospel facts, and, under pretence of a higher wisdom, transformed them into a phantasmagoria of its own creation; which attacked the fundamental doctrines of the Christian faith.[2] In waging this conflict, moreover, they labored under the very peculiar difficulty that there was as yet no universally recognized standard of truth to go by—no fixed canon of scripture, no fixed creed, no fixed court of appeal in matters of faith such as the council afterwards became.

What bulwark was to be reared against this innovating tide of speculation? That was true which was apostolic;[3] that was false—at least not authoritative—which could not claim apostolic sanction. This thought was applied by the fathers of the age specially in three ways.[4] They applied it (1) to an apostolic collection of scriptures—the idea of a New Testament canon. We have seen that the gospels were already read in Justin's day in the ordinary service of the church; collections of apostolic

---

[1] Apology 37, 50.

[2] The identity of the God of creation and the God of redemption, of the God of the Old Testament and the God of the New Testament, the true humanity of the redeemer, the reality of sin and atonement, and so on.

[3] Dr. Hatch has pointed out that the idea struck out by the church as giving it firm footing in this sea of controversy was that of the "apostolic."

[4] Thus Harnack.

letters were also very early formed.[1] Such collections, however, grew up naturally, informally, with a view to edification, and not with the idea of forming what we mean by a canon of scripture for the whole church. The conflict with Gnosticism gave a new turn to this conception. The first attempt at a formal canon of New Testament scripture we know of was the mutilated canon of Marcion. Other Gnostic and Ebionitic sects were flooding the church with apocryphal writings.

Under these circumstances, as well as to find a solid basis from which to repel the assaults of opponents, it was of the first importance for the church, not only to gather the true scriptures together, but to lay emphasis on that which gave them their claim to authority. This was their apostolic origin and character, that is, their origin either directly from apostles or from men immediately belonging to the first apostolic circles, and having apostolic sanction for their work. Thus sprang up in the latter part of the second century the conception of a definite canon of New Testament scripture—of a "New Testament," as it begins expressly to be called, which takes its place beside the "Old Testament" as of equal validity and authority with it. Lists are now drawn up of the sacred books;[2] and the fathers show the clearest consciousness of dealing with a code of writings of inspired character and authority. Tertullian is the first to use the name "New Testament," though the designation seems implied earlier in certain expressions of Melito of Sardis; Irenaeus usually speaks simply of the "scriptures."

The category of the apostolic was applied (2) to an apostolic "rule of faith"—the idea of a traditional creed. It was soon manifest that in controversy with Gnostics the appeal to scripture was not always so conclusive as it seemed. Even where scripture was not rejected the Gnostics had their own way of interpreting it. Their use of allegorical methods (to which the fathers themselves gave too much countenance) enabled them to get from the text as much support for their theories as they pleased. The question was no longer as to the canon of scripture, but as to the sense to be drawn from scripture when they had it. It was here that the fathers stepped back from the written

---

[1] 2 Peter 3:16; compare free use of epistles in Polycarp, and so on.
[2] For example, the canon of Muratori.

word to the constant and steadfast tradition of the truth which had been maintained in the church since apostolic days.

From earliest times the church had employed a simple baptismal confession. This had become enlarged till in the second century it assumed substantially the outline of our present Apostle's Creed. A form of this kind was certainly in use in the church of Rome before the middle of the second century; and the forms in use in other churches show, with variation and paraphrase, essential agreement. This form, gradually crystalizing into settled shape, was laid hold of by the church and erected into a "rule of faith," which, standing behind scripture, could be employed as a check on the wanton license of Gnostic interpretation. It was not intended to supersede scripture, but to corroborate it; still it marks the introduction of that principle of "tradition," as regulative of faith, which, at a further remove from the primitive source, became the parent of so many abuses.

Finally, this thought of the apostolic was applied (3) to an apostolic succession of office bearers in the church—the idea of a continuous historic episcopate, viewed as depository and guardian of the aforesaid tradition. It was not enough that there should be apostolic tradition; there must be some guarantee for the secure transmission and purity of the tradition. This was presumed to be found in the continuous succession of bishops from the days of the apostles. Lists of the succession of bishops in the greater churches are carefully given by the fathers in proof that this transmission of apostolic tradition is a possibility and reality. There is clearly here an unhistorical element; for it has already been shown that bishops, in the sense supposed, do not go back to apostolic days.[1]

---

[1] The bishops in Ignatius are never represented as successors of the apostles. It is in this form, that is, as a guarantee for the purity of tradition, that the doctrine of an "apostolic succession" of bishops first enters. It has not yet the sacerdotal associations of the next age. Already, however, there has now distinctly shaped itself, as the result of the above process, the idea of a catholic church, that is, a church resting on the "fides catholica et apostolica," and finding its unity in the episcopate, which is regarded also as the depository and guardian of its sacred tradition. From this time, accordingly, the term "catholic church"—already found in Ignatius, but simply in the sense of universal—gets into currency (Tertullian, Clement, Muratorian fragments, and so on). It

THE OLD CATHOLIC FATHERS (AD 180-250)

The chief interest of the period whose external history and internal development we have sought to describe is connected with the names of its great teachers. These form a galaxy of rare brilliance. The study of their works is at the same time the study of the theology and literature of the age.

IRENAEUS OF GAUL

The personal notices of this great father are scanty. He was born about AD 120, perhaps a little later; was a native of Asia Minor; in early life was a disciple of Polycarp, the disciple of John. In an epistle to his fellow pupil Flornius, who had lapsed into Gnosticism, he speaks of the vivid recollection he retained of Polycarp's discourses, and how they agreed with what was related in the scriptures. He was a presbyter in Lyons during the persecution under Marcus Aurelius in AD 177. The Montanist controversy was raging, and Irenaeus bore an intercessory letter on behalf of the Montanists from the martyrs to Eleutherus, the bishop of Rome.[1] After the martyrdom of the aged Pothinus, Irenaeus, as the fittest man, was chosen bishop in his place.[2] The only other occasion on which he comes into view is a few years later (AD 190-194) in connection with the action of Victor of Rome in the Quarto-Deciman controversy. The date of his death is uncertain (AD 202-203?).[3]

His one literary monument is his great work,[4] in five books, "Against Heresies," directed specially against the Valentinians (AD 180-190). It exists only in an early Latin translation; portions of the Greek, however, are preserved by other writers. The author's theological opinions are developed incidentally,

---

needs only the Cyprianic idea of the priestly character of its clergy to complete it.

[1] Eusebius 5.4.

[2] Lyons would appear at this time to have been the only bishopric in Gaul.

[3] All through Irenaeus showed himself a man of peaceful and conciliatory spirit—in marked agreement, Eusebius says, with his name ("peaceful").

[4] Besides fragments.

but sufficiently to show that Irenaeus had a theology of a very definite and organic character. The central thought in his conception of Christianity is the incarnation. Creation needs the incarnation for its perfecting. Only through the entrance of the Word (Logos) into humanity could man be led to his destination as a son of God. Irenaeus has no dubiety as to the eternal existence of the Word.[1] Redemption is brought under his favorite idea of a recapitulation of humanity in Christ. Christ is the compendium of the race; sums up the nature, the experiences, the history of mankind in himself. His obedience retracts the disobedience of the fall. As our head he wins for us a complete victory over Satan. He enters into our lot and doom as sinners, and ransoms us by his death.[2]

TERTULLIAN OF CARTHAGE

Tertullian is the first of the great Latin fathers, and founder of Latin theology. His general place in the history is about twenty years after Irenaeus. He follows Irenaeus closely in his antignostic polemic and doctrine of the church. The two men, however, are as different as can well be conceived. The calm, temperate spirit of Irenaeus bears no resemblance to the fiery, impetuous nature of the North African father. No impartial person will doubt his deep or sincere piety; yet the fire within him burned often with a murky flame. Tertullian was born at Carthage probably about AD 160. His father is said to have been a proconsular centurion, and he was educated for the law. His life till manhood was spent in heathenism, but its follies and pleasures left his soul unsatisfied. His conversion to Christianity may have been about AD 192. He probably became a

---

[1] "The Son has always existed with God, has always revealed the father, has always revealed the full Godhead" (Harnack).

[2] A trace only is discernible of the theory afterwards developed that Satan through the fall obtained rights over men which had to be respected. In eschatology Irenaeus is crudely Chiliastic (Antichrist, the first resurrection, the New Jerusalem, the 1,000 years' reign, and so on). His sacramental teaching conforms to the now well-established catholic type. The Eucharistic elements, for example, are "antitypes" of the Lord's body and blood; yet there is a real mystical union of these elements with the body and blood of Christ, so that in receiving them the communicant is nourished by the latter.

presbyter of the church at Carthage. We know that he was married, and that his wife also was a Christian.

The decisive event in his career was his conversion to Montanism (AD 202). Thereafter his relations with the church were embittered, and he withdrew from its communion.[1] It is doubtful, however, how far this withdrawal went. It is certain that Tertullian always regarded himself as belonging in a true sense to the catholic church, and there are evidences that towards the end of his life the asperities softened. His death is placed at AD 220-240. Whatever his faults of temperament, Tertullian's ability as a Christian advocate is second to none. His literary activity was prodigious. His pages sparkle with brilliant and original thoughts; are, indeed, for vigor, terseness and mastery of literary expression unsurpassed in patristic literature.[2] His writings are usually divided into those written before and those written after he became a Montanist, though it is doubtful to which class some are to be referred.

To the first period (AD 197-202) belong the tract "To the Martyrs" (AD 197), the "Apology" (AD 198-199), to which two books, "To the Nations," are related (possibly as an earlier sketch), the beautiful tract "On the Witness of the Soul,"[3] with a number of short treatises—"Tracts for the Times," as they have been happily called—dealing with questions arising out of the life of the time, and with practical subjects.[4] These shorter pieces especially exhibit a mixture of argument, wit, sarcasm, raillery, very characteristic of Tertullian. Though not yet a Montanist, his standard of judgment is always severe. The second period (after AD 202) reflects his changed attitude to the church, and shows Tertullian at his best and his worst. The resources of his rhetoric, his brilliant antitheses, his Christian zeal, his powerful and often convincing reasoning, command admiration; on the

---

[1] Against Praxeas 1.

[2] Cyprian's admiration of him was such that it is said a day never passed without his calling for some of his works, saying, "Give me the master."

[3] The germ of which lies in "the soul naturally Christian" of the Apology 17.

[4] For example, on "The Spectacles"; on "Idolatry"; on "The Attire of Women"; two treatises "To my Wife," discussing second marriage; on "Penitence," "Prayer," "Patience," and so on.

other hand, his faults of temper and argument are often glar-
ing. Here, again, we have to distinguish between his shorter
occasional pieces called forth by special circumstances,[1] and his
longer controversial works. The principal of those are his great
work, in five books, "Against Marcion," and his treatise "Against
Praxeas."[2] Reference should be made also to his forcible tractate "To Scapula" (the proconsul), in which, AD 212, he powerfully champions the cause of the whole of the Christians.

Tertullian's abiding services to the church are those which he
rendered as apologist and theologian. The "Apology" of Tertullian is by universal consent regarded as his masterpiece. It is
addressed to the emperor, and is a noble piece of pleading. The
opening chapters are introductory; they urge that Christianity
is hated because it is unknown. The body of the "Apology" is
divided into two parts—the first refuting the charges against
the Christians (first the popular calumnies of killing infants,
practicing incest in their assemblies, and so on, then the capital
charges of irreligion and disloyalty to the emperor); the second
describing in beautiful words the simple, spiritual, and orderly
character of the Christian worship, and the real nature of the
much maligned love-feast. The closing portion replies to objec-
tors, and reminds of coming judgment.

As a theologian Tertullian left his deep stamp on after thinking. He practically created the Latin ecclesiastical tongue, and
gave to theology many of the terms which have become its
permanent possession.[3] On the Trinity he followed the views of
the apologists in not attributing to the Son an eternal personal
existence. The Trinity is an internal divine "economy" or dispensation, with a view to creation and redemption. He follows
Irenaeus pretty closely on the doctrines of man and the incarnation. Man was made after the image of the future incarnate
One.[4] The earlier appearances of the Son to the patriarchs are

----

[1] For example, on "The Soldier's Crown," on "Flight from Persecution," on "The Veiling of Virgins," on "Single Marriage," on "Fasting,"
and so on.

[2] Other works, "Against Hermogenes," "Against the Valentinians,"
and so on.

[3] For example, one substance, three persons, satisfaction, merit, New
Testament, rule of faith, and so on.

[4] Christi futuri in carne.

"rehearsals" of the incarnation. Tertullian has a much deeper view of sin than obtained in the Greek church; but his ideas of penitential satisfaction obscure grace, and give a gloomy tinge to his theology.[1]

THE ALEXANDRIAN SCHOOL—PANTAENUS AND CLEMENT

Alexandria was, next to Athens, the city of the Greek world in which intellectual tendencies of every sort met and commingled. It was to be expected, therefore, that in this busy center the attempt would early be made to unite Christianity with what was best in the thought and culture of the time. This, accordingly, is what we see taking place in the famous catechetical school at Alexandria. It is characteristic of the Alexandrian school that it takes up a genial attitude to heathen learning and culture; regards Greek philosophy and science as in its way also a providential preparation for the gospels; seeks to meet an antichristian gnosis by a better gnosis, which grows out of faith and love. It is speculative, liberal, idealistic in spirit; in its scriptural methods allegorical, though not to the subversion of the history, as in the heretical Gnosticism.

Of the founder and first teacher of this school, Pantaenus (c. AD 180), we know very little. He was a Stoic philosopher, well trained in Greek learning, and the first, Origen says, who applied this learning in Christian instruction. His school was designed for catechumens, that is, those in training for baptism, but many heathens who desired instruction attended. Either before or after his catechetical labors he travelled widely in the East as an evangelist, penetrating as far as India,[2] and finding there, it is said, a copy of the Gospel of Matthew (in Hebrew), which had been left by Bartholomew. His most distinguished pupil was Clement, who succeeded him as head of the school in AD 189. Clement of Alexandria was born, probably at Athens, AD 150-160. Brought up in paganism—he speaks even of his initiation into the mysteries—he undertook a series of travels in pursuit of truth, but found no rest till he met with

---

[1] The words, "This is my body" in the supper are explained, "This is the figure of my body"; but a real presence in the elements is presupposed.

[2] Arabia Felix?

Pantaenus.[1]

His own genius gave new luster to the school over which he presided for thirteen or fourteen years, till the persecution of Severus (AD 202) compelled his withdrawal. From this time Clement is well-nigh lost sight of. He is supposed to have died about AD 220. Throughout he may be regarded as contemporary with Tertullian. Clement's genius is cast in a mould totally different from that of the other fathers we have named. He was, like Tertullian, a man of amazing learning, but he applied his learning in quite another way. He has none of the austerity of the Carthaginian father; but was soaring, poetic, idealistic, large and sympathetic in his views of truth. On the other hand, his power of reducing his ideas to logical order and connection is limited. His thought loves to roam free and unfettered, and his style in writing is exuberant and discursive.

Of the known works of Clement we are fortunate in possessing the three greatest—which, yet, in their connection form one work. They belong to the period of his work in Alexandria, and give a good idea of his instruction. They are entitled respectively "The Address to the Greeks" (aiming at conversion from paganism), "The Paedagogue" or "Tutor" (a manual of moral discipline, entering into minute details of conduct), and "The Stromata" or "Miscellanies" (initiating into the higher knowledge). These follow, he tells us, the method of the all-glorious Word, who first addresses, then trains, and finally teaches.[2] The "Stromata," while dealing largely with the relations of faith and knowledge, do not give much help in apprehending Clement's theology.[3] The central idea is the Logos (Word) as the enlightening source of all truth in humanity.[4]

---

[1] That "Sicilian bee," he says, "gathering the spoil of the flowers of the prophetic and apostolic meadow," engendered in his soul a deathless element of knowledge (Stromata 1.2).

[2] Paedagogue 1.1. The Word is the "Paedagogue."

[3] Had we possessed his "Outlines" (a lost work) we might have been in better case.

[4] The Logos is eternal, but the Trinitarian distinctions are so idealistically conceived as almost to lose their personal character. Even the sacraments are apprehended in a highly ideal way. Clement prepares for Origen by teaching a preaching in Hades for those who died without opportunity of repentance here (second probation), as well as for the

ORIGEN

Origen was the favorite pupil of Clement, as Clement had been the disciple of Pantaenus. We can hardly err in recognizing in him the greatest of the teachers of the early church—one of the greatest minds the church has seen in any age. Origen was born at Alexandria in AD 185. His parents were both Christians. He showed remarkable ability as a boy, committing to memory large portions of scripture, and often perplexing his father, Leonidas, by the questions he asked. His father reproved him, but in secret thanked God for such a son, and often, while he slept, kissed his breast as a temple of the Holy Spirit. When the persecution broke out (AD 202) his father was one of the first victims. Origen labored to support the family, and managed to collect a small library. His reputation was such that, on the withdrawal of Clement, he was induced, though only a youth of eighteen, to take the oversight of the school and give instruction in it (AD 203). The persecution still raged, and many of his early pupils suffered martyrdom. Origen, however, was nothing daunted, and his labors were crowned with remarkable success. To procure subsistence, as he would receive no payment, he sold his valuable collection of classical books.[1]

His period of labor in Alexandria lasted for twenty-eight years (AD 203-231). It was broken by visits to Palestine,[2] in the first of which he taught in the churches; in the second (extended to Achaia), AD 228-231, he was ordained presbyter.[3] These steps drew down on him the displeasure of the narrow minded bishop Demetrius, and compelled his departure from Alexandria. A

---

righteous through the law and philosophy, that is, just men, both Jews and gentiles, who died before the advent.

[1] He went further, and taking literally the injunction in Matthew 19:12, he performed an act of self-mutilation, which he lived bitterly to regret. In order better to qualify himself for his work, he took lessons in philosophy from Ammonius Saccas, the founder of the Neo-Platonic school. He learned Hebrew also to prepare him for his biblical studies. IIis course embraced arts and letters as well as studies properly theological. These preparatory studies he subsequently handed over to a colleague.

[2] AD 215-218.

[3] Shorter visits were paid in this and the subsequent period to Rome, Arabia, and so on.

council convened by the bishop excommunicated and deposed him (AD 231). The bishops in Palestine and elsewhere treated this sentence as null. The second period of his work was at Caesarea, where he opened a school on a still larger scale, and conducted it with even more brilliant success. His labors at Caesarea, broken only by a brief withdrawal during the persecution of Maximin (AD 236), continued for nineteen years (AD 231-250). Origen was apprehended, imprisoned and tortured in the persecution of Decius (AD 250). He was released in AD 251, but died from the effects of the torture in AD 253,[1] at the age of sixty-nine.

It is impossible to give more than an indication of this father's extraordinary literary labors. During his later residence at Alexandria he wrote many of his "Commentaries," and also his book on "First Principles"—our first work on systematic theology. A wealthy layman, Ambrose, provided him with the means of carrying on his labors on the most extended scale, gave him shorthand writers, and so on. A colossal work, which occupied him for twenty-eight years, was his "Hexapla," a collation of the Septuagint with the Hebrew text, and three other Greek versions (the Hebrew being printed also in Greek letters as a sixth column). The work, except the Septuagint part, has perished. To Caesarea belong "Homilies," treatises on "Prayer," "Martyrdom," and so on. In AD 249, in the reign of Philip, he wrote his great work in eight books, "Against Celsus"—the noblest apology of the early church. It has already been hinted that his expositions of scripture give large scope to the allegorical method.

As a theologian Origen shows a speculative genius hardly equalled. He distinguishes between what belongs to the rule of faith (to which he adheres) and points which the doctrine of the church leaves undetermined; and claims for his speculations on these points only tentative and provisional value. He emphasizes in the Trinity the "eternal generation" of the Son; on the other hand, lays such stress on the hypostatic distinction, and subordination of Son and Spirit to the Father, as almost to dissolve the divine unity. He speaks even of the Son in relation to the Father (absolute deity) as "a second God." As God,

---

[1] AD 254?

he thinks, must eternally have worlds on which to display his omnipotence, he teaches eternal creation. There is a preexistence of souls, and sin is explained by a fall of souls in this preexistent state. There was one pure soul that did not fall, but clave in love to the Logos. This is the soul of Jesus. Thus Origen explains the sinlessness of Christ. Redemption he regards under many points of view—among them that of a deception of Satan, who cannot retain the soul of Jesus, given him as ransom price for men. Origen is the first pronounced restitutionist in the church. All souls and worlds, he thinks, will yet be brought back to God.[1]

THE CHURCH OF ROME IN THIS PERIOD—HIPPOLYTUS AND CALLISTUS

Many circumstances combined to exalt the church of Rome in the second century to a position of exceptional preeminence.[2] This preeminence was, however, solely one of respect and honor. It did not mean that the church of Rome was as yet allowed any real authority or jurisdiction over other churches. The aim of the bishops of Rome, on the other hand, was to change this position of honor into one of actual authority. Every claim of this kind was, by other bishops, strenuously resisted. A case which makes this clear, and at the same time marks a stage in the claims of the Roman bishop, is that known as the Quarto-Deciman Controversy or dispute about the time of keeping Easter. In Asia Minor the churches began and finished their celebration on one day—the fourteenth day of Nisan, or day of the Jewish Passover, on whatever day of the week it might fall. They held that this was the custom handed down to them from the apostle John. Rome and the churches of the West, on the other hand, followed not the day of the month but the day of the week. They began on Friday of the Passover

---

[1] The daringness of some of these speculations involved the church in much after trouble (Origenistic controversies). Apart from his theological views, Origen is a valuable witness to Christian facts. He bears witness, for example, to the usage of the church in infant baptism, and traces the custom back to the apostles. Tertullian, on the other hand, advised delay.

[2] The political capital, antiquity and apostolic character of church, wealth and liberality of members, and so on.

week (Good Friday) and ended on the Easter Sunday morning. The matter was discussed in a friendly spirit between Polycarp, of Smyrna, and Anicetus, bishop of Rome (c. AD 155), without, however, a settlement being arrived at. It was the occasion of a sharp controversy in Asia Minor itself between Melito of Sardis and Apollinaris of Hierapolis (c. AD 170). Melito defended the Asiatic practice. But the most important stage in the controversy was in AD 190-194, when Victor, a haughty and imperious man, was bishop of Rome. Victor issued a mandate requiring conformity to the Roman practice; then, when protest was made, threatened the excommunication of the Asiatics. This assumption of authority was too much even for many who agreed with Victor in principle, and immediate remonstrances were made. The chief of these was from Irenaeus, who, in a letter to Victor, earnestly reproves him for his arrogance.[1]

The bishops next in succession to Victor were Zephyrinus (AD 200-218) and Callistus (AD 218-223), regarding whom (especially the latter) there is a curious story to tell which is best connected with the account of another great church father— Hippolytus. Hippolytus has had a most singular fate. A voluminous and learned writer, and one of the most conspicuous figures in the Roman church of his day, he seems afterwards to have dropped almost entirely out of view. Two interesting discoveries in modern times have restored him to our knowledge. First, his statue was dug up in Rome in 1551 (on the back of the chair his Easter cycle and list of his writings); and second, in 1842, his long-lost work, in ten books, "A Refutation of all Heresies," was recovered.[2] The first book had long been attributed to Origen, under the name "Philosophoumena;" the second and third books are wanting in the manuscripts, but the rest of the work is nearly entire. A valuable feature in the book is the original light it throws on the system of Basilides. But by far its most interesting service is its account of the state of the Roman church under the two bishops above named, and of Hippolytus' own relation to them.

---

[1] Irenaeus was successful in his protest, and the excommunication was not carried out. The Roman custom was ultimately affirmed at the Council of Nicaea (AD 325), though not till it had become generally accepted throughout the churches.

[2] Published in 1851.

Hippolytus in early life was a hearer of Irenaeus in Gaul or Rome. Later he headed a party of opposition in Rome to the bishops Zephyrinus and Callistus, whom he accuses at once of doctrinal heresy and of scandalous laxity in discipline.[1] Zephyrinus he describes as a weak and illiterate man, covetous and accessible to bribes, and in the latter part of his life completely under the influence of Callistus. The latter used him for his own purposes, and among other things inclined him to the adoption of the Patripassian heresy, then being actively disseminated in Rome. The account of Callistus is in the highest degree unfavorable. Originally the slave of a Christian master, he embezzled the funds of a banking business; fled, and, when about to be captured, tried to commit suicide; was sent to the house of correction; later, for a disturbance in the Jewish synagogue, was banished to the Sardinian mines, and so on. We next find him in the confidence of Zephyrinus, who set him over the cemetery ever since called by his name. On the death of Zephyrinus, he had influence enough to get himself appointed as bishop in his place.[2]

The difficulty is to know what position precisely Hippolytus himself occupied. He assumes the office of bishop and withholds that designation from Callistus; speaks of Callistus only as head of a school. A late and worthless tradition makes him bishop of Portus—the seaport of Rome. He was more probably really a rival bishop to Callistus, set up by his own party—the first of the long line of antipopes. Yet, all unwitting of his real history; the church later canonized him as a saint! The remaining fact of his life of which we can speak with certainty is that he and the bishop Pontianus were transported to Sardinia in the persecution of Maximin (AD 235). Some kind of reconciliation must have taken place, for the bodies of both were brought back to Rome about AD 236-237, and deposited in their respective sepulchers on the same day (13th August). Besides the work on heresies, we have from Hippolytus a treatise "Against Noetus," and minor works and fragments.

---

[1] Book 9.

[2] His scandalous administration is pictured in the darkest colors by Hippolytus.

CYPRIAN OF CARTHAGE—COMPLETION OF IDEA OF CATHOLIC CHURCH

Cyprian is the last of the old catholic fathers, and he marks the transition to the next period. Cyprian is not great as a theologian, but he is a great churchman. To him belongs the distinction of having placed the copestone on the edifice of the old catholic church which we have seen being built up by many hands from the days of Ignatius. His personal history presents us with a career of splendid self-sacrifice. Cyprian was born at Carthage, about AD 200, of noble and wealthy parents. Previous to his conversion he was distinguished as a teacher of rhetoric. He was won to Christ about AD 245 through the instrumentality of an aged presbyter, Caecilius, who directed him to the study of the Bible. Cyprian gave proof at once of the thoroughness and decision of his profession by taking Christ's command literally, and voluntarily selling his fine estate for the benefit of the poor.

Baptism followed rapidly on conversion, and was signalled by his adoption of the name of his spiritual father, Caecilius. In a writing of this period, "To Donatus," Cyprian gives a beautiful description of the effects of his conversion, and of the contrast between Christianity and heathenism in a moral respect. He was shortly after ordained a presbyter, and a little later—only two years after his baptism—was compulsorily raised by popular acclamation to the dignity of the bishop. His elevation gave deep offence to the presbyters who had been passed over. Five presbyters objected to his ordination, and to the jealousy thus created is to be traced most of his after troubles. Thus at the very beginning of his Christian course Cyprian found himself at the head of the clergy of North Africa.

In AD 250 the storm of the Decian persecution broke on the church, and Cyprian thought it prudent to withdraw for a time that he might better direct the affairs of the church, and prevent it from being deprived of its head.[1] He returned to Carthage in AD 251, when the persecution had ended through the death of the emperor. In AD 252 came the great pestilence, which afforded opportunity for a display of Christian devotion and

---

[1] Of the troubles which arose out of this persecution and the difficulties in which they involved Cyprian, we shall speak in the next chapter.

charity such as paganism was incapable of. A scheme was drawn up for the systematic visitation of the city; a ministry of help was organized; some undertook the work of nursing and burial; and through their unremitting efforts a general pestilence was averted. Under the Vallerian persecution, AD 257, Cyprian was banished to a city some forty miles distant. A year later (AD 258) a more severe edict was issued, and he was sentenced to death by beheading. The martyrdom took place on a level plain near the city in presence of a vast concourse of spectators, all of whom, even the pagans, did him reverence.

Cyprian, as said above, was less a theologian than a great church leader. The trying circumstances in which he was placed, and the oppositions he had to encounter, forced on him the task of strengthening to the utmost the bonds of church unity, and of seeking, in argument with his opponents, a dogmatic basis for that unity. The chief works in which this basis is set forth are his eighty-one epistles (a few not his), and, above all, his treatise on "The Unity of the Church"—the Magna Charta, as it has been called, of the old catholic and high church conception. Cyprian's doctrine of the church may be summed up in three points. (1) The unity of the church as represented by the episcopate.[1] (2) The priesthood of the clergy. The distinction of clergy and laity becomes absolute.[2] (3) With all this Cyprian held firmly

---

[1] Cyprian gives this a new grounding in basing it on the promise of Christ to Peter (Matthew 16:18-19). Peter, however, only represents the unity of the church in a symbolical way. It is not the bishop of Rome only, but the whole body of the episcopate, which inherits Peter's prerogatives.

[2] Cyprian is the first to give this conception fixed and definite shape. The way had long been preparing in the development of the idea of sacramental grace, and especially of the eucharist as a sacrifice. The sacrifice in the eucharist was originally the spiritual sacrifice of prayer and thanksgiving, or the offering up of the worshipper himself. The idea was extended to the gifts from which the elements of the supper were taken; then to the elements. Now that the idea was established of a real mystical presence of the Lord's body and blood in the elements, it was natural that the conception of the sacrifice should change. The sacrament becomes a real offering up of the body and blood of the Lord—a renewal of the sacrifice on the cross. Thus the idea of the sacrifice as a sin offering, and of the priest as an offerer at the altar (in the Jewish and Pagan sense), becomes established in the church. The clergy are a

the autonomy of each bishop in his own church.[1] From the above positions follows logically the conclusion which Cyprian now boldly draws, that out of this visible, episcopally organized church there can be no salvation.[2] Hence schism is the worst of sins; excommunication dooms the soul to perdition.

THE AGE OF THE GREAT PERSECUTIONS (AD 250-324)

It is a curious coincidence that the completion of Rome's millennium should also mark the beginning of its downfall. The Gothic invasions had commenced even in the reign of Philip; in that of Decius (AD 250-251) they spread frightful desolation through Rome's fairest provinces. The turning point in the history of the church is not less marked. Everything seemed going prosperously. It appeared as if an easy and peaceful victory were about to be achieved. But observant eyes, like Origen's, saw that this season of respite was only the calm before the storm of a great final struggle. The breaking of that storm was not long deferred. Hitherto there had been severe and distressing persecutions, but they had been more or less local and limited in range. Now the empire woke up to see that the very existence of paganism was at stake, and for the first time we have systematically planned and strictly universal persecutions.

THE DECIAN AND VALERIAN PERSECUTIONS

The Emperor Decius was a Roman of the old school. His two years' reign ended in a defeat by the Goths, in which he and his army perished miserably in a morass; but they were years fraught with important consequences for the Christians. Decius was a persecutor, not from impulse but from settled policy. He honestly believed that the salvation of Rome lay in the old

---

priestly class, mediating between the people and God, and conveying grace to the people from God.

[1] He resisted all arrogant pretensions on the part of the bishop of Rome. On the question of the rebaptism of heretics, for example, he came into violent collision with Stephen of Rome (AD 255-256), who wished to impose his own views on the churches of North Africa. The pope's unqualified primacy gets little help from the fathers of this age.

[2] Extra ecclesiam nulla salus.

institutions, and that Christianity, as a rival power, could not be too speedily or effectually crushed. He is credited with the saying that he would rather have a second emperor by his side than the bishop of Rome. He was therefore scarcely established in the empire when he launched the edict which inaugurated what is deemed the seventh persecution (AD 250). He does not seem at first to have desired the death of the Christians. His policy was to terrify them by citing them before tribunals and requiring them to recant; then, if they proved obstinate, to coerce them by imprisonments, confiscations, tortures, exile. It was only when these measures failed that the extremest tortures and death were inflicted on confessors, and especially on the bishops.

The persecution edict was sent throughout the empire and rigorously enforced. Christians who did not appear before the tribunal on an appointed day were to be sought after, and brought before a commission composed of the magistrate and five of the principle citizens. The edict fell like a thunderbolt on the church.[1] Multitudes in time of peace had joined the church who had no deep rooted piety; and these, especially the wealthier classes, now fell away in large numbers.[2] Special names had to be invented to designate the classes of the lapsed ("sacrificati," those who had sacrificed; "thurificati," those who offered incense; "libellatici," those who for payment obtained a certificate that they had sacrificed though they had not done so; and "acta facientes," those who without certificate pretended they had sacrificed). Many, however, did not apostatize, but submitted to be tormented with heat, hunger, and thirst in their prisons, stretched on the rack, torn with hooks, burnt with fire, and finally put to death.[3]

---

[1] The epistles of Cyprian, his "Treatise on the Lapsed," and a letter of Dionysius of Alexandria (Eusebius 6.41) give us vivid pictures of the persecution, but show also how ill-prepared the church was to meet it.

[2] Dionysius pictures them approaching the altar, pale and trembling, as if they were going to be sacrificed instead of to sacrifice, while the populace who thronged around jeered them.

[3] One of the first victims of the persecutions was the aged Fabian, bishop of Rome. For more than a year after this no bishop of Rome could be elected. Other distinguished sufferers were Babylus of Antioch and Alexander of Jerusalem, Origen's friend. Origen himself, it will be

It is, however, under the more important reign of the next emperor, Valerian (AD 254-260), that we come to what is usually numbered as the eighth persecution. Valerian was a man of unblemished virtue, and for the first four years of his reign was not unfavorably disposed towards the Christians.[1] The change seems to have been brought about by a dark minded man, Macrianus, who had acquired great influence over him. The reign of Valerian was the most calamitous the empire had yet experienced; this also had doubtless its effect. The persecution that ensued exceeded even that of Decius in severity. Its first stage was in AD 257, and went no farther than to remove bishops from their churches, and forbid Christian assemblies on pain of death; the second stage (AD 258) was far more drastic, decreeing that office bearers of the churches should immediately be put to death, persons of rank should be degraded, and, if they persevered, should be put to death, noble women and persons of lesser rank should suffer confiscation and banishment.[2]

EFFECTS OF PERSECUTIONS—SCHISMS OF FELICISSIMUS AND NOVATIAN

A delicate and difficult question for the church, as soon as the severity of the persecutions had abated, was the restoration of the lapsed. These formed a wide class, and among them were included many shades and degrees of guilt. Multitudes had little real sense of their sin in apostasy, and were indisposed to brook delay in restoration. The evil was aggravated by faction,

---

remembered, was imprisoned and tortured. The death of the emperor set him free. The persecution broke out again under his successor, Gallus (AD 251-254).

[1] His house is described by Dionysius as "filled with pious persons, and a house of God" (Eusebius 6.36).

[2] One of the first to suffer was again the bishop of Rome, Sixtus, who was beheaded in his episcopal chair. We saw that Cyprian suffered in this persecution. In Spain we read of a bishop and two deacons being burned alive in the amphitheater. The persecution came to an end with the captivity of Valerian in Persia (AD 260). How little all these persecuting edicts had done to destroy Christianity is shown by the fact that the first step of his frivolous son and colleague, Gallienus (AD 254-68), was to restore to congregations their right to worship, and give bishops permission to return to their charges. Christianity thus became once more practically a "religio licita."

and by a practice which had grown up of allowing confessors a right of intercession for the fallen, and even of granting certificates of peace with the church. In Carthage especially this privilege was abused beyond all bounds. The result was two schisms—one at Carthage, the other at Rome, the latter of which, at least, had important historical consequences.

Cyprian's view on the restoration of the lapsed tended to strictness; he was at any rate opposed to action till a council could be called to settle deliberately terms of readmission. It will be remembered that a party of opposition to Cyprian existed in Carthage—the result of jealousy at his ordination. The head of this party was a presbyter, Novatus, who had already shown his disregard for Cyprian by ordaining one Felicissimus as his deacon. These threw in their influence with the advocates of lenity, and received back all and sundry to church fellowship. Novatus shortly after went to Rome, where we find him assuming the opposite role of a leader of the strict party. Cyprian gradually softened in his views, but without effect on the opposition. Felicissimus openly revolted against his authority, and refused to receive a delegation which Cyprian had sent to inquire into the necessities of sufferers by the persecution. At a council held in AD 251 Felicissimus was condemned, and at a second council[1] milder rules were adopted. The party of Felicissimus now set up a bishop of their own, named Fortunatus, and the schism was complete. It seems to have had no permanent success.[2]

At Rome a much graver contest was being waged. Cornelius, the bishop elect, was opposed by Novatian, a man of somber temper and rigorous principles, who resisted all readmission of the lapsed to the church communion. He did not deny that the penitent might receive mercy from God, but held that the church had no power to grant it. Novatus, from Carthage, threw himself into this new strife, and, on the rejection of Novatian, persuaded his party not to accept Cornelius as their bishop, but to elect a bishop for themselves. Novatian was chosen opposition bishop, and a rival church was formed which developed into a great organization, spread into many

---

[1] AD 252.

[2] A third (Novatian) bishop was afterwards set up.

countries,[1] and continued for centuries, with a great reputation for piety.[2] Novatian was a genuinely able and learned man, as his work on "The Trinity" shows. Following the schisms, embittered disputes arose on the rebaptism of heretics. These, as formerly mentioned, brought Cyprian into collision with Stephen, bishop of Rome (AD 255-256). Cyprian, with the North African church, took the stricter view (insisting on rebaptism); Stephen took the milder. The more charitable view ultimately prevailed.

EMPIRE AND THE CHURCH TILL DIOCLETIAN—NEO-PLATONISM

The death of Gallienus in AD 268 left the empire in a state bordering on ruin. From this period a rapid succession of emperors held sway whose main task it was to clear the provinces from the barbarians that infested them. They were mostly men of obscure rank, of Illyrian extraction (hence known as the Illyrian emperors), and of great bravery and skill. The only one that need be mentioned here was Aurelian,[3] who achieved a series of brilliant triumphs in the east and west, but made himself odious by his pride and severity. He was zealous for the maintenance of pagan rites (was himself a devoted worshipper of the sun), and was on the point of subscribing an edict for the persecution of the Christians when he was cut off by conspirators. Some allege that the edict was actually issued. It is this, nevertheless, which is reckoned as the ninth persecution—a persecution, it will be seen, only on paper. The murder of the Emperor Numerian in AD 284 opened the way for Diocletian, with whom a new era in the empire begins.

During all this period (apart from the danger under Aurelian), as well as during the first nineteen years of the reign of Diocletian (till AD 303), the church enjoyed peace. This is known as the forty years' peace, and, while it lasted, the church continued to grow in numbers, wealth and influence, but also in worldliness and corruption. Large and magnificent churches began to be erected, greater splendor was introduced into the

---

[1] Gaul, Africa, Asia Minor, and so on.

[2] Epiphanius, for example, mentions that in Thyatira there were no catholics for a hundred and twelve years.

[3] AD 270-275.

services, church offices were multiplied, and so on. Christians were found in the highest positions in the palace. In the same proportion church discipline was relaxed, and the old evils from which the Decian persecution had done much to purify the church returned in full tide. Reference may be made here to a new form of opposition which had sprung up on the philosophical and literary side, namely, Neo-Platonism. This philosophical form of faith, while bitterly hostile to Christianity, is the strongest testimony to its influence.[1] The founder of this school, Ammonius Saccas of Alexandria,[2] was born of Christian parents, and, indeed, for a time himself professed Christianity.[3] The problem which Neo-Platonism set itself to solve was the union of the finite and the infinite; and its means of bridging the opposition of the two was "ecstasy."[4]

THE DIOCLETIAN PERSECUTION

The last and most violent of all the persecutions that overtook the Christians (the tenth persecution) was that in the reign of

---

[1] It no longer poured unqualified ridicule on Christianity, as Celsus had done, but dealt with it in an eclectic spirit, condemning only its exclusive claims. "We must not," said Porphyry, "calumniate Christ, but only pity those who worship him as God."

[2] Died AD 243.

[3] A trace of Christian influence may be seen in the Neo-Platonic doctrine of the trinity, which, however, has little in common with the Christian, but is wrought up from Platonic elements.

[4] The most illustrious teachers of the school after Ammonius were Plotinus (died c. AD 270) and Porphyry (died AD 304). Porphyry wrote a book entitled "Discourses against the Christians," of which fragments are preserved in the fathers who replied to it. Some of his objections to the books of scripture (for example, to the Book of Daniel) anticipate modern critical attacks. A literary opponent of a coarser stamp, generally reckoned to this school, was Hierocles, prefect of Bithynia (afterwards of Alexandria), a cruel persecutor of the Christians. His book, "Truth-loving Words to the Christians," attempts to disparage the character and miracles of Jesus by comparison with those of Aristaeus, Pythagoras, and the pagan miracle worker, Apollonius of Tyana. Eusebius wrote a reply to it. The school afterwards degenerated into theurgy and magic (for example, Jamblichus of Chalcis, who died c. AD 330). Its last famous teacher was Proclus of Constantinople, the commentator on Plato (died AD 485).

Diocletian (AD 303-313). Diocletian, the son of a slave, introduced changes into the organization of the empire of far reaching importance. He assumed personally the style of an Oriental
despot; divided the empire into two parts (West and East), with
an "Augustus" for each; changed the seat of the empire from
Rome to the new capitals, Milan (West) and Nicomedia (East);
further, subdivided the empire by associating with each "Augustus" a "Caesar," who was in due course to succeed to the higher
dignity. In pursuance of these arrangements, Diocletian (East)
associated with himself Maximian, in AD 286, a rude but able
soldier (West), and in AD 292 added, as the two Caesars, Galerius, originally a herdsman, and Constantius Chlorus, father of
Constantine the Great. To consolidate the relations Constantinus was required to put away his wife Helena (mother of Constantine) and become son-in-law of Maximian, while Galerius
became the son-in-law of Diocletian. Constantinus received
the rule of Gaul and Britain, and Galerius had Illyria.

If Diocletian did not molest the Christians during the first
nineteen years of his reign (his own wife, Prisca, and daughter,
Valeria, were reputed Christians) it was not from any love of
their religion. But Diocletian was a wary, politic man, and
knew better than most what a conflict with Christianity which
was to end in its suppression would mean. The real instigator
of the persecution was the low bred, ferocious Galerius. Diocletian long held back, but, plied with arguments by Galerius
and the pagan nobles, he at length gave way, and a persecution
was agreed on, to take effect on 23rd February, AD 303. There
was to be no halting or turning back, but measures were to be
taken for the entire suppression of Christianity. Proceedings
began at daybreak on the day named by the demolition of the
magnificent church at Nicomedia (one of the architectural ornaments of the city), and the burning of all copies of the scriptures
found in it. Next day an edict was issued giving the signal for a
general persecution. All churches were to be demolished; all
copies of the scriptures were to be burned; Christians holding
official positions were to be degraded and deprived of civil
rights; others were to be reduced to the condition of slaves;
slaves were to be made incapable of receiving their freedom.

The first edict (AD 303) was aimed, it will be observed, rather
at the churches and the scriptures (a new policy) than the persons

of the Christians; disobedience was punished by degradation, not by death. A second edict (AD 303) ordered all clergy, without option of sacrifice, to be thrown into prison. Some time after a third edict was issued, yet more severe. The clergy in prison were required to sacrifice; if they did not, they were to be compelled by every means of torture. Finally, in AD 304, a fourth edict extended this law to the whole body of the Christians. The most fearful tortures were inflicted on the Christians to compel them to submit, and though death was not mentioned in the edict, it was freely inflicted.[1] The sweeping severity of this persecution is apparent from the rehearsal of the edicts alone. Their publication, as in the Decian persecution, caused indescribable consternation. Immediately on the publication of the first, a soldier rashly tore it down with opprobrious words; for this act he was roasted over a slow fire. Fires that broke out in the palace were blamed on the Christians, and led to many being burned, beheaded and drowned. Formerly trusted chamberlains of the palace were put to death. Diocletian's own wife and daughter had to clear themselves by sacrifice.

Special panic was created by the order for the surrender and destruction of the sacred scriptures. The scenes of the Decian persecution were repeated in new forms. Multitudes hastened at once to give up their copies of the scriptures; some palmed off on the officers worthless and heretical writings; others, more enthusiastic, not only retained their scriptures, but boasted of their possession, and challenged the magistrates to do their worst. Those who for any reason gave up their scriptures were branded with the name traditors, and the antagonism to these afterwards gave rise to a new schism—that of the Donatists. The later edicts still further tried the faith and patience of the Christians. In Gaul and Britain, first under Constantinus, then under Constantine, the Christians enjoyed comparative peace. But throughout the rest of the empire the persecution raged with dreadful cruelty. Egypt and Palestine were specially afflicted.

In AD 305 Diocletian abdicated, but this rather made matters worse for the Christians. Galerius, the chief promoter of the persecution, was now emperor, and his creatures, Severus and Maximin, in West and East respectively, were entirely devoted

---

[1] As we see from Eusebius.

to his interests. The revolt of Maxentius in Italy (AD 306) was favorable to the Christians in so far as it was his interest to attach them to his side; and with the defeat of Maxentius by Constantine at the Milvian Bridge, AD 312, persecution in the West may be said to have ended. In the East, under the savage Maximin, it went on with intensified severity till AD 311, when a welcome relief came. In that year the arch-persecutor, Galerius, smitten with a dreadful internal disease, was moved to make peace with the Christians, and issued an edict of toleration, granting full liberty of opinion and worship. This was followed in AD 313 (after a provisional edict in AD 312) by the famous edict of Milan of Constantine and Licinius. Maximin himself, defeated by Licinius, likewise issued an epistle in which he granted full liberty of worship. One reason he gives for the persecution is that the emperors "had seen that almost all men were abandoning the worship of the gods, and attaching themselves to the party of the Christians."[1] Thus on every hand the persecution was admitted to have failed, and Christianity emerged triumphant.

CAREER AND CHARACTER OF CONSTANTINE—VICTORY OF CHRISTIANITY

To judge fairly of Constantine, distinction should be made between the period before he arrived at supreme power and the period that succeeded. In the early period his character and conduct stand before us in a most favorable light. The son of Constantinus Chlorus and Helena (said to be the daughter of an innkeeper), he was born at Naissus, in Dacia, probably in AD 274. After his mother's divorce he continued to reside at Nicomedia as a hostage for his father's loyalty. He joined his father in Gaul in AD 305, and was proclaimed emperor by the troops in Britain on the death of Constantinus in AD 306. Galerius, however, only granted him the rank of "Caesar." At the courts of Diocletian and Galerius he seems to have been a general favorite. His high reputation was maintained in Britain and in Gaul. He was tall and commanding in appearance, affable in manners, just and tolerant in his rule, pure in his personal morals. He was a man undoubtedly of large ambitions, but these rested on a conscious ability to rule.

---

[1] Eusebius 9.9.

From the first he was a protector of the Christians, and, as he sped on from victory to victory in their interests, it is perhaps not wonderful that in their eyes, and in his own, he should come to be regarded as a sort of second Cyrus—a special instrument raised up by God for the deliverance of his church. In AD 305 Maxentius, the son of Maximian, had (with his father) usurped the supreme power in Italy. His reign was one of intolerable oppression. A historical battle was fought between Constantine and Maxentius at the Milvian Bridge, about nine miles from Rome, AD 312, which issued in the defeat and drowning of the latter. It was on the march to this battle that Constantine had his famous vision of the cross, which some speak of as his conversion. He saw, or believed he saw, a cross in the sky, above the brightness of the sun, bearing on it the words "by this conquer." The same night Christ appeared to him in sleep, and directed him to make a standard of like pattern, which should be to him a token of victory.[1]

The Roman world was now divided between Constantine and Licinius (an "Augustus" of Galerius), and the final struggle could not be long delayed. In AD 313 the two emperors issued jointly the Edict of Milan, already mentioned. In AD 314 two battles were fought, in which Licinius was worsted. A truce of eight years followed. In this interval the mind of Constantine was clearing, and not a few of his laws show a Christian impress. Licinius, on the other hand, took the side of paganism, and the last war, in AD 323, was avowedly waged in the interests of the old religion and the old gods. "The issue of this war," said Licinius, "must settle the question between his god and our

---

[1] The incident was narrated on oath by Constantine to Eusebius. There is nothing improbable in the supposition that the emperor may have seen an appearance in the heavens which his excited imagination construed into a cross; or that in the agitation of his mind, on the eve of so critical a contest, he may have had such a dream as he describes. If his mind was already pondering the question of the acceptance of Christianity, this becomes the more probable. The sacred standard—the labarum—was at least made, and the monogram of Christ was displayed on shields and helmets of soldiers, and on gems and coins. Even yet, however, Constantine was very dimly instructed in the real nature of Christianity. Christianity, indeed, was never much more to him than a system of Monotheism and providence.

gods." The decisive victory at Hadrianople (AD 323), therefore, was well understood to be a victory for Christianity. In the following year[1] the Christian religion was established.[2]

THE DONATIST SCHISM

Even before arriving at full power Constantine had been asked to adjudicate in an ecclesiastical dispute arising out of the persecution in Carthage. Mensurius, bishop of Carthage, had given offence to the stricter party by evasive conduct when called on to surrender his scriptures and in other ways. They could accomplish nothing in his lifetime, but when his successor, Caecilian, was elected, in AD 311, they broke out in revolt under the leadership of one Donatus, accused Caecilian of having been ordained by a traditor Felix, and, at a synod attended by seventy bishops, set up a rival bishop in the person of Majorinus. Appeal was made (by the Donatists) to Constantine to have the question determined whether Felix was really a traditor; and a series of investigations were held (AD 313-316), including one by the Council of Arles (AD 314), and a final inquiry by the emperor himself (AD 316)—all with the same result of clearing Felix and upholding Caecilian. Majorinus died in AD 315, and was succeeded as bishop by a second and greater Donatus, from whom the sect specially takes its name. Donatus proved utterly irreconcilable, and Constantine was provoked to order the party into banishment. This edict he recalled next year (AD 317). Donatism continued to spread, and, by the end of Constantine's reign, was able to summon a synod of two hundred and seventy bishops. It became a rallying point for all the forces of discontent in the district, and gave rise to outrageous manifestations in the roaming bodies of Circumcellions (or "round the cottages"), whose violence spread terror through the country. The better Donatists, of course, repudiated these abuses. The party was still powerful in the days of Augustine (fifth century).

---

[1] AD 324.

[2] The nature of this settlement, and some of the later events of Constantine's reign, on which dark shadows rest, are touched on in the next section.

ESTABLISHMENT OF CHRISTIANITY—CONSTANTINE'S LATER YEARS

The Christians not unnaturally were as men that dreamed at the great revolution which had taken place in the state of their affairs. By one turn of the wheel they saw themselves raised from the lowest depths of abasement and suffering, and their religion placed on the throne of the empire. When, however, we speak of the establishment of Christianity by Constantine, we must beware of importing into that phrase the associations of modern alliances of church and state. On the one hand, the position of the church in its relation to the empire was very different from that held by the pagan religion. The old Roman religion was part of the state; it had no independent existence, no rights, no jurisdiction of its own. Its officers were state officials, and the emperor himself was Pontifex Maximus. In fact the Roman state establishment was not abolished till the reign of the emperor Gratian, near the end of the century (AD 382).

The Christian church was in quite a different position. It had grown up independently of the state, and possessed a vast organization of its own. It had its own office bearers, its own laws, its own canons of discipline, its own councils, and so on. It was an "imperium in imperio" which the state did not create, but could only recognize. On the other hand, no formal alliance was entered into between church and state such as we are familiar with in modern times. The establishment of Christianity was not an act done at once, but grew up from a series of proclamations, letters, edicts, enactments, gifts, appeals in disputes, meetings of councils, and so on, and only gradually took shape as time went on. The following are some of the chief heads: (1) There were proclamations of the emperor, publicly announcing himself a Christian, restoring their liberty to the Christians, ordering restitution of property, and recommending the Christian religion to his subjects. (2) The emperor encouraged everywhere the building and repairing of churches, contributing liberally from his own funds to the expenses. (3) He extended his Christian legislation and increased the privileges of the clergy. One important measure was the legalizing of the decisions of the church in civil disputes where parties preferred to take their case before the bishops. Another was the conferring on the church the right to receive bequests. (4) The public acts of the state were purified from pagan associations, and conformed to Christian principles. A law had already been passed in AD 321 enforcing the civil observance of Sunday ("dies solis") to the extent of suspending all legal business and military exercises on that day. (5) The emperor exercised the authority which the church conceded to him of summoning councils for the settlement of doctrinal disputes, and otherwise took part in ecclesiastical affairs. The chief example of this was the summoning of the great Council of Nicaea, in AD 325, to decide the Arian controversy. (6) While Christianity was thus protected and privileged, paganism was tolerated, or suffered to dwindle away under the shadow of royal disfavor, except in special instances, where rites of a licentious character were forcibly suppressed.[1]

It does not fall within the limits of this sketch to recount the later events of Constantine's reign. Even in this later period it is just to acknowledge that Constantine is distinguished by many great and striking qualities. His life remains unstained by private vices; he maintained, with slight exception, the policy of toleration with which he set out; he took a sincere interest in the progress of the Christian cause, and labored to the best of his knowledge and ability for the peace and unity of the church.[2] On the other hand, it is not difficult to see in him a growing elation and complacency in himself as an instrument chosen by God to fulfil his purposes—a consciousness not sufficiently tempered by the feeling of personal unworthiness. With this tendency to self-elation went a strong dash of personal vanity and growing love of splendor, seen not only in the adornment of his person in robes of Oriental sumptuousness, but in the gratification of expensive tastes in building.[3]

---

[1] The above were no doubt substantial advantages to the church; yet through them the church was drawn into the sphere of earthly politics, and the ill-defined boundaries between civil and ecclesiastical jurisdiction led to the gravest evils. The victory of the church in the state marks at the same time the beginning of an era of secularization and declension, from which Monasticism was a species of reaction.

[2] Even the dark domestic tragedies of his life in AD 326 are too much wrapped in mystery to enable us to apportion fairly what measure of blame attaches to him.

[3] The most conspicuous example of this was the rearing of his new

THE CHURCH OUTSIDE THE EMPIRE—MANICHAEISM

The gospel by the time now reached had penetrated into many countries outside the bounds of the Roman Empire. There had long been Christians in Arabia; a Gothic bishop was present at the Council of Nicaea; Armenia, under Tiridates, at first a violent persecutor, had been persuaded to receive the gospel from Gregory the Illuminator about AD 302; Georgia received Christianity about AD 326. Persia, too, had large numbers of Christians, who were soon to undergo a fierce persecution. The gospel found its way into Ethiopia[1] through two captive youths, Edesius and Frumentius, one of whom afterwards became the bishop of the church.[2] In connection with Persia, notice must be taken of the rise in the latter part of the third century of the form of heresy known as Manichaeism. In general, Manichaeism is a mixture of Persian dualism with ideas borrowed from Christianity and Gnosticism.[3] The rise of Manichaeism was coincident with the accession of a new Persian dynasty (the Sassanidae), and of a great revival of Zoroastrianism.

The founder of the sect, Mani, was a young and talented Persian, who, under Sapor I (AD 240-272), conceived the idea of

and splendid capital—Constantinople (dedicated AD 330). The lavish expenditure on this city and on the gorgeous establishment of his court involved him in the necessity of imposing heavy taxation on his subjects, so that his reign came to be regarded as despotic and oppressive. Even on the subject of his blameworthy self-exaltation account should be taken of the temptations to which he was exposed, and of the extravagant adulation he received from the Christians around him. One of the most remarkable facts in his career is that while the patron of Christianity, the friend of bishops, judge of their controversies, president in their councils, a preacher and exhorter to Christian living, he himself did not receive baptism till the last days of his life (AD 337). We may, despite it all, find much in Constantine not unworthy of the great repute he has always had in the church.

[1] Abyssinia.

[2] Under Athanasius.

[3] Its fantastic ideas might seem to put it beyond serious consideration; but it is to be remembered that it had fascination enough to enslave for nine years even such an intellect as Augustine's, and that, despite persecution, it went on propagating itself for centuries, giving rise to sects in the Middle Ages, which were no small trouble to the ruling powers (Paulicians, Cathari, and the like).

bringing about a fusion of the Zoroastrian and Christian religions.[1] He had to flee, and in the course of extensive travels[2]
evolved his religious scheme into definite form. Returning to
Persia on the death of Sapor, he met at first with a flattering
reception, but finally was denounced as a heretic and flayed
alive (AD 277). The system is a piece of extravagant mythology
from first to last. It starts with the dualistic conception of a
kingdom of good (light) and a kingdom of evil (darkness). The
kingdom of evil invades the kingdom of good, and bears off
from it a portion of its light substance. It is these particles of
light imprisoned in the chaotic elements of this lower world
which give to the latter its mingled character. They suffer
acutely, it is supposed, in being thus held in material bonds.[3]
Mani formed a church, with two grades of members: (1) the
auditors, or outer circle; and (2) the elect, or sacerdotal caste,
the "perfect" of the Manichaean sect. These did no work, but
were maintained by the auditors.[4]

THEOLOGY—THE MONARCHIAN HERESIES

As the second century was the period of the Gnostic heresies, so
the third century is preeminently the period of what are known
as the Monarchian heresies. We have reserved a brief connected account of these to the present point. They arose partly
as a reaction against the doctrine of the trinity, developed by
the Apologists and old catholic fathers, which seemed to put in
jeopardy the unity ("monarchia") of God; and partly as a protest against the subordinationist doctrines of certain of the
fathers, which seemed to imperil the Christian interest of the

---

[1] The dates in Mani's life are quite uncertain.

[2] India, and so on.

[3] The Manichaeans spoke of this as the crucifixion of the eternal
Christ throughout creation. Creation (organization) is an expedient for
their liberation. Man is created by the evil powers that the higher elements might be more securely bound; but the concentration aids, instead of retarding, the process of evolution. Redemption is through a
higher power (the "primeval man"), identified with the spirit of the
sun, or Mithras. The end of the development is the total separation of
the light from the darkness.

[4] Augustine wrote elaborate refutations of the system.

true divinity of the Son. The simplest form of reaction against trinitarian views is an Ebionitic, humanitarian, or purely unitarian view of Christ, and this we find developing itself in the end of the second century and beginning of the third.[1] More remarkable was the type of Monarchianism produced by the christological interest. Here the aim was to make sure that in Christ men had no secondary or derived being, but the absolute God; and this was thought to be secured only by the assertion that in Christ the Father himself had become incarnate and suffered. Hence the name Patripassians given to this party.[2]

The defect of these theories was their failure to do justice to the trinitarian distinction plainly involved in the New Testament doctrine of God. This fault was met in the modalistic trinitarianism of Sabellius—the most completely evolved and longest enduring of these Monarchian heresies. Sabellius[3] is first met with in Rome under the episcopate of Zephyrinus (AD 202-218) as an adherent of Cleomenes. He was excommunicated by Callistus (himself a Patripassian). His heresy had a powerful revival in North Africa about AD 260, and reappeared in the fourth century as a reaction against Arianism (Marcellus).

---

[1] Of Jewish Ebionitism we spoke in the second chapter. In the gentile church we have an early form of Monarchianism in the "Alogi" (deniers of the Logos), an obscure sect of Asia Minor, about AD 170, who rejected the Gospel of John. At Rome pure unitarianism was represented in the Theodotians, under Victor and Zephyrinus (AD 190-218), and the Artemonites, a few years later. Christ, in this view, was "mere man." The Artemonites were replied to in a book called "The Little Labyrinth," by Caius, a Roman presbyter, who adduces against them the testimony of ancient hymns.

[2] The oldest representative of it we know of was Praxeas, at Rome (about AD 177-190), against whom Tertullian wrote a treatise. Praxeas tried to explain that Christ, according to the flesh, was "Son," but the divine element in him was the "Father." He stayed himself upon the words, "I and my father are one" (John 10:30). A more subtle form of the same doctrine was taught under succeeding episcopates by Noetus (about AD 200) and his disciple Cleomenes. Noetus affirmed the capacity in God of existing in different modes. As ingenerate, God was Father; as generate, he was Son. Hippolytus wrote against Noetus. Both Tertullian and Hippolytus accuse the Roman bishops of the period of sympathy with this error. Origen, at a synod in Arabia (AD 244), had the satisfaction of recovering Beryllus, of Bostra, from a similar heresy.

[3] A Libyan?

In principle its solution is the substitution of a trinity of revelation for a trinity of essence; a trinity of modes or aspects of the one divine Being for a trinity of persons. The one God ("Monas") expands and contracts in successive revelations, as the arm may be outstretched and drawn back again. God revealed in the Law is the Father, in Jesus Christ is the Son, in the indwelling in believers is the Spirit. The incarnation is thus a passing mode of God's manifestation.[1]

This yields the transition to the last phase of Monarchian doctrine, that is, the dynamical unitarianism of Paul of Samosata, bishop of Antioch, AD 260-270. Paul was a vain, ostentatious, theatrical man, of whom many discreditable things are related. He held, like the earlier Unitarians, that Christ was mere man, but affirmed a union of the divine Logos (or reason) with Christ in a degree predicable of no other. Through his interpenetration by the divine power Christ advances by "progressive development" till he becomes God, or is raised to divine rank. Deity here only means that Christ was deemed worthy for his peculiar excellence of divine honors—not that he became God in nature. It was apotheosis; deification by favor. Two influential synods were held at Antioch on the subject of Paul's heresy (AD 264 and 269), at the second of which he was condemned. He held, however, by his palace and dignities till forcibly expelled three years later (AD 272).

CHURCH TEACHERS AND LITERATURE OF THE PERIOD

The church teachers of this period are not men of the mental stature of the great fathers of the previous age, but they are interesting characters, and took an active part in the church life of their day. Among the Greek writers, the chief interest centers in the school of Origen—the Alexandrian school—graced by such names as Dionysius of Alexandria, Gregory Thaumaturgus, Firmilian of Cappadocia, and Pamphilus of Caesarea. Dionysius of Alexandria has already been before us as a witness to the facts of the Decian persecution. He was a man of the utmost mildness and conciliatoriness of disposition, and on this

---

[1] Pushed to its issue, it means nothing more than a dynamical presence of God in the soul of Christ.

account his advice and mediation were much sought after in the various disputes of the church. He was born about AD 190 of wealthy parents, and in early life was brought to faith in Christ. He attached himself to Origen; was made presbyter in AD 233; became head of the catechetical school in Alexandria; in AD 247 or 248 was elected bishop. He suffered loss and exile in the Decian and Valerian persecutions, but returned at the peace under Gallenius. He died AD 265. A good many fragments of his works and some of his letters remain to us.

Not unlike Dionysius in some respects was a second great pupil of Origen—Gregory Thaumaturgus (the wonder worker). Gregory's original name was Theodorus, and his surname was given him on account of the repute he came to have as a miracle worker. The accounts of these miracles, however, are late. In a "Panegyric on Origen," delivered when leaving the school at Caesarea, he gives a full account of his life up to that time. He was born at Neo-Caesarea, in Pontus, about AD 210, of noble and wealthy parents. Led accidentally to Caesarea in Palestine, he was arrested by the genius of Origen, and became his most devoted disciple. His soul became knit to Origen, as he says, like the soul of Jonathan to David. He remained with Origen five years (AD 233-238). About AD 240 he became bishop of his native city, and had such success that, at his death about AD 270, it is said there were only seventeen pagans remaining. His evangelizing activity was incessant, but he erred in too great concession to pagan customs. Like all Origen's pupils, Gregory was a man of liberal, candid, cultured mind, actuated by a strong love of truth, and of earnest and glowing piety. Several of his genuine writings remain to us.

Firmilian, bishop of Caesarea in Cappadocia, was one of the most influential bishops of his time, but does not seem to have written much. Origen took refuge with him during the persecution of Maximin in AD 235. A letter to Cyprian denouncing Stephen of Rome is all we have from his pen. Mention must be made finally of a member of the school of Alexandria who did splendid service to the cause of sacred learning in the end of the third century—Pamphilus of Caesarea, founder of the famous library in that city, and friend of Eusebius. Pamphilus was a native of Phoenicia, and, like the others named, came from a wealthy family. He studied at Alexandria under Pierius, and there contracted an unbounded admiration for Origen. Removing to Caesarea, he devoted himself to the great task of his life—the collection and copying of manuscripts of the scriptures, of commentaries, and other works of value. The literary treasures thus amassed were of priceless worth, and furnished Eusebius with ample material for his literary undertakings. In the fifth year of the Diocletian persecution Pamphilus was thrown into prison, and was finally martyred, with eleven others, in AD 309.[1]

Origen, however, had also his opponents, of whom the principal was Methodius, bishop of Olympius, in Lycia (later of Tyre), who perished under Maximin about AD 311. We have from him a mystical dialogue in praise of virginity, "The Banquet of Ten Virgins." Only fragments remain of his attacks on Origen's views of creation, pre-existence, the resurrection, and so on. It was formerly mentioned that the Alexandrian theologians were speculative, idealizing, Platonizing, allegorizing in their tendency, liberal in their whole attitude to culture. Before the century closed, however, we note the beginnings of another school—the Antiochian—which was to have a long and influential history as the rival of the Alexandrian. This second school is marked from the commencement by a sober, matter-of-fact tendency, a preference of Aristotelianism to Platonism, and an adherence to a strictly grammatical and historical method of exegesis. Its founder was Lucian, who, like the heretical bishop Paul, was a native of Samosata. Lucian himself fell under suspicion of unsound views, and was separated from the church during three episcopates. He was restored to the church, carried on his school with distinguished success, and finally crowned his career by a heroic martyrdom in AD 311 or 312. His method was predominatingly exegetical, and his style of exegesis was grammatical and literal. His school is the reputed fountainhead of the Arian heresy. Later it had such distinguished representatives as Chrysostom, Theodore of Mopsuestia, and Theodoret.[2]

---

[1] He wrote in conjunction with Eusebius an elaborate work, "The Defence of Origen." So intense was Eusebius' appreciation of this good man—"the holy and blessed Pamphilus," as he calls him—that after his martyrdom he adopted his name as part his own.

[2] A creed attributed to Lucian was presented to a Council of Antioch in AD 341.

The Latin writers of the period may be more summarily alluded to. Commodian (about AD 250) wrote "Instructions for Christian Living," and an apologetic poem against Jews and gentiles, both in rude Latin hexameters. A little earlier Julius Africanus (died about AD 240), the first Christian chronographer, had drawn up a work, in five books, setting forth the course of sacred and profane history till the reign of Elagabalus. The two Latin writers who belong properly to our period are Arnobius and Lactantius, both apologists in the time of the Diocletian persecution. The apology of Arnobius, a teacher of rhetoric, "Against the Nations," is in seven books, and, as might be expected in a recent convert, is not very mature in Christian doctrine. It is, however, an able, learned, and convincing defence of the Christians from many of the objections brought against them, and an effective enough exposure of the folly of idolatry. Arnobius lays stress on the unique and well attested character of Christ's miracles and the excellence of the Christian morality. Lactantius is reputed the most classical and elegant of all the Christian writers. His apologetic work, "The Divine Institutes," in seven books, was, in its finished form, dedicated to Constantine. He wrote also a work, "On the Death of the Persecutors," narrating the judgments of God on the persecutors of the Christians from Nero onwards. He died in old age, about AD 330.

A last name to be noticed is that of the Greek writer and great church historian, Eusebius of Caesarea, who, though he belongs properly to the next age, yet begins his activity in this. He is indeed the link between the old and the new order. He was born probably about AD 260. His early associations are with Caesarea, of which city he became bishop about AD 315. He held this position till his death in AD 339 or 340. Eusebius was a man of extraordinary learning and industry, and his works form a little library of themselves. They are of all classes: historical, apologetic, exegetical, critical, doctrine, orations, and so on. Reference need only be made here to his "Ecclesiastical History," extending from the birth of Christ to the defeat of Licinius in AD 323; his two apologetic works, the "Evangelical Preparation" (fifteen books), and the "Evangelical Demonstration" (twenty books, ten extant); his "Chronicle" (based on Julian Africanus, part in Jerome's translation); and his "Life of

Constantine," a panegyric rather than a biography, yet important for facts. The works of Eusebius are often desultory and
ill-arranged; he has little independent merit as a theologian,
and inclines to laxity of opinion; he plays the courtier with too
much success to "our pious emperor"; yet his writings are invaluable as sources of information, and for the extracts they
preserve. In the use of authorities he shows himself most accu-
rate, painstaking and faithful—a virtue of the first rank.

POINTS IN CHURCH CONSTITUTION AND WORSHIP

The chief matters requiring to be glanced at here may be gathered up under a few heads. (1) Church buildings—These became
common in the course of the third century, and were greatly
multiplied after the victory of Constantine. The model usually
followed was that of the "Roman basilica." The basilica was a
building of oblong shape, which served the double purpose of a
hall of justice and place of concourse. The body of the building
consisted of a central portion or nave and side aisles, one or
more, separated off by pillars. At the upper end, in a semicircular recess, were the praetor's chair, the seats of the judges,
and in front the altar, where incense was burned and oaths were
taken. This form of building readily adapted itself to Christian
purposes.[1] The larger churches stood in a court or atrium,
surrounded by colonnades. The doors opened into a vestibule
or narthex, which was as far as penitents were permitted to
approach. The congregation assembled in the nave, or broad
middle part of the church. At the upper end a railed-off portion
was reserved for the choir and inferior orders of clergy—the
chancel (from, "cancellus", a railing). Here also on one side
stood the pulpit ("ambo"). Finally, the semicircular part ("apse")
formed the special sanctuary. The praetor's seat became the
bishop's throne; around him sat the presbyters and deacons;
the altar in front became the communion table (now also called
altar), and so on. In the more splendid churches all the parts,
doors, pillars, apse and galleries, were finely adorned.[2]

---

[1] The description of the church of Tyre, in Eusebius 10.4, may be
compared.

[2] In contradiction to later practice the church was sometimes so
placed that the rising sun might strike upon its front (so at Tyre).

(2) Development of church offices and service—In the third century church offices became greatly multiplied. The clergy were now divided into two groups—the greater orders ("ordines majores"), consisting of bishops, presbyters and deacons; and the lesser orders ("ordines minores"), consisting of subdeacons, readers, acolytes (attendants on the bishop), exorcists, precentors, door keepers, catechists, and so on. The distinction between clergy and laity was now firmly established. If we may trust the oldest liturgies,[1] the church service had by the end of the third century become highly liturgical and elaborate. The service was now divided into two parts—catechumens, penitents, and so on, being dismissed before the Eucharistic celebration began. The Eucharistic service itself was highly complex and ornate, including long prayers, responses, prescribed actions of the priest. The clergy had distinctive vestments.

Festival days were now observed—especially Easter and Pentecost. The whole period between these feasts was apparently observed as a time of gladness. Music in the church was more highly developed. We have met with references to hymns, and there were now regular choristers and conductors. Baptism was generally connected with the above feast days, and certain rites had gradually become connected with the original ceremony.[2] The practice of exorcism had also become a part of the ritual. Shortly before baptism the creed was imparted to the catechumen as a sort of password.[3] Baptism in grave cases of sickness was administered by sprinkling (clinical baptism). The discipline of the church was also made more elaborate. This followed from the prominence given to the idea of penance for the removal of post-baptismal sin.[4]

---

[1] For example, that in the so-called "Apostolical Constitutions" from fourth century.

[2] For example, trine immersion (thrice dipping of head), the sign of the cross on the forehead and breast, giving the baptized person milk and honey, unction on the head, a white robe, and so on.

[3] Symbol.

[4] Penitents were now regularly classified into weepers (who prostrated themselves at church doors imploring restoration), hearers (who were allowed to hear the scripture lessons and sermon), kneelers (who were admitted to the prayers, but in a kneeling posture), and standers (who were allowed to take part in the whole worship standing). The

(3) Development of church councils—Meetings of this kind sprung up informally in the latter half of the second century. They were at first quite local, one bishop inviting other bishops and clergy to confer with him on matters of common concern, and their decisions had no binding force on other churches. In these early councils presbyters and laymen took part as well as bishops; latterly only bishops appear to have voted. As councils assumed a more regular character they came to be distinguished into different kinds. (a) There was the parochial council of the bishop and the clergy of his city. (b) There were provincial councils, attended by the clergy of a whole province. These were generally held in the metropolitan city, and the bishop of that city presided. (c) Tertullian speaks of councils of a whole region ("regionis")—national councils. (d) Finally, when the empire became Christian, and the emperor himself undertook the summoning of councils, there became possible councils of the whole church—ecumenical councils.[1]

(4) Gradations of rank in the episcopate itself—These sprung from the meetings of councils and other causes in the state of the church. The bishops of the metropolitan cities soon attained from their position a higher rank than other bishops, and were known as "metropolitans." The sanction of the metropolitan came ultimately to be necessary to the validity of the election of another bishop. This was followed in the fourth century by the elevation of the bishops of certain churches deemed worthy of special honor to the wider jurisdiction of patriarchs. Such churches were Antioch, Alexandria and Rome, to which Constantinople (as new Rome) and Jerusalem were subsequently added—five in all. This, however, carries us beyond our special limits.[2]

---

course of probation was often three or four years.

[1] The first of these was the Nicene (AD 325). In reality these were almost exclusively Greek councils. The decrees of the councils were now compulsorily imposed by the emperors. As examples of councils may be mentioned those in Asia Minor about the Montanists and Easter, those in North Africa on heretical baptism, those in Antioch about Paul of Samosata, the Council of Arles against the Donatists, the Council of Elvira in Spain (AD 306), and so on.

[2] Our sketch has brought us to the triumph of Constantine, and formal adoption of Christianity as the religion of the empire. Ere, however,

---

this consummation was reached, the Arian controversy had broken out (AD 318), and the church was in flames from within, to the unconcealed delight of the pagan onlookers, and the intense chagrin of the emperor, who had hoped to find in this monotheistic faith a bond of peace in his dominions. The Nicene Council itself (AD 325) did little more than open new controversies, with which for half a century the world and church were filled. Narrow minded imperial interference made matters ever worse. Over all the storms looms the noble figure of Athanasius, who appears already upon the scene before our period closes. To him the church owes nearly all its real guidance in the distractions of the age that follows. "Athanasius contra mundum." On the verge of this new era we cease our tale.

SIX LECTURES
ON THE ANTE-NICENE FATHERS

WRITTEN BY

FENTON JOHN ANTHONY HORT
Hulsean Professor and Lady Margaret's Reader
in Divinity in the University of Cambridge

EDITED BY

BRENT WALTERS
Curator, Ante-Nicene Archive
Dean, College of Early Christian Studies

London: Macmillan and Co.

1895

San Jose: The Ante-Nicene Archive
Bibliographics Incorporated

1993

CONTENTS

INTRODUCTION

The lectures which I hope to deliver this term are intended to have for their subject "Some early fathers of the church." In this description of the proposed subject the word "fathers" means simply what it means in common usage, the Christian writers of the early Christian centuries. In one literal sense they might be called fathers, namely, as being the parents of the Christian thought and belief and life of later centuries, which, however modified and altered by the inward and outward changes arising in the course of time, retain always down to the present day important features inherited from the peculiar circumstances of the centuries which followed the Apostolic age. But, although it is important to remember that our own thoughts, and the thoughts of all Christians everywhere, have been in a great measure thus shaped for us by the thoughts of the early fathers, it is not on account of this fact that we call them fathers, but rather in gratitude and veneration for them as the patriarchs of Christendom, speaking to us still out of that early dawn of the Christian period of history, and often speaking to us out of the fiery trial of persecution.

But it would be a misuse of this legitimate reverence to treat the words of the fathers as oracles appointed to dictate to us what we ought to believe. If we read their words with an open and teachable mind, we shall often find there abundant help and instruction, but the responsibility will always lie upon us of weighing and testing what we read, to the best of our power. We must not be surprised if we sometimes find much dross, for each age has its own limitations and vagaries, and, besides these, each man in each age has his own limitations and vagaries, some more, some less. Again it is not really possible to measure the comparative worth of the fathers, one with another, merely by their comparative antiquity. There is no doubt a peculiar freshness in the best writings of quite the earliest time, the only time which can with any propriety share with the Apostolic age the much misused and slippery epithet "primitive." But the greatest of the fathers belong to later times, and different later times, when in doctrine and in institutions and in various other things pertaining to Christian life, great and unavoidable changes had taken place, changes that were on the whole for good and belonging to healthy growth, but also by no means free from loss, from injurious one-sidedness, and from corruption. In what we call the age of the fathers there was anything rather than a uniform state of things. Movement was at that time more rapid than probably at any later time of Christian history.

There are several comparatively distinct subjects which might properly enough be lectured about or written about in connection with the fathers. They might serve as a thread for speaking about church history generally, or about the history of doctrine, of course in either case within the limits of their own time. Or again they might, with more obvious fitness, be taken as the heads of the corresponding history of Christian litera- ture. The time at our disposal will not however allow us to follow any of these lines, unless it be incidentally and to a small extent. I wish rather to do what I can towards putting before you the leading fathers of the earliest centuries as living men, the children of a particular time, and to give some account of the purpose and character of their chief works, illustrated by translated extracts which may help towards the formation of individual impressions that may remain associated with their respective names.

It is well to keep in mind throughout that only a small part of the actual Christian literature of the early centuries is now preserved to us. Not only many books, but all the books of many authors, have completely perished. Of others we possess only scanty fragments. On the other hand, when we observe the neglect or even dislike with which the Ante-Nicene Christian literature, with very limited exceptions, was regarded by most of the Christian theologians of later days, we can hardly be too thankful that so much has been preserved; and moreover that what has been preserved has so representative a character, that is, supplies us with substantial and important examples of different times, different schools, and different churches. Again it is a striking and encouraging fact that so many lost works, or lost portions of works, belonging to this period have come to light within the last forty years. Nor is there any reason to believe that we have come to the end of discoveries of this kind.

CLEMENT OF ROME

The fathers of whom I propose to speak today belong to the small group to which it has been usual for above two hundred years to give the rather unmeaning name of Apostolic Fathers, that is, preeminently Clement of Rome, Hermas, Ignatius, and Polycarp.[1] We begin then with Clement of Rome.[2] The apparent time when the epistle was written and the apparent personal position of Clement are both remarkable. Some thirty years had passed, what is counted a generation, since the persecution of Nero, some twenty-five years since the fall of Jerusalem, the greatest as well as most awful of events for all Christians. For the empire, after all the frightful turmoil which had followed the death of Nero, a happier time had already begun with the accession of Vespasian.[3]

Vespasian's son Titus had succeeded, and then his other son Domitian, his reign being the one exception to the comparative brightness of the series of eight. Always capricious and suspicious, the emperor showed these qualities in an extreme form about the years AD 95-96, the last of his life. Among his victims were his own first cousin and niece's husband, Flavius Clemens, the father of the two reputed heirs to the empire. This Clemens was executed, and his wife exiled, both apparently as having become Christians. The Clement who wrote our epistle was, it would seem, a freedman or freedman's son

---

[1] In the opinion of many the earliest extant Christian writing outside the New Testament is the remarkable little manual of Christian morals and ecclesiastical instruction calling itself the "Teaching of the Twelve Apostles," now familiarly known as the "Didachè," which was discovered and published a few years ago. It may however be considerably later: and at all events it lies too near the edge of our subject to need more than this passing word of notice.

[2] The little that is really known about him will be best found in Dr. Lightfoot's admirable edition, and still more in the "Appendix" which he published eight years later, in which he has carefully sifted the mass of ancient legend and modern speculation which has gathered round Clement's name. Some pages of his Philippians are also worth reading in the same connection.

[3] A period Dr. Merivale says "distinguished by the general prosperity of the administration, the tranquil obedience of the people, and (with a single exception) by the virtue and public spirit of the rulers."

in their household, and had in this manner received his name. Everything in his letter shows that he must have been long a Christian himself, so that his mind would naturally be saturated, as we find it, with the language and ideas of the Old Testament, the only scriptures, properly so called, for Christians at this early time, even if he was not previously, as is possible, a Jew of the dispersion. His precise position in the Roman church is difficult to ascertain.[1]

The epistle itself starts with a salutation resembling those of the apostolic epistles, beginning, "The church of God which sojourns at Rome to the church of God which sojourns at Corinth." The first words of the letter itself show the state of things at Rome. "Because of the sudden and quickly succeeding misfortunes and calamities happening to us, brethren, we deem that we have been somewhat slow in giving attention to the matters that are in dispute among you." Thus the epistle was written during or soon after the persecution which fell on the Roman Christians in those last months of Domitian's reign, the first persecution of which we have any knowledge after the persecution of Nero and the immediately following time of confusion.

The purpose of this the first extant writing of a Christian father is the promotion of peace, the restoration of a divided and disorderly Christian community to the concord and order implied in the very idea of church membership. At the outset the Roman church commends warmly the previous temper and conduct shown by the Corinthian church, and then especially those ways of theirs to which the present state of things stood

---

[1] Two or three generations later, when the early constitution of the European churches had been forgotten, he was placed in the series of early bishops of Rome. But, as Dr. Lightfoot has shown (Philippians, page 218, eighth edition), it is difficult to reconcile his holding such an office with the language of the epistle itself, or with other indications as to the constitution of the church of Rome at a somewhat later time. But he must certainly have been a man of importance and influence in the church to be entrusted with the duty of writing such an epistle, even if he was not the Clement to whom the book of Hermas' Visions (to which we shall come shortly) was to be sent for sending on to the cities away from Rome, that task, it is said, having been entrusted to him.

in the strongest contrast.[1] In place of all this had now come what is called a vile and unholy sedition (or quarrel, στάσις), kindled by a few headlong and self-willed persons to a pitch of madness which had brought their honorable name into disgrace.[2] It had arisen, we read further on, from contumacy shown against some of the elders of the church, who had been thrust aside without having deserved it.[3]

This conduct is traced back to "an unrighteous and impious jealousy" (ζῆλος),[4] a jealousy of which examples are given as leading to great crimes and misfortunes in the times of the Old Testament, and now again as leading to the martyr deaths of Peter and Paul and many others of those who are called "elect." These admonitions the Roman church then takes up as addressed equally to themselves: "we are in the same arena, and the same contest awaits us." "Let us hearken to his majestic and glorious purpose, and coming as suppliants of his mercy and graciousness let us fall down [before him] and turn to his compassions, abandoning the laboring that is vain and the strife and the jealously that leads to death."[5] Then follow examples of those "who have ministered perfectly to God's majestic glory" by obedience or faith or in other like ways, beginning with Enoch, Noah, and Abraham, the words of the Old Testament being copiously cited as well as the lives of its holy men.

> The humility therefore and the submissiveness of so many and so great men, who have thus obtained a good report, have through obedience made better not only us but also the generations which were before us, even them that received his oracles in fear and truth. Seeing then that we have been partakers of many great and glorious doings, let us hasten to return unto the goal of peace which has been handed down to us from the beginning, and let us look steadfastly unto the Father and Maker of the whole world, and cleave

---

[1] Lightfoot, Clement of Rome, Appendix, page 346.
[2] Chapter 1.
[3] Chapters 44, 47, 57, and so on.
[4] Chapter 3.
[5] Chapter 9.

unto his splendid and excellent gifts of peace and ben-
efits. Let us behold him in our mind, and let us look
with the eyes of our soul unto his long suffering will.
Let us note how free from anger he is towards all his
creatures. The heavens are moved by his direction
and obey him in peace. Day and night accomplish the
course assigned to them by him, without hindrance
one to another. Moreover, the inscrutable depths of
the abysses and the unutterable statutes of the nether
regions are constrained by the same ordinances. The
basin of the boundless sea, gathered together by his
workmanship into its reservoirs, passes not the barri-
ers wherewith it is surrounded; but even as he ordered
it, so it does. For he said, "So far shall you come, and
your waves shall be broken within you." The ocean
which is impassable for men, and the worlds beyond
it, are directed by the same ordinances of the Master.
The seasons of spring and summer and autumn and
winter give way in succession one to another in peace.
The winds in their several quarters at their proper
season fulfil their ministry without disturbance; and
the ever-flowing fountains, created for enjoyment and
health, without fail give their breasts which sustain
the life of men. Yes, the smallest of living things come
together in concord and peace. All these things the
great Creator and Master of the universe ordered to
be in peace and concord, doing good unto all things but
far beyond the rest unto us who have taken refuge in
his compassionate mercies through our Lord Jesus
Christ, to whom be the glory and the majesty forever
and ever. Amen.[1]

Then follows a series of chapters of religious exhortation in
the same lofty strain, ending with texts thus introduced.

This is the way, dearly beloved, wherein we found
our salvation, even Jesus Christ the high-priest of our
offerings, the guardian and helper of our weakness.

---

[1] Lightfoot, Clement of Rome, Appendix, pages 355 and following.

Through him let us look steadfastly unto the heights of the heavens; through him we behold as in a mirror his faultless and most excellent visage; through him the eyes of our hearts were opened; through him our foolish and darkened mind springs up unto the light; through him the Master wills that we should taste of the immortal knowledge; who being the brightness of his majesty is so much greater than angels, as he has inherited a more excellent name. For so it is written; "Who makes his angels spirits and his ministers a flame of fire"; but of his Son the Master said thus; "You are my Son, I this day have begotten you. Ask of me, and I will give you the gentiles for your inheritance, and the ends of the earth for your possession." And again he says unto him; "Sit on my right hand, until I make your enemies a footstool for your feet." Who then are these enemies? They that are wicked and resist his will.[1]

The original subject of the epistle returns in a fresh exposition of the necessity and divineness of order. "The great without the small cannot exist, neither the small without the great" (according to the wise Greek proverb). "All the members breathe together and join in one [common] subjection that the whole body may be saved." This spirit of order is traced in the Mosaic legislation, and in the office and work of the apostles who received the gospel for us from Jesus Christ, even as he was sent forth from God.[2] Again and again the original evil state of things at Corinth is touched on, and then always there is a return to the setting forth of the right spirit which would make such scandals impossible. In these later chapters there is special insistence on love as, so to speak, the deepest root of the matter, as it had been set forth by St. Paul in writing to that same Corinthian church. The demand which it makes for self-suppression and self-surrender is illustrated by examples both from among God's saints of old and from among heathens who

---

[1] Lightfoot, Clement of Rome, Appendix , page 364.

[2] The details of what is said about the appointments of elders or men having oversight by the apostles would need more time to discuss than we can give.

sacrificed themselves for their fellow-citizens. "These things have they done and will do, that live as citizens of that commonwealth of God for belonging to which there is no regret."[1]

As the end of the epistle draws near, the Romans by the mouth of Clement declare themselves now guiltless of the sin of the Corinthian malcontents, should it be persevered in; and break forth in a prayer equally memorable for its own sake and for the large borrowings from it which are found in various later Greek liturgies. It begins with asking that we may hope on your name, and so on.

> Grant unto us, Lord, that we may set our hope on your name which is the primal source of all creation, and open the eyes of our hearts, that we may know you, who alone abides Highest in the highest, Holy in the holy; who lays low the insolence of the proud, who scatters the imaginings of nations; who sets the lowly on high, and brings the lofty low; who makes rich and makes poor; who kills and makes alive; who alone is the Benefactor of spirits and the God of all flesh; who looks into the abysses, who scans the works of man; the Succor of them that are in peril, the Savior of them that are in despair; the Creator and Overseer of every spirit; who multiplies the nations upon earth, and has chosen out from all men those that love you through Jesus Christ, your beloved Son, through whom you did instruct us, did sanctify us, did honor us. We beseech you, Lord and Master, to be our help and succor. Save those among us who are in tribulation; have mercy on the lowly; lift up the fallen; show yourself unto the needy; heal the ungodly; convert the wanderers of your people; feed the hungry; release our prisoners; raise up the weak, comfort the faint-hearted. Let all the gentiles know that you are God alone and Jesus Christ is your Son and we are your people and the sheep of your pasture.[2]

---

[1] Chapter 54.

[2] Lightfoot, <u>Clement of Rome</u>, Appendix, page 376.

The prayer for the Christian community presently expands into universality;[1] and then, in the true spirit of St. Paul and St. Peter, specially makes supplication for the rulers of the Roman empire,

> You through your operations did make manifest the everlasting fabric of the world. You, Lord, did create the earth. You that are faithful throughout all generations, righteous in your judgments, marvellous in strength and excellence, you that are wise in creating and prudent in establishing that which you have made, that are good in the things which are seen and faithful with them that trust on you, pitiful and compassionate, forgive us our iniquities and our unrighteousness and our transgressions and shortcomings. Lay not to our account every sin of your servants and your handmaids, but cleanse us with the cleansing of your truth, and guide our steps to walk in holiness and righteousness and singleness of heart and to do such things as are good and well-pleasing in your sight and in the sight of our rulers. Yes, Lord, make your face to shine upon us in peace for our good, that we may be sheltered by your mighty hand and delivered from every sin by your uplifted arm. And deliver us from them that hate us wrongfully. Give concord and peace to us and to all that dwell on the earth, as you gave to our fathers, when they called on you in faith and truth with holiness, that we may be saved, while we render obedience to your almighty and most excellent name, and to our rulers and governors upon the earth. You, Lord and Master, have given them the power of sovereignty through your excellent and unspeakable might, that we knowing the glory and honor which you have given them may submit ourselves unto them, in nothing resisting your will. Grant unto them therefore, O Lord, health, peace, concord, stability, that they may administer the government which you have given them without failure. For you, O heavenly Master,

---

[1] "Give concord and peace both to us and to all that inhabit the earth."

King of the ages, give to the sons of men glory and honor and power over all things that are upon the earth. Do you, Lord, direct their counsel according to that which is good and well-pleasing in your sight, that, administering in peace and gentleness with godliness the power which you have given them, they may obtain your favor. O you, who alone are able to do these things and things far more exceeding good than these for us, we praise you through the high-priest and guardian of our souls, Jesus Christ, through whom be the glory and the majesty unto you both now and for all generations and forever and ever. Amen.[1]

The epistle closes with a few more quiet sentences on its principal theme, and with the commendation of two members of the Roman church sent as bearers of the letter, "faithful and prudent men, that from youth to old age have walked blamelessly among us, who shall also be witnesses between you and us."[2]

HERMAS OF ROME

After Clement of Rome we come to Hermas of Rome. We need not trouble ourselves about his precise date, which is much disputed. At earliest he was a contemporary of Clement, at latest half a century later. He was a brother, possibly an elder brother, of Pius, who was bishop of Rome about the middle of the second century. He was evidently a layman, apparently

---

[1] Lightfoot, Clement of Rome, Appendix, pages 377 and following.

[2] The unaffected loftiness of this epistle of Clement of Rome, and its position at the head of post-biblical Christian literature, have been a temptation to give it a somewhat disproportionate amount of time. What is called the second epistle of Clement, really an anonymous homily, a generation or two later in date, may be left alone, though important for the history of doctrine. It is rather eccentric in character, though less so than the early epistle which bears the name of Barnabas. Whoever may be the author of that epistle, he was certainly not the Barnabas of the New Testament; and though full of points of interest to advanced students, the epistle is one which for our purpose may be passed over with little loss.

engaged in commercial pursuits. By birth, according to his first
words, he was a slave. His book, which from an early time was
called "The Shepherd," was read in various churches in the first
centuries; and the Latin translation, which till lately was the
only form known of it, had a certain popularity in Western
Europe in the Middle Ages, so that it is even found in or after
the Old Testament in several manuscripts of the Latin Bible. It
has often been compared to the "Pilgrim's Progress," and with
good reason. It contains in an imaginative form the thoughts
and broodings of a simple-minded devout man, on whom the
evil that he feels within him and sees around him lies as a
heavy burden, more especially evil which he cannot help recognizing within the church itself, the holy society of God's own
chosen people. Repentance is perhaps the idea that he cherishes
most. He is entirely free from bitterness or arrogance; and the
messages which he delivers he delivers not as from himself but
as entrusted to him by one or other kind of divine messenger.

The first part of the book consists of five Visions. In the first
he receives a rebuke for a sinful thought of his own; and then
presently for his tolerating the misdeeds of his children, which
had brought loss upon him. The speaker in the latter part of
this vision is an aged lady in bright apparel, sitting on a seat of
snow white wool; who in the second vision is revealed to him
to be not, as he supposed, the Sibyl, but the church. The third
vision, a very striking one, is chiefly of a tower in process of
building upon the waters, made of squared shining stones, that
is, again the church, built of men (living stones, as St. Peter
would say) who fit rightly into their place, other stones being
partially or wholly cast away. In the fourth vision a great
monster from whose mouth proceed fiery locusts is seen and
interpreted to be the great tribulation, which is approaching to
try the faint-hearted and double-minded that they may be purified for God's use. The fifth vision in a manner includes the
rest (above three-fourths) of the book. It begins thus:

> When I had been praying in my house, and had seated
> myself on the bed, there came in a certain man of glo-
> rious appearance, in the guise of a shepherd, clothed
> in a white (goat's) skin, and having a wallet on his
> shoulders and a staff in his hand. And he greeted me,

and I returned his greeting. And straightway he sat down beside me and said to me, "I have been sent by the angel of highest dignity, that I may dwell with you the remaining days of your life."

The shepherd presently bids him write down the commandments and the parables which he would declare to him. He is then described as the shepherd, the angel of repentance. Thenceforth he reappears several times, almost to the end of the book.

Then come twelve Commandments, as they are called. The first is a short one,

First of all believe that God is one, he who created and frames all things, and made all things out of what is not, [bringing them] into being, and contains all things, but alone is uncontained. Trust him therefore and fear him, and fearing practice self-restraint. Keep these things, and you shall cast from yourself all wickedness, and put on every virtue of righteousness, and shall live to God, if you keep this commandment.

The subjects of the other commandments are truthfulness, chastity, long suffering, the ways and the angels of good and of evil, right and wrong fear, right and wrong abstinence, the need of faith for prayer, the evil of a gloomy spirit, the true and the false prophet, good and evil desire.

After the twelve Commandments come ten (or more strictly nine) Parables or Similitudes. They are almost wholly taken from country scenes and agricultural or pastoral occupations, specially from vines and other trees. Perhaps the most interesting is the eighth. The angel shows Hermas "a great willow tree, overshadowing plains and mountains, and under the shade of the willow had come all that have been called by the name of the Lord." This mighty tree which overshadowed plains and mountains and all the earth, is explained to be the law of God which was given "to go forth into all the world: and this law is the Son of God proclaimed unto the ends of the earth; and the peoples that are under the shade are they that heard the proclamation and believed on him." These last words refer to the next incident of the parable:

> There stood an angel of the Lord glorious exceedingly,
> in height above the willow tree, holding a great reaping
> hook, and he cut down branch after branch from the
> willow, and gave to the people that were overshad-
> owed by the willow. . . . And after that all had received
> their twigs, the angel laid aside his reaping hook, and
> the tree was sound just as I had seen it before.

Presently the angel asks back the twigs, and receives them
one by one, some withered and gnawed as by a moth, others
withered only, others half withered, others half withered and
cracked, and so on in various gradations to those which were
wholly green and clothed with fresh shoots and fruit. Those
who had held these last were crowned with palm-leaves. This
is perhaps the most remarkable example of the just and truth-
ful habit of mind which leads Hermas in various places to mark
the various gradations in which good and evil are actually
mixed in the hearts and lives of men. The shepherd invites
Hermas to join in planting the other twigs, which in various
degrees had lost their greenness, if perchance some of them
might live when they have been duly watered: for, said the
shepherd, "He that created this tree wills that all should live
who have received branches from this tree." With these words
we may part company from Hermas.

IGNATIUS OF ANTIOCH

Last week we had for our subject the two earliest Christian
fathers belonging to the Roman church, Clement of Rome the
writer of the epistle sent by the church of Rome to the church
of Corinth, and Hermas the writer of the book of Visions,
Commandments, and Parables which takes the name "The
Shepherd" from the prominent part played in it by the angel of
repentance, who appeared to Hermas in the guise of a shepherd. Today we proceed to the others of the fathers commonly
called "Apostolic," who have special claims to be remembered.
These are Ignatius of Antioch and Polycarp of Smyrna.
    The names of these cities remind us at once that we are pass-
ing into very different worlds from that world which immediately surrounded Clement and Hermas; and one at least of the

two Eastern fathers, Ignatius, is singularly unlike his two brethren of the West. Ignatius was bishop of the Christian church at
Antioch. Beyond this bare fact we know nothing of his life and
work before the last journey to which his letters belong. We
can see from the letters that he had been condemned to death
as a Christian of Antioch and sent off under a guard of ten soldiers, to suffer death at Rome. The course taken was, in part
at least, through Asia Minor and then through Macedonia.
Arrived at Smyrna, he was welcomed not only by the church of
the city and its bishop Polycarp, but also by the delegates of the
churches of three other cities lying along what we should now
call the loop line of road which he had not traversed, and especially the church of the great capital, Ephesus.

During this short stay at Smyrna he wrote these letters
(which have been preserved) to these three churches which he
had been obliged to pass unvisited, and a fourth of a different
character to the church of Rome, the goal of his journey, the
place where he expected and desired to suffer martyrdom. We
next find him at Alexandria Troas, the seaport from which he
was to sail for Europe. There he had the happiness of being
overtaken by two deacons from the neighborhood of his own
Antioch, and receiving news of the cessation of the persecution
which had caused his own condemnation. There also he wrote
three more letters, to the church of Smyrna which he had just
left, to Polycarp its bishop, and to the church of Philadelphia
which he had been allowed to visit on his way to Smyrna. Thus
the seven letters are made up, which are now in our hands.

Of the European part of his course we have traces in Polycarp's epistle, to which we shall come just now. The church of
Philippi received him warmly, and at his request sent a letter of
greeting to the church of Antioch through Polycarp, as he had
asked those other churches to do to which he had written after
receiving the good tidings from Syria. The Philippian Christians at the same time took the opportunity to ask Polycarp for
copies of any letters of Ignatius in his possession. Of what
followed we know nothing beyond the bare fact that Ignatius
suffered martyrdom at Rome. Two different narratives exist
professing to describe his martyrdom: but they are fabrications
of late date. It is morally certain that the manner of death
would be by the fangs of wild beasts, and that the place of it

would be the vast Flavian amphitheater which for many centuries has been called the Colosseum. Anyone who may have the good fortune to visit Rome and stand within the ruins of that wonderful pile will do well to think of Ignatius, and the testimony which he bore. The time of Ignatius' martyrdom is known on less clear evidence than could be wished. The probabilities however are in favor of about AD 110.[1]

We must now turn to the substance of the letters themselves. It is impossible not to shrink in some degree from any attempt to analyze them, as almost a cold-blooded thing to do. Nothing in early Christian literature is at all like them; nothing else has the same intensely personal character. It may be that their peculiarity is in part owing to difference of race: we seem to hear a Syrian speaking to us, not a Greek, much less a Roman, though Ignatius is a Roman name. But a strong personal individuality is there too .[2] The thought that underlies every word is the thought that the writer is a man sentenced to death, to death for the name of his Lord. The thought brings with it a sense of keen and yet utterly humble exultation. As he passes through the cities of Asia, his constant impulse is towards close fellowship between himself and the various churches in their midst, and again between these and his own church of Antioch. By word and by letter he is constantly striving to make them sharers in his own fervor of martyrdom, and to make himself a sharer in all that concerned their welfare.

Here and there we find warnings against doctrinal errors to the influence of which these Asiatic churches were exposed, apparently of two types only; one, the early form of what is commonly called "Docetism," the tendency so to dwell on our Lord's divine nature as to regard his body as a mere unreal appearance; the other the subordination of the Christian faith to Judaism, somewhat as in the days of St. Paul. This latter evil was specially rife at Philadelphia, where the Judaizers seem to have raised opposition against Ignatius himself as he passed

---

[1] The time fixed by Lightfoot in general terms.

[2] Utterly unlike as they likewise are in other ways to all the apostolic epistles, they have here and there a certain affinity of spirit to the second Epistle to the Corinthians, the most individual of all St. Paul's epistles.

through. But a larger part of the letters is taken up with practical exhortations, especially to unity of spirit, unity of worship,
unity of organization. Even at this early time the churches
evidently had many members who had become careless about
Christian fellowship, and neglectful of the means by which
alone it could be preserved in warmth and vigor.

To take one significant example, it would seem that many
of the Asiatic Christians had got into a habit of celebrating the
Holy Communion in a loose and haphazard way, meeting
together in little private knots of people, rather than in the
central congregation as members of one great body. In this as
in all matters Ignatius endeavored to revive and strengthen
internal an external fellowship by exhorting the members of
the church to gather dutifully round its duly appointed officers
who were organized in a compact body of three orders, the
bishop at the head, the presbytery or college of elders who
formed his council, and the deacons or servants (διάκονοι) who
were chiefly occupied in the arrangements for the relief of the
poorer members of the church. Ignatius' language on these subjects, sometimes startling enough at best, becomes at least more
intelligible when this practical purpose of his is remembered.[1]
Having a keen sense of the immediate evil, he eagerly has re-
course to that external remedy which lay immediately ready to
his hand.

But it is poor work attempting to describe the words of a
man like Ignatius. A few extracts will give a truer impression
of him. We will begin with one of the elaborate salutations
which head his letters, that to the Philadelphians.

> Ignatius, who is also Theophorus, to the church of God
> the Father and of Jesus Christ, which is in Philadelphia
> of Asia, which has found mercy and is firmly estab-
> lished in the concord of God and rejoices in the passion
> of our Lord and in his resurrection without wavering,
> being fully assured in all mercy; which church I salute
> in the blood of Jesus Christ, that is eternal and abiding
> joy; more especially if they be at one with the bishop
> and the presbyters who are with him, and with the

---

[1] See Lightfoot, Philippians, pages 234 and following, and elsewhere.

deacons that have been appointed according to the mind of Jesus Christ, whom after his own will he confirmed and established by his Holy Spirit.[1]

Writing to the Ephesians he says,

> I know who I am and to whom I write. I am a convict, you have received mercy: I am in peril, you are established. You are the high-road of those that are on their way to die unto God. You are associates in the mysteries with Paul, who was sanctified, who obtained a good report, who is worthy of all felicitation; in whose footsteps I would fain be found treading, when I shall attain unto God; who in every letter makes mention of you in Christ Jesus. Do your diligence therefore to meet together more frequently for thanksgiving to God and for his glory. For when you meet together frequently, the powers of Satan are cast down; and his mischief comes to nought in the concord of your faith. There is nothing better than peace, in which all warfare of things in heaven and things on earth is abolished. None of these things is hidden from you, if you be perfect in your faith and love toward Jesus Christ, for these are the beginning and end of life—faith is the beginning and love is the end—and the two being found in unity are God, while all things else follow in their train unto true nobility. No man possessing faith sins, and no man possessing love hates. The tree is manifest from its fruit; so they that profess to be Christ's shall be seen through their actions. For the work is not a thing of profession now, but is seen then when one is found in the power of faith unto the end. It is better to keep silence and to be, than to talk and not to be. It is a fine thing to teach, if the speaker practice. Now there is one teacher, who spoke and it came to pass: yes and even the things which he spoke in silence are worthy of the Father. He that truly possesses the word of Jesus, is able also to hearken unto his silence, that he may be perfect; that through his

[1] Lightfoot, Apostolic Fathers, part 2, volume 2, section 1, page 559.

speech he may act and through his silence he may be known.[1]

And again a little earlier,

> And pray also without ceasing for the rest of mankind (for there is in them a hope of repentance) that they may find God. Therefore permit them to take lessons at least from your works. Against their outbursts of wrath be meek; against their proud words be humble; against their railings set your prayers; against their errors be steadfast in the faith; against their fierceness be gentle. And be not zealous to imitate them by requital. Let us show ourselves their brothers by our forbearance; but let us be zealous to be imitators of the Lord, vying with each other who shall suffer the greater wrong, who shall be defrauded, who shall be set at nought; that no herb of the devil be found in you: but in all purity and temperance abide in Christ Jesus, with your flesh and with your spirit.[2]

For a comprehensive passage on unity we may take this from the "Epistle to the Magnesians."

> Seeing then that in the aforementioned persons I beheld your whole people in faith and embraced them, I advise you, be zealous to do all things in godly concord, the bishop presiding after the likeness of God and the presbyters after the likeness of the council of the apostles, with the deacons also who are most dear to me, having been entrusted with the diaconate of Jesus Christ, who was with the Father before the worlds and appeared at the end of time. Therefore do you all study conformity to God and pay reverence one to another; and let no man regard his neighbor after the flesh, but love one another in Christ Jesus always. Let there be nothing

---

[1] Lightfoot, Apostolic Fathers, part 2, volume 2, section 1, page 543.
[2] Lightfoot, Apostolic Fathers, part 2, volume 2, section 1, page 542.

among you which shall have power to divide you, but be united with the bishop and with them that preside over you as an example and lesson of incorruptibility. Therefore as the Lord did nothing without the Father, [being united with him,] either by himself or by the apostles, so neither do you anything without the bishop and the presbyters. And attempt not to think anything right for yourselves apart from others; but let there be one prayer in common, one supplication, one mind, one hope, in love and in joy unblameable, which is Jesus Christ, than whom there is nothing better. Hasten to come together all of you, as to one temple, even God; as to one alter, even to one Jesus Christ, who came forth from one Father and is with one and departed unto one.[1]

These passages are from letters to churches, the six Asiatic churches to which he wrote. We may take also a few words from the beginning of his one letter to a single man, Polycarp the bishop of Smyrna.

Ignatius who is also Theophorus, unto Polycarp, who is bishop of the church of the Smyrnaeans, or rather whose Bishop is God the Father and Jesus Christ, abundant greeting. Welcoming your godly mind which is grounded as it were on an immovable rock, I give exceeding glory that it has been vouchsafed me to see your blameless face, whereof I would fain have joy in God. I exhort you in the grace wherewith you are clothed to press forward in your course and to exhort all men that they may be saved. Vindicate your office in all diligence of flesh and of spirit. Have a care for union, than which there is nothing better. Bear all men, as the Lord also bears you. Suffer all men in love, as also you do. Give yourself to unceasing prayers. Ask for larger wisdom than you have. Be watchful, and keep your spirit from slumbering. Speak to each man severally after the manner of God. Bear the maladies

---

[1] Lightfoot, <u>Apostolic Fathers</u>, part 2, volume 2, section 1, page 547.

of all, as a perfect athlete. Where there is much toil, there is much gain.[1]

I have kept till last the "Epistle to the Romans," which is of different character from the rest. This was the church which was to receive him last; at Rome he was to die. To the Roman Christians he pours forth his inmost thoughts about his martyrdom. The exhortation which he has to address to them is chiefly that they will do nothing to hinder him in attaining this object of his desire. It is probable enough that among them were to be found persons of much influence with the emperor, who might thus have been able to save his life. But this is what he most anxiously deprecates. It must be confessed that much of the language here used about martyrdom is out of harmony with the teaching of the Lord and his apostles. Taken up by men of a lower type of mind and character, it led but too naturally to the mere frenzy of self-destruction, under the name of martyrdom, against which some of the wiser fathers had afterwards to protest. But reverence is due even to the extravagances of such as lofty soul as that of Ignatius.

> Ignatius, who is also Theophorus, unto her that has found mercy in the bountifulness of the Father Most High and of Jesus Christ his only Son; to the church that is beloved and enlightened through the will of him who willed all things that are, by faith and love towards Jesus Christ our God; even unto her that has the presidency in the country of the region of the Romans, being worthy of God, worthy of honor, worthy of felicitation, worthy of praise, worthy of success, worthy in purity, and having the presidency of love, walking in the law of Christ and bearing the Father's name; which church also I salute in the name of Jesus Christ the Son of the Father; unto them that in flesh and spirit are united unto his every commandment, being filled with the grace of God without wavering, and filtered clear from every foreign stain; abundant greeting in Jesus Christ our God in blamelessness.

---

[1] Lightfoot, Apostolic Fathers, part 2. volume 2, section 1, page 567.

Forasmuch as in answer to my prayer to God it has been granted to me to see your godly countenances, so that I have obtained even more than I asked; for wearing bonds in Christ Jesus I hope to salute you, if it be the divine will that I should be counted worthy to reach unto the end; for the beginning verily is well ordered, if so be I shall attain unto the goal, that I may receive my inheritance without hindrance. For I dread your very love, lest it do me an injury: for it is easy for you to do what you will, but for me it is difficult to attain unto God, unless you shall spare me. For I would not have you to be men pleasers but to please God, as indeed you do please him. For neither shall I myself ever find an opportunity such as this to attain unto God, nor can you, if you be silent, win the credit of any nobler work. For if you be silent and leave me alone, I am a word of God; but if you desire my flesh, then shall I be again a mere cry. No, grant me nothing more than that I be poured out a libation to God, while there is still an alter ready; that forming yourselves into a chorus in love you may sing to the Father in Jesus Christ, for that God has vouchsafed that the bishop from Syria should be found in the West, having summoned him from the East. It is good to set from the world unto God, that I may rise unto him. I write to all the churches, and I bid all men know, that of my own free will I die for God, unless you should hinder me. Let me be given to the wild beasts, for through them I can attain unto God. I am God's wheat, and I am ground by the teeth of wild beasts that I may be found pure bread [of Christ]. Rather entice the wild beasts, that they may become my sepulchre and may leave no part of my body behind, so that I may not, when I am fallen asleep, be burdensome to anyone. Then shall I be truly a disciple of Jesus Christ, when the world shall not so much as see my body. Supplicate the Lord for me, that through these instruments I may be found a sacrifice to God. I do not enjoin you, as Peter and Paul did. They were apostles, I am a convict; they were free, but I am a slave this very hour. Yet if I shall suffer, then am I a freedman of Jesus Christ, and I shall rise free in him. Now I am learning in my bonds to put away every desire. Remember in your prayers the church which is in Syria, which has God for its shepherd in my stead. Jesus Christ alone shall be its bishop. He and your love. But for myself I am ashamed to be called one of them; for neither am I worthy, being the very last of them and an untimely birth: but I have found mercy that I should be someone, if so be I shall attain unto God. My spirit salutes you, and the love of the churches which received me in the name of Jesus Christ, not as a mere wayfarer; for even those churches which did not lie on my route after the flesh went before me from city to city. Now I write these things unto you from Smyrna by the hand of the Ephesians who are worthy of all felicitation. And Crocus also, a name very dear to me, is with me, with many others besides.[1]

POLYCARP OF SMYRNA

Polycarp, we have seen, was the chief person with whom Ignatius was brought in contact on his journey as a condemned prisoner through Asia Minor. There are other proper names in tolerable abundance in the Ignatian letters: but they belong to men now forgotten, and even in that day none of them can have had the prominence of Polycarp. His own one extant writing belongs to this very time: that is, it was written after Ignatius had not only left Asia Minor but Philippi also, but when as yet no tidings had come from Italy as to what had befallen him at Rome. This writing is a letter to the Philippians in answer to that which they had written on Ignatius' departure. To it were appended copies of the letters written by Ignatius to Smyrna and other churches, and these copies are probably the source of our present collection.

The letter itself has no such vivid personal interest as those of Ignatius. The good Polycarp was a much more commonplace

---

[1] Lightfoot, <u>Apostolic Fathers</u>, part 2, volume 2, section 1, pages 555 and following.

person. But apart from its connection with Ignatius, his letter has a great value of its own, partly as showing what manner of thoughts on Christian faith and practice the bishop of a great Asiatic city cherished at that early date, partly also as showing what writings of the apostles he possessed and revered and drew upon (and that copiously) to give point and authority to what he had to say. The letter is for the most part made up of brotherly admonition, partly to the Philippian church at large, partly to its deacons, partly to its elders. There is no mention of any bishop, any more than there is in Ignatius' "Epistle to the Romans." Apparently this concentration of church government had not yet at this time spread from Asia into Europe. We may take a short chapter from near the beginning (after the salutation), and another from near the end.

I rejoiced with you greatly in our Lord Jesus Christ, for that you received the followers of the true love and escorted them on their way, as befitted you—those men encircled in saintly bonds which are the diadems of them that be truly chosen of God and our Lord; and that the steadfast root of your faith which was famed from primitive times abides until now and bears fruit unto our Lord Jesus Christ, who endured to face even death for our sins, whom God raised, having loosed the pangs of Hades; on whom, though you saw him not, you believe with joy unutterable and full of glory; unto which joy many desire to enter in; forasmuch as you know that it is by grace you are saved, not of works, but by the will of God through Jesus Christ.[1] . . . For I am persuaded that you are well trained in the sacred writings, and nothing is hidden from you. But to myself this is not granted. Only, as it is said in the scriptures, "Be angry and sin not" and "Let not the sun set on your wrath." Blessed is he that remembers this; and I trust that this is in you. Now may the God and Father of our Lord Jesus Christ, and the eternal high priest himself, the God Jesus Christ, build you up in faith and truth, and in all gentleness and in all

---

[1] Lightfoot, Apostolic Fathers, part 2, volume 2, section 2, page 1051.

avoidance of wrath and in forbearance and long suffering and in patient endurance and purity; and may
he grant unto you a lot and portion among his saints,
and to us with you, and to all that are under heaven,
who shall believe on our Lord and God Jesus Christ
and on his Father that raised him from the dead. Pray
for all the saints. Pray also for kings and powers and
princes, and for them that persecute and hate you, and
for the enemies of the cross, that your fruit may be
manifest among all men, that you may be perfect in
him.[1]

This meeting with Ignatius must have come somewhere
towards the middle of Polycarp's long life. His importance for
us depends in no small degree on that longevity of his.[2] Born
somewhere about the time of the destruction of Jerusalem by
Titus, he lived in early life near St. John and it may be one or
two more of the twelve. Of this converse in early youth he used
to rejoice to tell in his later years. This we learn from a striking
passage from a letter of Irenaeus which has happily been preserved. He wrote,

I can tell the very place in which the blessed Paul used
to sit when he discoursed, and his goings out and his
comings in, and the stamp of his life, and his bodily
appearance, and the discourses which he held towards
the congregation, and how he would describe his intercourse with John and with the rest of those who had
seen the Lord, and how he would relate their words.
And whatsoever things he had heard from them about
the Lord and about his acts of power and about his
teaching, Polycarp, as having received them from eye-
witnesses of the life and word would relate altogether
in accordance with the scriptures.[3]

---

[1] Lightfoot, Apostolic Fathers, part 2, volume 2, section 2, page 1055.
[2] As Dr. Lightfoot has expounded with peculiar force, he bridges the
long and comparatively obscure period between the close of the Apostolic age and the great writers of the latter part of the second century.
[3] Lightfoot, volume 1, page 429. Eusebius, History 5.20.

But from that midpoint of Polycarp's life formed by the passing of Ignatius we are able not only to look back to his youth but
also forward to his extreme old age. Somewhere about the
middle of the second century he made a journey to Rome to
take counsel with Anicetus the bishop (for by that time episcopacy was regularly established at Rome) about various matters
of church usage, but especially about the time of celebrating the
Paschal festival, as to which the churches of Asia Minor differed
from those of the West. They remained in perfect amity, though
the differences of usage continued, and Anicetus paid Polycarp
the honor of setting him in his own place to preside over the
Eucharistic service at Rome. Not long after the old man's
return, something like forty-five years after Ignatius' death for
conscience sake, he too in his turn was called to give his life in
bearing witness to the truth. A probably genuine narrative of
his martyrdom still survives, being a letter from the church of
Smyrna to one or more churches in Phrygia. Everyone, I suppose, has somewhere or other read the answer which he is
recorded to have made when the magistrate, anxious to spare
him, besought him to revile the Christ, and so obtain release.
"Fourscore and six years have I been his servant; and how can I
blaspheme my king that saved me?" Let us read also his last
words when he had been tied to the stake, true last words of a
true father of the church.

> So they did not nail him, but tied him. Then he, placing
> his hands behind him, and being bound to the stake,
> like a noble ram out of a great flock for an offering, a
> burnt sacrifice made ready and acceptable to God,
> looking up to heaven said; "O Lord God Almighty, the
> Father of your beloved and blessed Son Jesus Christ,
> through whom we have received the knowledge of
> you, the God of angels and powers and of all creation
> and of the whole race of the righteous, who live in
> your presence; I bless you for that you have granted
> me this day and hour, that I might receive a portion
> amongst the number of martyrs in the cup of [your]
> Christ unto resurrection of eternal life, both of soul
> and body, in the incorruptibility of the Holy Spirit.
> May I be received among these in your presence this

day, as a rich and acceptable sacrifice, as you did prepare and reveal it beforehand, and have accomplished
it, you that are the faithful and true God. For this
cause, yes and for all things, I praise you, I bless you, I
glorify you, through the eternal and heavenly high-
priest, your beloved Son, through whom with him and
the Holy Spirit be glory both now [and ever] and for
the ages to come. Amen."[1]

JUSTIN MARTYR

Last week we finished those of the fathers who are called
Apostolic Fathers. We considered two of them who were also
martyrs, though at a long interval of time, one a bishop of Antioch who was conducted through Asia Minor to perish by the
fangs of wild beasts at Rome, the other a bishop of Smyrna
who welcomed him on his way to death, collected his letters
and wrote about him at the time, journeyed himself in extreme
old age from Asia Minor to Rome to confer about difference of
church usages, came peacefully home, and then before long
was himself called to perish at the stake in his own Smyrna
because he too would not deny his Lord. We come today to a
third martyr, one who conventionally bears the title of martyr
almost as if it were part of his name.

Justin was born at Flavia Neapolis close to Sychem in
Samaria, but, it would seem, of heathen parentage. His "Dialogue," to which we shall come presently, is represented as
having had its scene laid at Ephesus. Eventually Justin would
seem to have been much at Rome, at that time a special place
of resort for those who took an active part in religious movements: and there he suffered martyrdom. The genuine works
of his which have come down to us in their original form are
at most three in number, without counting a little treatise
against heresies, lost in its original form, but apparently in
great part copied by Irenaeus.[2] They are two "Apologies," as

---

[1] Lightfoot, Apostolic Fathers, part 2, volume 2, section 2, page 1064.

[2] Several others bear his name in manuscripts, but are certainly by
other authors of various ages, some quite late. Early in the fourth century his name was attached to a partially different list of writings, the

they are called, defending Christians against heathen misrepresentations and heathen persecutions; and a "Dialogue" with a Jew named Trypho in which the faith of Christians is vindicated against Judaism.

It is hardly necessary to say that Justin's "Apologies" have nothing whatever to do with courteous excuses, that is, with the modern English sense of the word "apology." It is simply the common Greek word to denote any kind of defence against any kind of accusation, in a court of justice or anywhere else. Justin's "Apologies" were not quite the earliest of which we have any knowledge; but, so far as we do know, their predecessors were of less permanent value. Justin's first and longest "Apology" is addressed to the Roman emperor (Antoninus Pius), and his two adopted sons, one of them the philosopher Marcus Aurelius, to the sacred Senate and all the people of the Romans. The time is two or three years before the middle of the second century. Justin writes, he says, on behalf of them who out of every race of mankind are the subjects of unjust hate and contumely, being himself one of them.

He begins by appealing to the names "pious" and "philosopher" borne by the rulers. He says,

> Reason instructs those who are truly pious and philosophers to honor and cherish that only which is true, refusing to follow mere opinions of the ancients if they are bad ones: for sober reason instructs us not only not to follow those actions or decisions which have been unjust, but the lover of truth is bound in every way, and with disregard of his own life, to choose to say and do such things as are just, though he be threatened with death for so doing.

He protests against condemnation of Christians for the mere name, without anything evil being proved against them. He repudiates the vulgar imputation of atheism, pointing out how the same charge had been brought against Socrates, and had

---

genuineness of which we have no means of testing. But the books of his which we do possess are so valuable from several points of view that we have every reason to be satisfied.

caused his death. That crime he attributes to the inspiration of the demons, whom he identifies with the gods of the heathen, and whom he represents as similarly inspiring the attacks upon Christians. As regards such gods as these, he confesses atheism, but not as regards the most true God, the Father of right, and temperance and the other virtues, himself free from all mixture of evil; and his Son and the prophetic Spirit.

As regards the lives of Christians, he courts the fullest enquiry, demanding that any found guilty of misconduct be duly punished, but for his crimes. not for being a Christian. Then follow several chapters on the true service of God, on the divine kingdom for which Christians look, and on their living as ever in God's sight; and this is followed by free quotation from the Sermon on the Mount, and other similar passages from gospel records; and by reference to Christ's own authority for the faithful loyalty which Christians practised towards the emperors. But it would take far too long to give even a slight sketch of the contents of the "Apology." At every step we find attempts to trace analogies between Christian beliefs on the one hand and Greek philosophy or Greek mythology on the other.[1]

The doctrine of the divine Word or λόγος received from scripture he connected with the Stoic doctrine of the Word or Reason (λόγος) a seed of which is inborn in all men, and thus he was enabled to recognize the workings of God in the ages before the Word became incarnate. He also appeals largely to the testimony of the Jewish prophets; but on this subject he is hampered by his habit of looking chiefly to supposed literal fulfillments of verbal predictions and by a want of perception of the true nature of prophecy. The last few chapters contain a valuable account of baptism as then practised,[2] and then of the conducting of the newly-baptized person to the assembly of "the brethren," followed by the offering up of prayers for him and "for all others everywhere," and by the joining of all in the feast of thanksgiving or Eucharist, of which he gives a further explanation. He proceeds,

---

[1] This was no mere diplomatic "ad hominem" accommodation, but connected with Justin's own deepest convictions.

[2] That is, adult baptism, for nothing is said of infant baptism.

And we from that time forward always have each other in remembrance; and we that are wealthy give help to all that are in need, and we are in company with each other always. And for all that we partake of we bless the Maker of all things through his Son Jesus Christ and through the Holy Spirit.

Last he describes the Sunday service including the Eucharist, and the distribution of the offerings among orphans and widows, the sick and the needy, prisoners and sojourners from other lands.

The second or shorter "Apology" is probably a sort of appendix to the first. It begins with a complaint how Urbicus the city prefect (or mayor, as we should say) had condemned three Christians in succession to death, without any crime on their part. Justin declares that he too is expecting a similar fate, perhaps by the false accusations of the cynic Crescens who went about declaiming against the Christians. In what follows Justin speaks still more explicitly than before of the seed of the Word which had been implanted in the wiser and better heathen, causing them to be persecuted, not Socrates only but Musonius and other Stoics: but they all differed, he explains, from Christ, because what with them was in part only was with him complete and whole. He says,

Whatsoever things therefore have been said well in any men's words belong to us Christians: for we worship and love next to God the Word who comes forth from the unborn and unutterable God, since for our sakes also he has become man, that becoming also a partaker of the things that affect us he might also accomplish for us a cure. For all those writers were able to see but dimly through the seed of the Word inborn in them the things that are. For a seed of a thing and imitation of it granted according to capacity is one thing, and quite other is that which graciously gives itself to be imparted and imitated.

The other work of Justin, a much larger one, is the "Dialogue with Trypho":

While I was walking one morning in the walks of the Xystus, a certain man, with others in his company, having met me, said, "Hail, O philosopher!" And immediately after saying this, he turned round and walked along with me; his friends likewise turned round with him. And I for my part addressed him, saying, "Well, what is it?" And he replied, "I was taught," says he, "by Corinthus the Socratic in Argos, that I ought not to despise or neglect those who wear this dress, but to show them all kindness, and to associate with them, if so be some advantage might arise from the intercourse either to some such man or to myself. It is good, moreover, for both, if either the one or the other be benefited. On this account, therefore, whenever I see anyone in such dress, I gladly approach him, and now for the same reason, have I willingly accosted you; and these accompany me, in the expectation of hearing for themselves something profitable from you."

"But who are you, best of mortals?" So I replied to him in jest.

Then he told me simply both his name and his race. "Trypho," says he, "I am called; and I am a Hebrew of the circumcision, escaped from the war lately carried on there, and now spending my days in Greece, for the most part at Corinth."

"And in what" said I, "would you be profited by philosophers so much as by your own lawgiver and the prophets?"

"What?" he replied. "Do not the philosophers make their whole discourse on God? and are they not continually raising questions about his unity and providence? Is not this truly the duty of philosophy, to investigate concerning the Divinity?"

"Yes," said I, "so we too have supposed. But the most have not even cared about this, whether there be one or more gods, and whether they take thought for each one of us or not, as if this knowledge contributed nothing to our happiness; no, they moreover attempt to persuade us that God takes care of the universe as a whole with its genera and species, but not of me and you, and each individually, since otherwise we would surely not need to pray to him night and day. But it is not difficult to understand the upshot of this; for fearlessness and licence in speaking result to such as maintain these opinions, doing and saying whatever they choose, neither dreading punishment nor hoping for any benefit from God. For how could they? They affirm that the same things shall always happen; and, further, that I and you shall again live in like manner, having become neither better men nor worse. But there are some others, who, having supposed the soul to be immortal and immaterial, believe that though they have committed evil they will not suffer punishment (for that which is immaterial is insensible), and that the soul, in consequence of its immortality, needs nothing from God."

And he, smiling gently, said, "Tell us your opinion of these matters, and what idea you entertain respecting God, and what your philosophy is."

"I will tell you," said I, "what seems to me; for philosophy is in fact the greatest possession, and most honorable before God, to whom it leads us and alone commends us; and these are truly holy men who have bestowed attention on philosophy. What philosophy is, however, and the reason why it has been sent down to men, have escaped the observation of most; for there would be neither Platonists, nor Stoics, nor Peripatetics, nor Theoretics, nor Pythagoreans, this knowledge being one. I wish to tell you how it has become many-headed. It has happened that those who first handled it, and who were therefore esteemed illustrious men, were succeeded by those who made no investigations concerning truth, but only admired the perseverance and self-discipline of the former, as well as the novelty of the doctrines; and each thought that to be true which he learned from his teacher: then, moreover, those latter persons handed down to their successors such things, and others similar to them; and this system was called by the name of him who was styled the father of the doctrine. Being at first desirous of

personally conversing with one of these men, I surrendered myself to a certain Stoic; and having spent a
considerable time with him, when I had not acquired
any further knowledge of God (for he did not know
himself nor did he say that this was a necessary part of
teaching) I left him, and betook myself to another, who
was called a Peripatetic, and as he fancied, shrewd.
And this man, after putting up with me for the first few
days, requested me to fix a fee, in order that the intercourse might not be unprofitable to us. Him too for
this reason I abandoned, believing him to be no philosopher at all. But as my soul was still yearning to hear
the peculiar and choice part of philosophy, I came to a
Pythagorean, very celebrated—a man who thought
much of his own wisdom. And then, when I had an
interview with him, willing to become his hearer and
disciple, he said, 'What then? Are you acquainted with
music, astronomy and geometry? Do you expect to
perceive any of those things which conduce to a happy
life, if you have not been first informed on those points
which wean the soul from sensible objects, and render
it fitted for objects which appertain to the mind, so
that it can contemplate that which is honorable in its
essence and that which is good in its essence?' Having
commended many of these branches of learning, and
telling me that they were necessary, he dismissed me
when I confessed to him my ignorance. Accordingly I
took it rather impatiently, as was to be expected when
I failed in my hope, the more so because I deemed the
man had some knowledge; but reflecting again on the
space of time during which I would have to linger over
those branches of learning, I was not able to endure
longer procrastination. In my perplexity it occurred to
me to have an interview with the Platonists likewise,
for their fame was great. And so I conversed much
with one who had lately settled in our city—a man of
intelligence, holding a high position among the Platonists—and I made progress, and gained ever so much
increase day by day. And the perception of immaterial
things quite overpowered me, and the contemplation

of ideas furnished my mind with wings, so that in a little while I supposed that I had become wise; and such was my stupidity, I expected forthwith to look upon God, for this is the end of Plato's philosophy."

"And while I was thus disposed, when I wished at one time to be filled with great quietness, and to shun the tramp of men, I used to go to a certain field not far from the sea. And when I was near that spot one day, which having reached I purposed to be by myself, a certain old man, by no means contemptible in appearance, showing a meek and grave disposition, followed me at a little distance. And when I turned round to him, having halted, I fixed my eyes rather keenly on him."

Then Justin recounts how the old man, after much discourse on philosophy, and especially that of Plato and Pythagoras, guided him to the prophets and the Christ of whom they prophesied. He concluded,

"'But pray that before all things, the gates of light may be opened to you; for these things are not perceptible to the eyes or mind of all, but only of the man to whom God and his Christ shall give the power to understand.' When he had spoken these and many other things, which there is no time for mentioning at present, he went away, bidding me follow them up; and I saw him no more. But straightway a fire was kindled in my soul; and a love of the prophets, and of those men who are friends of Christ, possessed me; and while revolving his words in my mind, I found this philosophy alone to be safe and expedient. Thus, then, and for this reason, I am a philosopher. Moreover, I would wish that all with a resolution similar to my own would never separate themselves from the words of the Savior. For they possess an awe in themselves, and are sufficient to abash those who turn aside from the path of rectitude; while the sweetest rest comes to those who carefully practise them. If then, you have any care for yourself, and seek after salvation and put your trust in God, you may come to know the Christ of

God, and become perfect, and so be happy."

When I had said this, my beloved friend, those who were with Trypho laughed; but he, smiling said, "I approve of your other remarks, and admire the eagerness with which you study divine things; but it were better for you still to abide in the philosophy of Plato, or of some other man, cultivating endurance, self-control, and moderation, rather than be deceived by false words, and follow the opinions of men of no reputation. For if you remain in that mode of philosophy, and live blamelessly, a hope of a better destiny were left to you; but when you have forsaken God, and reposed confidence in man, what safety still awaits you? If, then, you are willing to listen to me (for I have already considered you a friend), first be circumcised, then keep as the law has ordained the sabbath, and the feasts, and the new moons of God; and, in a word, do all things which have been written in the law: and then perhaps you shall have mercy from God. But Christ—if he has indeed been born, and exists anywhere—is unknown, and does not yet even recognize himself, and has no power until Elias come to anoint him, and make him manifest to all. But you, accepting a vain report, invent a Christ for yourselves, and for his sake are now inconsiderately perishing."

"I excuse and forgive you, my friend," I said "for you know not what you say, but have been persuaded by teachers who do not understand the scriptures; and you speak, like a diviner, whatever comes into your mind. But if you are willing to listen to an account of him, how we have not been deceived, and shall not cease to confess him—although men's reproaches be heaped upon us, although the most terrible tyrant compel us to deny him,—I shall prove to you as you stand here that we have not believed empty fables, or words without any foundation, but words filled with the Spirit of God, and big with power, and flourishing with grace."[1]

---

[1] Justin Martyr, "Dialogue with Trypho," from pages 85-97 in Rev. G.

Some of Trypho's companions depart with jeers, and then the dialogue begins in earnest. It ranges over the various points of difference between Judaism and the Christian faith of that time, and large masses of the Old Testament are naturally quoted and discussed. But we must be content with the auto-biographic sketch, for such it doubtless is, which forms the introduction. Of course we must not expect that that story of passing from philosopher to philosopher is a complete account of the course of Justin's conversion.[1] But the name which he commonly bore, Justin philosopher and martyr, was entirely appropriate. He is the first prominent representative of what was to be the characteristic of many fathers of the church both Greek and Latin, the construction of a theology out of the biblical elements of the faith in combination with this or that gentile philosophy of the loftier sort.[2]

IRENAEUS

We must now turn to a different region from any in which we have as yet paused.[3] Irenaeus, one of the greatest of the fathers, belongs to different countries; but he must always be chiefly associated with South-East France, the scene of his principal labors and episcopal authority. There is however a prelude to his work which must not be passed over. Marseilles

Reith's translation ("Ante-Nicene Christian Library").

[1] In his second "Apology" he speaks strongly of the impression made on him by the virtues of the Christians while he was in his Platonist stage, and we may be sure that this impression acted powerfully on him.

[2] How soon Justin's anticipations of martyrdom were fulfilled is not known with certainty. There is fair evidence however that the interval was not long. A short and simple narrative of his examination before the prefect still survives, and is almost certainly genuine. He and his companions died by the headsman's sword.

[3] We possess other Greek "Apologies" written later in the same century. The most individual of them is by Tatian, an erratic disciple of Justin's, the compiler of a famous "Diatessaron" or composite gospel narrative formed by putting together small fragments of the four gospels. He was by birth a Syrian, not a Greek, and his fiery nature bursts forth in his "Apology" in bitter hatred and contempt for all that was Greek. The other "Apologies" have a value of their own, but are far below Justin's in force and freshness.

was a Greek colony of great antiquity; and from it the Greek language and culture spread not only along the coast but for a considerable distance up the Rhone. How the gospel first found its way there we do not know: but there is some evidence of a connection between the churches of Western Asia Minor and those of the Rhone. Now the historian Eusebius has preserved for us the greater part of a letter which begins thus:

> The servants of Christ who sojourn in Vienne and Lyons in Gaul to the brethren throughout Asia and Phrygia who have the same faith and hope of redemption with us: peace and grace and glory from God the Father and Christ Jesus our Lord.

The purpose of the letter is to describe a grievous persecution which had fallen upon them, Pothinus the bishop, a man of ninety years of age, being among the victims. The story of Christian heroism, especially as shown by the slave girl Blandina, has hardly an equal in literature: but it must be read as a whole, and it is of considerable length. While some of these Christians of Lyons and Vienne were in prison, they wrote various letters, among others one to Eleutherus, bishop of Rome, "on behalf of the peace of the churches."[1] The bearer of the letter was an elder of Lyons, Irenaeus by name; and the writers of the letter warmly commend him to Eleutherus, as one who was zealous for the covenant of Christ. How long he had been in Gaul, we know not; but he came from Asia Minor, where as we know from the passage read previously he had listened eagerly to the aged Polycarp, and his reminiscences of his intercourse in youth with men who had seen the Lord.[2]

Later in life he addressed himself to Rome for another mission of peace. The importance which the church of Rome derived from its position in the central city of the empire was gradually fastening itself to the person of its bishop, and

---

[1] That is, probably to urge toleration for the votaries of the new enthusiastic movement proceeding from Phrygia which we know under the name Montanism.

[2] There is also some evidence that he was at Rome at the time Polycarp's death, and heard there the sound as of a trumpet proclaiming "Polycarp has suffered martyrdom."

assumed exaggerated proportions when the arrogant Victor
was its bishop. The differences between the Asaiatic and the
Roman customs as to the time of keeping the Paschal festival
had now become aggravated into a deadly strife, and Victor
endeavored to impose the Roman custom on all churches. Irenaeus was now a follower of the Roman custom: but this did
not prevent his writing a strong letter of remonstrance to Victor
in the name of the Christians of Gaul. This incident occurred
somewhere in the last few years of the second century. After
this we hear no more of Irenaeus on any tolerable authority.
He may or may not have lived into the new century. Essentially he is the best representative of the last half, and especially
the last quarter, of the second century.

Besides minor works, chiefly epistles, of which we have only
fragments, we possess entire Irenaeus' great work, the "Refutation and Overthrow of the Knowledge (Gnosis) falsely so
called." Only a small proportion of it is preserved in Greek:
but it is a great thing that the ancient Latin version is completely preserved. Thus far I have said nothing about the theologians who are now called "Gnostics." Unfortunately not
many fragments are preserved of their own writings; so that
our knowledge of them comes chiefly from opponents who saw
truly the impossibility of reconciling their main principles with
the historical gospel, but who as a rule had but a dim sense of
the real meaning of their speculations, and a very imperfect
sympathy with the speculative difficulties which led to them.
The so-called Gnostic systems were various attempts to interpret history and nature by a medley of Christian ideas with the
ideas and mythologies suggested by various Eastern religions.
The most definite types of so-called "Gnosticism" were further
shaped by Greek influence, and it is in this form that they chiefly
came into collision with the ordinary churches.

Their great time was about the middle of the first half of the
second century: but they lasted on in one shape or another for a
considerable time. The great leaders had passed away before
Irenaeus wrote: but even in Gaul his flock was troubled by
some of the successors; and it was no superfluous task that he
undertook when he set about an elaborate refutation.[1] But it is

---

[1] Doubtless he had other predecessors besides Justin. Thus Papias

a striking fact that, while his censure of the so-called Gnostic systems is always unreserved and pitiless, he is unconsciously influenced by the new thoughts which they had brought forward. The Christianity which he proclaims has a comprehensiveness such as no earlier Christian father known to us could ever have dreamed of. His doctrine of the Word is a true expansion of St. John's doctrine, a rich application of it to bring order into the retrospect of the spiritual history of mankind: and so his vision of the future is inspired by the thought which he loves to repeat out of the Epistle to the Ephesians, how that it was the eternal purpose of the Father to sum up all things in Christ (ἀνακεφαλαιώσασθαι, "recapitulare").

Two passages must suffice, though many are tempting to read. The first shall be a familiar one from the second book, on our Lord's taking upon him all the ages of man up to adult manhood.

> He was thirty years of age when he came to the baptism, thenceforth having the full age of a teacher, when he came to Jerusalem, that he might rightly be able to receive the title of "Teacher" from all. For to seem one thing, and be another, was not his way, as is said by those who represent him as being in appearance only: but what he was, that he also seemed. Being therefore a Teacher, he had likewise the ages of a Teacher, not rejecting nor transcending man, nor breaking the law of the human race in himself, but hallowing every age by its likeness to himself. For he came to save all through himself; all, I mean, who through him are born anew unto God, infants, and little children, and boys, and youths, and elders.

---

had written "Expositions of the Lord's Oracles" to correct and supersede the fantastic interpretation of our Lord's parables and other discourses by which some of the so-called Gnostics endeavored to find authority for their speculations. Nor was he the only "elder," to use the often recurring title, whom Irenaeus was thankful to quote and sometimes to transcribe at considerable length. Doubtless, if so large a proportion of the Christian literature of the preceding half century had not perished, we should have found yet clearer evidence of the width of his reading.

Accordingly he came through every age, with infants becoming an infant, hallowing infants; among little children a little child, hallowing those of that very age, at the same time making himself to them an example of dutifulness, and righteousness, and subjection; among young men a young man, becoming an example to young men and hallowing them to the Lord. So also an elder among elders, that he might be a perfect Teacher in all things, not only as regards the setting forth of the truth but also as regards age, at the same time hallowing also the elders, becoming likewise an example to them. Lastly he came also even unto death, that he might be the first begotten from the dead, himself holding the primacy in all things, the Author of life, before all things, and having precedence of all things.[1]

The other passage shall be from the end of the book, the end also of the millennial speculations which filled Irenaeus as they did other men of that age. If some of the thoughts are difficult to follow, yet they manifestly deserve to be listened to and pondered.

In clear vision then did John see beforehand the first resurrection of the righteous, and the inheritance of the earth during the kingdom (reign): to the same effect also did the prophets prophesy concerning it. For thus much the Lord also taught, in that he promised that he would have a new mixing of the cup in the kingdom with the disciples. And the apostle too declared that the creation should be free from the bondage of corruption to enter the liberty of the glory of the sons of God. And in all these [events], and through them all, the same God, even the Father, is shown forth, who fashioned man, and promised the inheritance to the fathers, who prepared it for the resurrection of the righteous, and fulfills the promises for his Son's kingdom, afterward bestowing as a Father things which neither eye has seen, nor ear heard, and which have

[1] Irenaeus, page 358, Stieren.

not ascended into the heart of man. For one is the Son, who accomplished the Father's will; and one the human race, in which the mysteries of God are accomplished, which angels desire to see, and have not power to explain the wisdom of God, through which the being which he fashioned is brought into conformity and concorporation with the Son; that his offspring, the first begotten Word, might descend into the creature, that is into the being that [God] fashioned, and be received by him; and that the creature again might receive the Word, and ascend up to him, mounting above the angels, and come to be after the image and likeness of God.

HIPPOLYTUS

In Justin the Samaritan, who taught and who died a martyr's death at Rome, we have had before us the most characteristic of the Greek apologists of the second century, a man who went about clad only in the traditional philosopher's cloak, and who pleaded the cause of the Christians against the assaults of magistrates and populace on the ground that their faith and conduct should commend itself to philosophers and lovers of right reason. In Irenaeus, the disciple of Polycarp at Smyrna, who became bishop of Lyons and took an active part in promoting the peace of the church when endangered by the intolerance of Victor, bishop of Rome, we have had the first great theologian, in the strict sense of the word, whose writings are to any great extent preserved to us. His great refutation of the leading doctrines of the teachers called Gnostics, is a still imperfectly worked mine of great thoughts on God's dealings with mankind through the ages, founded on the idea of the Word before and after the incarnation.

A few words are due to a disciple of Irenaeus, who forty years ago would have been commonly reckoned an obscure and unimportant father, namely Hippolytus. Shortly after that date there was published from a manuscript then lately brought to Paris an elaborate Greek account and refutation of early heresies, chiefly "Gnostic," which it was soon recognized could not well have any other author than Hippolytus. There is no real doubt about the matter, though, for quite intelligible reasons, a few still hold otherwise. The author writes as a bishop, and Hippolytus is sometimes called bishop of Rome, sometimes bishop of Portus, the commercial port of Rome.[1] The treatise itself is one of much value for the extracts which it gives from Gnostic writings. But of more general interest is the narrative of some of the inner history of the Roman church under two successive bishops. After every allowance has been made for the partisanship of the writer, the picture is not an agreeable one. But this lies outside our proper subject.

Of the part taken by Hippolytus it is enough to say that he regarded Callistus and the dominant authorities of the Roman church as dangerously lax in their admission of penitents to communion, and he likewise accused them of favoring a doctrine not far from Sabellianism, while he himself, from the manner in which he expounded the doctrine of the Word, a doctrine which evidently had little meaning for them, was accused by them of setting up two Gods to be worshipped. The end of the story seems to be supplied by a curious early Roman record which states that "Pontianus the bishop" (the second after Callistus) and "Hippolytus the presbyter were banished to Sardinia, to the island of deadly climate." Perhaps, as has been suggested, the Roman magistrates took this way of enforcing peace in the Christian community, by getting rid of the two leaders together.[2]

---

[1] What he really was, is still an open question. The most commonly received view is that which was suggested by Döllinger, that for at least a certain time Callistus and Hippolytus were respectively recognized by different parties in the Roman church as each the only true and lawful bishop of Rome, though eventually Callistus alone was officially acknowledged as having been bishop.

[2] From another record forming part of the same document we learn that the Roman church in the middle of the fourth century kept on the same day the festival of Hippolytus in one cemetery and of Pontianus in another, both evidently as martyrs. Apparently they had both perished in the mines of Sardinia, and their bodies been received back in peace together. According to a somewhat confused tradition Hippolytus before his death had advised his followers to return to the communion of the Roman church authorities. In the fourth and later centuries the strangest and most contradictory legends of his martyrdom became current. By a singular good fortune a contemporary memorial of him has

Hippolytus was one of the three most learned Greek fathers of his time, mostly the early part of the third century.[1] Hippolytus' writings chiefly fall under two heads, doctrinal treatises of a controversial kind, and books connected with the study of scripture, either actual commentaries or essays at constructing some sort of scripture chronology. His defence of the Gospel and Apocalypse of St. John against certain contemporary gainsayers might be reckoned under either head. He was especially interested in the books of Daniel and Revelation, and in some of the questions which they suggest.[2] All that remains of him however, with the exception of the great treatise on heresies, itself far from complete, makes up only a small volume. This is the more remarkable as the fame of his writings spread far and wide through the East, though the story of his life was unknown outside Rome or else forgotten.

CLEMENT OF ALEXANDRIA

Hippolytus, following Irenaeus, has conducted us well into the third century.   We must now go back half a generation or so to make acquaintance with a different region and a different way of apprehending Christianity and its relation to the world, though no doubt to a certain extent anticipated by Justin Martyr. Alexandria at the mouth of the Nile had long been a special home of Greek learning and philosophy, a place where the culture of Egypt, Asia, and Europe met together. But of still greater

———————

been preserved, such as we possess for no other early father whatever. Above three centuries ago a large part of an ancient sitting statue was dug up near Rome, and in due time recognized by the very interesting inscriptions on the base to have been no other than Hippolytus, though his name does not appear, and to have been erected shortly after his death. In the great hall of the Christian Museum at St. John Lateran, as you walk up between two lines of early Christian sarcophagi of the highest interest for their carving, you are faced by this great statue of Hippolytus looking down upon you from the platform at the end.

[1] Of one of them Julius Africanus, of whom only fragments remain, I propose to say no more. To Origen we shall come presently.

[2] To him they were by no means questions of idle curiosity; for in the new hostility of the Roman state, as shown in the persecution of Septimius Severus, he supposed that he saw a fulfillment of Apocalyptic prophecy.

moment was the nature of the Judaism which had arisen in the midst of the vast Jewish population of the city, a Judaism almost wholly detached from the legal influences which dominated the Judaism of Palestine, and aiming especially at the comparison and harmonizing of the Old Testament, and especially the Pentateuch, with the better forms of Greek philosophy.[1]

We know almost nothing of Alexandrian Christianity in its earlier days: but evidently it took its shape in no small degree from the type of Judaism which was already current in the place. In the middle part of the second century we hear of a Christian catechetical school at Alexandria, probably for the instruction of the highly educated converts who joined the church. The second name preserved to us from the list of its heads or chief instructors is that of the Sicilian Pantaenus, best remembered now as having gone on a missionary journey to India. Among his pupils was Clement of Alexandria, the father who next claims our attention, and who often speaks of him, chiefly only under the title "the elder," with enthusiastic affection. Clement himself is said to have been an Athenian and probably was so. Profoundly Christian as he is, there is no father who shows anything like the same familiarity with the ancient classical literature of Greece, especially the poetical literature.[2]

There is reason to suppose that after a time he became a colleague of Pantaenus in the catechetical school, and at all events when Pantaenus died he succeeded him, probably somewhere

---

[1] Of this Graecized Judaism we have invaluable examples in Philo's writings.

[2] It is not clear whether he was of Christian or of heathen parents: but we know from himself that he travelled in early life, and came under the influence of at least six different Christian teachers in different lands, whom he calls "blessed and truly memorable men." In Greece he met the first, an Ionian, (probably from western Asia Minor): two others in Magna Graecia, the Greek-speaking south part of Italy, one from middle Syria and another from Egypt. Whether he went to Rome, as one would expect, does not appear: at all events he refers to no teacher met there. From Italy he crossed to the East, and there he learned from an Assyrian, supposed to be Justin's scholar Tatian, and from another, in Palestine, one of Jewish birth. The last, he says, in order, but virtually the first, he found lurking in Egypt, and there he rested. He had found Pantaenus.

about the year 200. He was now or soon after a presbyter of the church. But two or three years later through a change in the policy of the Emperor Septimius Severus a persecution broke out, which fell with much severity on Alexandria; and the teachers of the catechetical school, evidently including Clement, took refuge elsewhere. A few years after this we have a glimpse of him through a scrap of a letter of his pupil Alexander, fortunately preserved by Eusebius. Alexander was at this time apparently bishop of a Cappadocian church; certainly he was in prison for conscience sake; and he wrote a congratulatory letter out of his prison on their recent choice of a new bishop, sending it by Clement whom he calls "the blessed presbyter, a man virtuous and well tried": who by the providence of God was then with him and had established and increased the church. Clement cannot have lived much longer.

In another letter to Origen, written before 216, Alexander again speaks affectionately of Clement as of Pantaenus, both as now departed. These testimonies are of value as showing that Clement's withdrawal from the approaching persecution was due to no selfish cowardice, but to such rightful avoidance of useless sacrifice of life as had been commanded by our Lord himself when he bade the apostles, "When they persecute you in one city, flee into another." For Alexander knew what martyrdom meant. He was made bishop of Jerusalem under very peculiar circumstances, partly in consequence of what were regarded as divine monitions, partly on account of what he had bravely endured in the persecution. It was the same to the end of his life. In the year 250 he was brought before the magistrates in the Decian persecution, and thrown into prison, and there he died.

Clement's chief writings form a connected series. First comes the "Hortatory Address to the Greeks"; the purpose is to show that the Christian faith accomplishes what the heathen religions and philosophies vainly sought. It is too florid in style, and overloaded with superfluous illustrations. But it is inspired by the purest Christian fervor, and, apart from details, its general drift is at once lofty and true. Next comes the Παιδαγωγός or "Tutor." The Tutor is not, as we might have guessed, the book itself; nor is he a man. It is none other than Christ the Word of the Father, the Tutor of mankind, educating them

always in love and for their benefit, sometimes by gifts, sometimes by chastisements. The purpose of the book is the guidance
of the youthful convert from heathenism in habits belonging to
Christian morality.

The heads of this morality are not vague generalities, but
practical and concrete enough; for example, meat and drink,
and sumptuous furniture, behavior at feasts, laughter, bad
language, social behavior, use of perfumes and garlands, sleep,
marriage duties, dress and ornaments, use of cosmetics, use of
baths, exercises.[1] The permanent interest of these discussions
is very great. Often as we may have to dissent from this or
that remark, the wisdom and large-mindedness with which the
"Paedagogus" is written are above all praise. On the one hand
there is an all-prevading sense that the gospel is meant to be at
once a moulding and a restraining power in all the pettiest
details as in the greatest affairs of life: on the other hand there
is no morbid jealousy of the rightful use of God's good gifts,
and no addiction to restrictions not commanded by morality, or
not required for self-discipline.

The third treatise of the series is commonly known by the
name στρωματεῖς.[2] Various writers had used this name for
books of the nature of miscellanies. By Clement it is in strictness used only of the seven different books of the great treatise,
Στρωματεύς. His descriptive title, if less quaint, is more really
interesting, "Gnostic jottings" (or "notes") "according to the
true philosophy." The Alexandrian convert from heathenism
needed instruction not only in the outward behavior proper to
the Christian life but also in the deeper grounds of the Christian morality and religion. In the schools of ordinary Greek
philosophy he would learn the value and the dignity of wisdom
and knowledge; and now he had to be taught that, whatever
might be said to the contrary by unwise Christians, these things
had a yet higher place under the gospel: for the Christ whom it
proclaimed was not only the Savior of mankind in the simplest

---

[1] Alexandria seventeen centuries ago was clearly not so very different a place from towns better known to us.

[2] "Stromata," common in modern books, is incorrect. A στρωματεύς
was a long bag of striped canvas, in which bedclothes (στρώματα) were
kept rolled up.

and most obvious sense, but also one in whom lay hid the treasures of wisdom and knowledge.

Clement was not made timorous by the association of the word γνῶσις, "knowledge," with the sects called heretical of those whom we now call Gnostics. No, it rather urged him to claim for the church a word and an idea which could not be spared. If St. Paul had spoken of a Christian gnosis falsely so called, he had thereby implied that there was a right Christian gnosis, a gnosis truly so called; and this is what Clement set himself to defend and in part to provide. It is a leading idea of Clement that the divinely ordained preparation for the gospel ran in two parallel lines, that of the Jewish law and prophets and that of Greek philosophy. His exposition of it is somewhat damaged by his following an old but quite unfounded common-place of Jewish apologetics, much repeated by the fathers, that the Greek philosophers borrowed largely from the Old Testament. But the idea itself enabled him to look out both on the past history of mankind and on the mixed world around him with a hopeful and helpful faith.

The treatise is a very discursive one. The leading heads are such as these:—faith, Christian fear, love, repentance, endurance, martyrdom, the true doctrine of marriage, teaching by signs and allegories, the attribution of human feelings to God in scripture. There is much comparison of Christian teaching on these themes with that of Greek philosophers and also of leading Pseudo-Gnostics, usually in a candid and discriminating manner. But it is no merely theoretical knowledge that is here celebrated. The true Gnostic, according to Clement, is:

He who imitates God in so far as is possible omitting nothing pertaining to such growth in the divine likeness as comes within his reach, practising self-restraint, enduring, living justly, reigning over his passions, imparting of what he possesses, doing good by word and deed to the best of his power. He, it is said, is greatest in the kingdom of heaven who shall do and teach in imitation of God by showing free grace like his, for the bounties of God are for the common benefit .[1]

---

[1] Clement of Alexandria, Stromateis 2, page 480, Potter.

The fourth treatise of the series, written after Clement left Alexandria, was called Ὑποτυπώσεις, "Outlines." The greatest part of it unhappily is lost, though a fair number of difficult but peculiarly interesting fragments of it have been preserved. Its subject was apparently fundamental doctrine, while it also contained expository notes on various books of the Bible, including St. Paul's epistles and four out of the Catholic epistles. What remains enables us to see that this first great attempt to bring the gospel into close relation with the whole range of human thought and experience on other lines than those of the Pseudo-Gnostics contained, as was natural, various theological crudities which could not ultimately be accepted; while it must also have been rich in matter of permanent value.[1]

We must now bid farewell to Clement of Alexandria. He was not, as far as we know, one of those whose writings have exercised a wide or a powerful influence over subsequent theology. Large portions of his field of thought remained for long ages unworked, or even remain unworked still. But what he at once humbly and bravely attempted under great disadvantages at the beginning of the third century will have to be attempted afresh with the added experience and knowledge of seventeen Christian centuries more, if the Christian faith is to hold its ground among men; and when the attempt is made, not a few of his thoughts and words will probably shine out with new force, full of light for dealing with new problems. A comparatively simple passage from the "Stromateis" on faith, knowledge, love, will sufficiently illustrate his way of writing.

> Knowledge (that is, Christian knowledge, gnosis) is so to speak a perfecting of a man as a man, accomplished through acquaintance with divine things, in demeanor and life and word, harmonious and concordant with itself and with the divine Word. For by it faith is perfected, this being the only way in which the man who has faith becomes perfect. Now faith is a kind of inward good, and even without seeking God, it confesses

---

[1] In addition to the great series of four, Clement wrote several minor treatises now almost wholly lost, except a tract on the question "What rich man can be saved?" It contains the well-known beautiful story of St. John and the young man who became a bandit.

that he is and glorifies him as being. Hence a man must start from this faith, and when he has made increase in it must by the grace of God receive as far as he can the knowledge (gnosis) concerning him. . . . Not to doubt about God but to believe is the foundation of gnosis, while Christ is both at once the foundation and the structure built upon it, even as through him is both the beginning of things and their [several] ends. And the things that stand first and last, I mean faith and love, do not come by teaching; but gnosis transmitted by tradition according to the grace of God is entrusted as a deposit to those who show themselves worthy of the teaching; and from gnosis the dignity of love shines forth, out of light into light. For it is said "To him that has shall more be added"; to faith shall be added gnosis, and to gnosis love, and to love the inheritance.[1]

I will only add half-a-dozen pregnant lines from another "Stromateis," expounding by a memorable image the true relation between man and God in prayer. He says,

As men attached at sea to an anchor by a tight cable, when they pull at the anchor, draw not the anchor to themselves but themselves to the anchor, even so they who in the gnostic life draw God to them (that is, so it seems to them) have unawares been bringing themselves towards God.[2]

TERTULLIAN

The last father whose life and writings came before us was Clement of Alexandria. In him ancient Christian theology in some important respects reaches its highest point. There were after him greater as well as more influential theologians: but with all his very manifest defects there was no one whose vision of what the faith of Jesus Christ was intended to do for

---

[1] That is, (I suppose) the fulness of divine Sonship. Clement of Alexandria, Stromateis 7, page 864, Potter.

[2] Clement of Alexandria, Stromateis 4, page 633, Potter.

mankind was so full or so true. His great pupil Origen, and one or two of Origen's own pupils, who worthily carried on the tradition of Alexandrian theology, will I hope come before us next time. Meanwhile we must turn aside today to a region geographically not remote from Egypt, but in other respects curiously unlike Egypt as regards the Christian theologians whom it bred in the earlier centuries.

The Roman proconsular province of Africa, approximately what we now in church history for clearness' sake call "North Africa," was a remarkably insulated region, being shut off from the interior and from the coasts to the East by vast deserts.[1] The most important part of it answers roughly to the modern Tunis, Carthage being the capital. The Mediterranean divided it from Sicily and Italy: but there was close intercourse with Rome by water. Unhappily we know nothing of the foundation or earlier history of the North African churches. But there is good reason to believe that they first created a Latin Bible. They also probably contributed largely to the creation of the church organization which became prevalent in the West. They certainly created the distinctively Latin theology, which, developed especially by Augustine, and again by great theologians of the Middle Ages, and again by the leading Continental Reformers of the sixteenth century, has dominated men's thoughts in Western Europe respecting God and man, both for good and for evil. We have to consider today the first two great fathers known to us from the North African churches, probably the first two great fathers whom they produced, Tertullian and Cyprian.

Nearly all that we know about Tertullian is gleaned from his own writings, and that is not much. He was probably born somewhere about the middle of the second century, and himself a native of North Africa. At Carthage he would have the fullest opportunity for acquiring the best culture of the time. Next to Rome, it was the second city of the Western Empire in size and importance; perhaps also the most corrupt city of the West as well as the chief center of the Latin cultivation and literature.[2] Tertullian's writings show what full use he made of these opportunities, as regards Greek and Roman literature. His

---

[1] As Mommsen has pointed out.
[2] As Mommsen says.

occupation was that of an advocate; and the usual course of a lawyer's training in rhetoric would naturally lead him to spend some time at Athens and at Rome in youth. To an intelligent young lawyer Rome would be a very attractive place just then, on account of the distinguished Roman jurists of the time. All this time Tertullian was assuredly a heathen, and apparently a man of vicious life, as he states himself, and as the foulness which ever afterwards infested his mind too painfully confirms.

How he became a Christian he never tells us directly: but it is tolerably clear that he is reciting his own experience when he more than once speaks of the moral impression produced on beholders by Christian martyrs. So in a famous passage of the "Apologeticum"[1] addressed to the heathen:

> We multiply every time that we are mown down by you: the blood of Christians is seed. . . . That very obstinacy which you reproach us with is a teacher. For who when he beholds it is not impelled to examine what are the inner contents of the matter?

Again:

> Everyone looking on such endurance, smitten as with a kind of scruple, is both enkindled to examine whence it proceeds, and, when he has discovered, himself also at once follows the truth.

Within the last few years it has become possible to surmise with some probability what the martyrdoms were which thus changed the course of Tertullian's life. We now know that the year 180, the first year of the Emperor Commodus, was the year when seven men and five women from the African town of Scilla were martyred at Carthage. The Acts of their martyrdom are still extant.[2]

Seventeen years later there was again persecution. Apparently the Christians, or some Christians, refused to take part

---

[1] Tertullian, Apology 50.
[2] See Lightfoot's <u>Apostolic Fathers</u> (second edition), Ignatius, volume 1, pages 524 and following.

in the public festivities, probably involving idolatrous usages, which greeted the final victory of the Emperor Septimius Severus over other claimants of the imperial authority; and accordingly the existing laws seem to have been put in force against Christians, though probably not by the emperor himself. At least three of Tertullian's writings are memorials of this time; his great "Apologeticum," a brilliant and elaborate defence of Christians from the charges of all kinds brought against them, abounding in interesting matter of many kinds, and for its own purpose effective; yet all written with an exuberant cleverness which is too often merely painful. This book was addressed to the governors of provinces, another the "Ad nationes" to the heathen peoples generally, a third "Ad martyres" to the Christian prisoners in North Africa.[1]

Taking a second leap of fourteen or fifteen years more, we come to another apologetic book of Tertullian's, addressed to the Proconsul Scapula. Severus had died at York in February 211, and persecution broke out afresh quite early in his successor Caracalla's reign. Thus we have Tertullian coming forward as an apologist at two distinct and distant crises. But, if he was an energetic defender of the church, he also became a hardly less energetic assailant of the church. Jerome writes of him,

> Till middle life he was a presbyter of the church;[2] but, having afterwards fallen away to the doctrine of Montanus through the envy and contumelies of the clergy of the Roman church, he refers to the new prophecy in many books:

Jerome then enumerates certain books, now lost, which he calls specially written against the church. The statement is crude in form, and evidently colored by reminiscences of Jerome's own

---

[1] To this crisis also belong the "Acts of Martyrdom of Perpetua and Felicitas," which, if not written by Tertullian himself, as some think, at all events proceed from that set of North African Christians of which he was the leader, and show clear signs of a Montanistic feeling. Of all the genuine Acts of martyrdom that have been preserved to us these are the most interesting.

[2] This by the way is the only evidence we have, though it is probably sufficient, that Tertullian was ever more than a layman.

quarrels with the Roman clergy of a century and a half later: but the substantial facts were probably to be found in those books now lost. There are sufficient echoes of them in the existing books.[1]

The story which we have just been reading carries us to what was doubtless the governing interest of Tertullian's life, his relations to what is called "Montanism." This, you will remember, was an enthusiastic popular religious movement, originating in the uplands of Phrygia. It was the erratic form taken by a great impulse towards reformation which went through various churches late in the second century, partly due to a survival from an earlier stage of Christianity, but still essentially a reaction and an innovation. Briefly, its characteristics were these; first, a strong faith in the Holy Spirit as the promised Paraclete, present as a heavenly power in the church of the day; secondly, specially a belief that the Holy Spirit was manifesting himself supernaturally at that day through entranced prophets and prophetesses; and thirdly, an inculcation of a specially stern and exacting standard of Christian morality and discipline on the strength of certain teachings of these prophets.[2] To these three characteristics of Montanism may be added two others, fourthly, a tendency to set up prophets against bishops, the new episcopal organization being probably favorable to that large inclusiveness of Christian communion in which the Montanists saw only spiritual danger; and fifthly, an eager anticipation of the Lord's second coming as near at hand, and a consequent indifference to ordinary human affairs.

Now it was the rigorous moral legalism of Montanism that probably first attracted Tertullian. With a man of vehement and ill-disciplined character, as he was, and always, remained,

---

[1] Everyone must be struck by the parallelism with the story of Hippolytus, all the more when it is remembered that he and Tertullian were contemporaries. In more respects than one they must have had strong mutual sympathies, though Hippolytus, as far as we know, kept clear of those special eccentricities which, as we shall shortly see, were the fundamental cause of Tertullian's eventual separation from the great body of the church.

[2] An increase in the numbers and prosperity of the church having brought an increase of laxity, it was not unnatural that attempts should be made to stem it by a rigorous system of prohibitions.

conversion from heathenism might naturally be accompanied by a violent rebound: and traces of this are seen in what are apparently his earliest writings; and then after a time we find him drawn on from Montanist morality and discipline to belief in the Montanist prophets, and to the ecstatic type of inspiration which they represented, and to their peculiar form of devotion to the Paraclete. But all this time he is simply a partisan within the church, not in any way separated from it. But there is a third stage in which he writes clearly as the member of a different body, claiming to be made up of "men of the Spirit," while he sneers at the members of the great church (the worldly church, he would say) as being only "psychici," "men of the soul." In what manner he and his "men of the Spirit" became finally detached from the church; whether they seceded or (more probably) were expelled, we do not know.[1]

Besides Tertullian's apologetic writings, nearly all of which have been already noticed, he was the author of a number of tracts of greater or less length addressed to Christians on various subjects belonging to morality or religion; for example, theatrical representations, idolatry (that is, as mixed up with various trades and public occupations), the soldier's chaplet (the laurel crown which he held to be implicated in idolatry), flight in persecution, "scorpiace" (martyrdom), prayer, patience, baptism, repentance, two books to his wife (against second marriage of women), adornment of women, exhortation to chastity (against second marriage of men), monogamy, modesty ("Pudicitia," chiefly on the question of admitting penitents), fasting, against the "Psychici," veiling of virgins, and the cloak (that is, the philosopher's cloak, as now worn by Christians).

Besides these more or less practical writings, there are eight or nine more of a strictly doctrinal character, chiefly intended directly or indirectly for the confutation of Pseudo-Gnostics or other supposed heretics; but including a very important treatise against Praxeas in which the doctrine of the Trinity is defended against the Roman Sabellians against whom Hippolytus wrote.

---

[1] Personal squabbles, such as Jerome speaks of, may well have been mixed up with intolerances on either side, or on both. The time when this took place was probably some twenty years more or less from the beginning of the century. Jerome tells us that Tertullian is said to have lived to an extreme old age. This is all that we know.

Three of the treatises bear the titles "On the Flesh of Christ," "On the Resurrection of the Flesh," "On the Soul." Much the longest is the treatise against Marcion in five books, probably founded on earlier Greek writings. In spite of its reckless scurrility of tone, it contains many passages both beautiful and true. The most popular however of all these doctrinal works, and virtually a preface to them, is one entitled "On the Prescription of Heretics." The main drift of this most plausible and most mischievous book is this: you try to argue with heretics and to convince them, and you do no good: you discuss scripture with them and appeal to its authority, and again you do no good: the only way to overcome them is to shut them up sharply with what the Roman law calls prescription, and tell them our belief is the belief of the churches which trace back their origin to the apostles, and therefore it must be the true belief.[1]

To understand him rightly we must remember that under the Roman lawyer was probably hidden the man of Carthaginian, that is, the Phoenician blood. As in the case of Tatian, his utter want of sympathy with Greek and Roman greatness is probably due to the inborn sense of alien race. To the same source may perhaps be also traced his violence, his passion for bitter antagonisms. But it is a relief to read the touching words in which, writing on patience, he bewails his own want of it.

It will be a kind of solace to dispute about that which it is not given me to enjoy, like sick men, who, since they

---

[1] It was pardonable enough that Tertullian should not have in mind the living growth of belief which had been always going on in these very churches. But it is another thing to find him making war on all free action of the mind and conscience in the things of faith, and assuming that there are no depths of divine truth beyond the doctrines which men have been able to formulate for public acceptance. His compliant is not only against "heretics" but also against "nostri": he names no names, but what he says seems specially directed against Clement of Alexandria. It grieves him much that an appeal is made to our Lord's words, "Seek and you shall find, knock and it shall be opened to you"; which he explains away by a series of ingenuities, beginning with the assertions that having been uttered early in our Lord's ministry, while he was as yet imperfectly known, they ceased to be true afterwards, and that they were addressed to the Jews alone. This is a sufficient illustration of Tertullian's characteristic defects.

are removed from health, do not know how to cease
speaking about its advantages. So I poor wretch,[1]
always sick with the heats of impatience, must needs
sigh after and call after and discourse about that
health of patience which I fail to possess. . . . Patience
is so set at the head of the things of God, that no one
can observe any precept, or perform any work well
pleasing to the Lord, if he be a stranger to patience.

Apart from the infectiousness of his intolerance, Tertullian
did serious injury to the church of his own age and of later ages
by beginning the process of casting the language of theology in
the moulds supplied by the law courts. In the Bible legal images
take their place among a variety of other images; but that is
quite another thing from the supremacy which legal conceptions of spiritual things acquired through the reckless use of
legal phraseology. But, when the worst is said, Tertullian remains one of the greatest of the fathers, always needing to be
read with the utmost caution, but almost always amply worth
reading; not the less perhaps because it needs some labor to
extract the meaning from his closely condensed and epigram-
matic sentences. He is a man of true genius; and not that only
but also a man of warm and passionate Christian feeling; and
moreover one who, despite the obstacles created by his own
theories, had a keen eye for many not obvious aspects of truth,
which presented themselves to him for the most part in sudden
flashes, and so by their frequent contradictions reflect the
moods of a fiery soul, itself always full of contradictions.
    As a sample of his more quiet controversial vein, in which he
is something much better than controversial, we may take a
few words of his on the creation of man, in refutation of
Marcion's theory that the God of creation and of the law was
only a just God, not a good God.[2] The exaggerations here and
there do not spoil the general drift.

Meanwhile the world consisted of all good things,
thereby sufficiently showing beforehand how much
good was in store for him for whom this whole [sum of

---

[1] "Miserrimus ego."
[2] Tertullian, Against Marcion 2. 4.

things] was being prepared. Lastly, who could be worthy to inhabit the works of God but his own image and likeness? That also was wrought by Goodness. . . . Goodness spoke [the words], Goodness fashioned man out of slime into such a substance of flesh built up into so many qualities out of one matter, Goodness breathed [into him] making him a soul that was living, not dead. Goodness set him to enjoy and reign over all things, and moreover to give them names. Goodness yet further bestowed fresh enjoyment on man, that, although a possessor of the whole world, he should dwell in a specially pleasant region by being shifted into paradise, already out of a world into a church. The same Goodness provided also a help for him, that nothing good might be wanting; for it is not good, God said, that man be alone: he knew that man would profit by the sex of Mary and thenceforward of the church.[1] But even the law which you blame, which you twist into themes of controversy, it was Goodness that enacted it for the sake of man, that he might cleave to God, for fear he should seem not so much free as abandoned, on a level with his minions the other living creatures who had been cast loose by (from?) God and were free through his scorn of them; but that man alone might have the boast of having been alone worthy to receive a law from God, and that being a reasonable living creature with a capacity for understanding and knowledge, he might be held in likewise by that very liberty which belongs to reason, being subject to him who had subjected to him all things. And in like manner it was Goodness that wrote on this law the counsel of observing it, "In the day that you eat thereof, you shall surely die," for it graciously showed the issue of transgression, for fear ignorance of the danger should help towards neglect of obedience. . . . I call on you therefore to recognize thus far the goodness of our God as shown by works that were good, by blessings that were good, by acts of indulgence, by acts

---

[1] In this curious limitation the Montanist speaks.

of providence, by laws and forewarnings that were good and gracious.

CYPRIAN

Jerome tells us that once in North Italy he had met an old man who told him how when he was quite young he had in like manner seen at Rome a man of great age, formerly a notary of Cyprian's and had heard from him how Cyprian was accustomed to pass no day without reading something of Tertullian's, and how he used often to say to him, "Give me the Teacher," meaning Tertullian. This curious little reminiscence links together the two greatest men in the North African church before Augustine. Strictly speaking Cyprian was not a theologian, while he was a great ecclesiastical ruler. His writings show hardly any appropriation of the deeper elements in Tertullian's thoughts, those in which he claims affinity to Greek theology, perhaps partly due to borrowing from it: but the Roman legalism, which was so potent an ingredient in Tertullian's ways of thinking and speaking, acquired still greater force in its guidance of a man of simpler and more direct mind like Cyprian, accustomed through life to derive his thoughts of social order from the provincial administration of the Roman Empire, and when he had become a Christian bishop, writing almost always under the impulse of grave practical responsibilities.

The depth and purity of his own religious feeling makes itself felt almost everywhere in his writings: yet the conceptions of the church and its institutions which he sets forth, and which thenceforward dominated Latin Christianity, were indeed most natural under their circumstances of time and place, but not less truly involved injurious limitations and perversions of the full teaching of the apostles. We have the great good fortune of possessing a large amount of Cyprian's correspondence during the last ten years or so of his life, and also a memoir of him by his deacon Pontius. We have also from his pen about a dozen tracts on religious or disciplinary subjects. He bears well the testing of his inner self which these materials render possible. There is nothing petty and nothing ungoverned about him. He is always pursuing high ends according to the best of his lights with entire self devotion and seldom failing in patience and gentleness. He lived habitually in accordance with what he wrote in his early tract to his friend Donatus.[1]

> To God belongs whatever power we have. From that source we draw our life, from that source we draw our strength, from that source is taken and embraced the energy by which, while still placed here, we discern beforehand the signs of the things to come. Let only there be fear to guard innocence, that the Lord, who by the visitation of the heavenly mercy has graciously shone into our minds, may be held fast through righteous conduct as the guest of a mind that delights him, lest the security thus received breed heedlessness and the old enemy steal in anew. . . . The Spirit streams forth incessantly, overflows abundantly: let only our breast be athirst and open: as is [the measure] of faith to receive that we bring to it, such is [the measure] of inflowing grace that we drink in.

Cyprian was apparently converted to the gospel in middle life. He was what we should call a country gentlemen, and at the same time a man of good Latin education. Not long after he became a Christian he sold his estates, wholly or in part, to give the proceeds to the poor; though ultimately they were restored to him by the liberality of friends. Very early after his baptism he was admitted to the presbyterate, and shortly afterwards, while still accounted a neophyte, he was elected bishop of Carthage. He was evidently popular with the laity, with whom the election seems to have chiefly rested. His social position by itself could hardly have won for him such a mark of confidence: doubtless he was already before his conversion known as a man of virtuous life and high public spirit. It was no light task that was laid on him by his election. Persecution had slumbered for about a generation, and as a consequence various abuses had sprung up in the church, the bishops and clergy not excepted. But after a year and a half came the persecution of Decius, the same persecution in which Alexander bishop of Jerusalem perished in prison.

---

[1] Cyprian, To Donatus 4.5.

Its fires were not without a purifying effect on the Christian community: but it shortly gave rise to a difficult question of discipline which much exercised Cyprian, the treatment of those who had "lapsed" or fallen away under terror of death or torments. On the one hand there was a strong party of mere laxity at Carthage, on the other a strong party of unswerving and undiscriminating severity at Rome; and the controversy was complicated by purely personal elements, Cyprian's election not having been by any means universally acceptable. Of course it would be impossible to give now a narrative of the complicated transactions at Carthage and at Rome. It must suffice to say that Cyprian took an intermediate and carefully discriminative course, and that his policy was at last substantially adopted, though presently he was constrained by the force of circumstances, and especially a lesser persecution under Gallus, to accept a more indulgent set of rules than at first.

Presently North Africa was invaded by a terrible pestilence from the East which lasted on for long years afterwards. Cyprian instantly stood forward to organize his Christian flock for measures of help and relief, pecuniary and personal, insisting strongly on the duty of helping heathens as well as Christians in the spirit of true Sonship, following the example of him who sends his rain and sunshine on all alike. Presently a fresh controversy arose when Stephen became bishop of Rome. The former controversy had left behind it an unhappy schism, the followers of Novatian having split off from the church at large in the name of stricter discipline. The question now was whether persons having received Novatianist baptism, and subsequently joining the church, needed to be baptized over again, or only to be received with laying on of hands. On this point Cyprian threw all his strength into the stricter theory, which had been falling into disuse in the West; and induced a large synod of North African bishops to support it unanimously; while Stephen upheld the view that ultimately became fixed in the West, condemning such a repetition of baptism: only unfortunately he upheld it with much violence and intolerance.

Stephen died in August 257. In the same month a fresh persecution began under Valerian, and Cyprian was at once banished, though treated with remarkable respect and forbearance by the heathen authorities; and in his banishment he devoted himself to plans for help of other sufferers. But in about a year the persecution assumed a more terrible form. Xystus bishop of Rome was beheaded as he sat preaching in his episcopal chair in one of the Roman cemeteries, and Cyprian returned to Carthage to await his now inevitable doom. The trial took place. The sentence was read "It is decreed that Thascius Cyprianus be executed by the sword." The record then proceeds "Cyprian the bishop said, 'Thanks be to God.'"

ORIGEN

In the last two lectures the fathers who have come before us have all belonged to Africa. It will be the same today. We return now from North Africa, and the two great fathers whom at this early time it brought forth for Latin theology, to Egypt and to the most characteristically Greek theology. If the influence of Clement of Alexandria over the later times of early Christianity was less than we might have expected, the same cannot be said of his great pupil Origen. Not only had he the veneration of devoted disciples for several generations; but the theologies built up in the succeeding centuries of the age of the fathers would, as far as we can see, have been very different from what they actually were, had it not been for the foundations laid by him. Above all, his influence as an interpreter of the Bible, direct and indirect, has been both wide and lasting. In the ancient church three men stand out above all others as having left a deep mark by their independent interpretation of Scripture. The other two are Theodore of Mopsuestia (late in the fourth century), the highest representative of the school of Antioch, and (a generation later) Augustine the North African, the primary teacher of the Latin West.

Not the least interesting fact however in the history of the influence of Origen as an interpreter is the way in which his thoughts and often his words were appropriated and handed on by Latin fathers, and especially the three greatest Latin fathers of the fourth century, Hilary of Poitiers (theologically the greatest of them all), Ambrose and Jerome.[1] The permanent

---

[1] In this manner, as well as by direct translations of some of Origen's works, Origenian ideas, penetrating down through various channels,

value of his interpretation of scripture is much lessened by the fact that, in common with most ancient interpreters outside the school of Antioch, he shows an excessive devotion to allegorical senses: yet along with this mere fancifulness we find in him evidence of a genuine and profound study of the words of scripture. For all his great and lasting influence, Origen's name has been by no means surrounded with the halo of conventional glory which has traditionally adorned fathers inferior to him in every way. Some of his speculations were doubtless crude and unsatisfactory: but these are but trifles beside the vast services which he rendered to theology; and accordingly, every now and then, from Athanasius onwards, he has received cordial words of vindication from men who were able to recognize goodness and greatness, in spite of an unpopular name.

Unlike the fathers whom we have been lately considering, Clement of Alexandria, Tertullian, Cyprian, Origen had the blessing of Christian parentage, and received from his father Leonides a careful education both in the ordinary Greek culture of the day and in the study of scripture, becoming the pupil of Clement. He was not seventeen when that persecution of about the year 202 under Septimius Severus occurred which drove Clement from Alexandria, and Leonides was thrown into prison. Origen himself, being restrained by a device of his mother's from rushing to join him in the anticipated martyrdom, wrote to him entreating that no care for his family should be allowed to shake his constancy. On his father's martyrdom, with confiscation of goods, he provided for his own and his mother's and six brothers' wants by teaching, except that he was lodged by a lady of wealth. Some heathens came to him for instruction, including Plutarchus, who was martyred, and Heraclas, who became bishop of Alexandria; and thus he was led to take up, though in an informal way, the dropped work of the catechetical school. After a time he was placed formally at its head by the bishop Demetrius.

---

supplied a by no means insignificant element in the very miscellaneous body of traditional interpretation which prevailed till the fresh and open study of the meaning of scripture was restored, chiefly by the revivers of learning just before the Reformation and by some of the reformers themselves.

For some twelve years he went on without other interruption than a short visit to Rome and another to Arabia, lecturing to large audiences as a layman, living a sternly rigorous and self-denying life. To this time belongs the rash act of self-mutilation always associated with his name, suggested to him by a misunderstanding of the real drift of one of our Lord's sayings. Meanwhile he labored to fit himself for his work more and more. On the one hand he studied Hebrew; on the other he attended the lectures of the most eminent heathen philosophers, that he might be "better able to understand the thoughts of those" who came to him for help. The work increased so much that he associated with himself his convert Heraclas. At length about the year 215 he was driven by tumults to leave Alexandria, as Clement had done, and took refuge for a considerable time at Caesarea, the Greek or Roman capital of Palestine. Alexander, now bishop of Jerusalem, of whom we heard a fortnight ago, and the bishop of Caesarea joined in inviting him to preach (ὁμιλεῖν) to the assembled congregation. On receiving a remonstrance from Demetrius at their permitting a layman to preach before bishops, they cited various precedents in defence of their action. But Demetrius refused to give way, and fetched Origen back to Alexandria in a peremptory way. After his return he was persuaded by Ambrosius, now a friend, formerly a convert of his from some Pseudo-Gnostic sect, to undertake commentaries in writing, for which purpose Ambrosius provided shorthand writers.

But after Origen had taught at Alexandria for about a quarter of a century, his career there came to a painful end. The churches of Achaia, being much distracted by what were called heresies (of what kind, is not related), invited him to come to their help. He started without obtaining license from Demetrius (but under what circumstances we do not know), and took his way through Palestine. There he was ordained presbyter by the bishop of Caesarea, with Alexander's knowledge and approval. He then completed his journey to Greece, making sojourns at Ephesus and Athens, and at length returned home. His reception there is a sad one to read of. Demetrius assembled "a synod of bishops and of certain presbyters," by whom he was forbidden to teach or even reside in Alexandria. They did not agree to reject his ordination, as apparently Demetrius wished: but this too he obtained from a subsequent smaller meeting of bishops alone. Our too fragmentary authorities do not tell us quite clearly the ground of condemnation. Apparently it was the ordination of one who was mutilated, though it is also possible that doctrinal differences and it may be even personal jealousies were unavowed motives of action.[1]

Origen left Alexandria forever, and though beloved disciples of his own succeeded Demetrius as bishop, apparently no attempt was made to undo the banishment. Gentlest, humblest, and most peace loving of men, Origen would be the last to disturb the peace of the church for his own sake. Accordingly for the third time he betook himself to the friendly Caesarea, and there in the great seaport beside the Mediterranean he made his permanent home for the rest of his life, above twenty years. Being welcomed and cherished by the two Palestinian bishops of whom we heard before, he carried on his literary work as a Christian theologian with the help of Ambrosius, and at the same time resumed oral instruction, partly by expository sermons of a comparatively simple kind in church, partly by more advanced lectures to students and philosophical enquirers, as at the catechetical school of Alexandria. With this period are specially connected the names of two illustrious disciples, Firmilianus and Gregory of Neocaesarea.[2]

---

[1] There is reason to believe that the Roman church supported the action of Demetrius; but it was entirely ignored by the bishops of Asia; those of Palestine, Arabia, Phoenicia (that is, probably North Syria) and Achaia being specially mentioned.

[2] Firmilianus was apparently already bishop of the Cappadocian Caesarea, the capital of the inland regions of Eastern Asia Minor, when this recorded intercourse with Origen took place, though it may well have begun at an earlier time. Sometimes he used to get Origen to come to visit him in Cappadocia to instruct his churches; sometimes he used to make stays in Palestine to have the personal benefit of hearing Origen discourse. A man of still greater eminence in the years after the middle of the third century was Gregory bishop of Neocaesarea in Pontus. According to his own narrative he had travelled to Palestine to educate himself as an advocate by study at Beirut, where there was a famous school of Roman law; but before fixing himself there he had travelled on to Caesarea with his sister, whose husband held an official post there. Beirut however was soon given up.

Gregory of Neocaesarea fell (with his brother) under the spell of Origen's teaching and personal presence, and remained under his instruction for five years. On his departure he delivered an address in expression of his gratitude, and this address is still extant. In it he describes how he first came under Origen, and how Origen dealt with him and with other pupils. First came a training in the faculties of the mind, a pruning away of wild growths of opinion for opinion's sake, an enforcement of clear thinking and exact speaking. Then came the study of the visible order of nature, founded on the study of geometry. Thirdly, came Christian ethics as founded on godliness, which he called the beginning and the end of all the virtues. Having passed through these preliminary stages of mental discipline, Origen's pupils were encouraged to read freely in the works of Greek poets and philosophers, and then, thus prepared, to enter on the study of Christian theology proper, more especially in its primary source, the Bible. Such was the method of Origen's regular teaching at Caesarea.[1]

Our first glimpse of Origen was as a boy, encouraging his father to face martyrdom without hesitation, undistracted by any anxieties for his helpless family. A third of a century later a similar task fell to his lot. The emperor Alexander Severus, who had been friendly to the Christians, and with whose mother Mamaea Origen had had some intercourse, had come to a violent end, and his murderer and successor Maximinus entered on a persecution of such Christians, it would seem, as had stood in special favor with Alexander. Origen was apparently saved by a Christian Cappadocian lady, Juliana, who kept him out of harm's way. But Ambrosius and a presbyter of Caesarea were imprisoned, and to them Origen wrote an exhortation which we still possess. But fifteen years later, or less, he had to suffer

---

[1] But he did not refuse invitations to leave home for awhile, and give help to other churches. Some time, we know, he spent at Athens. Twice he was asked to come into Arabia to help in neutralizing false doctrines which had arisen there. In each case, instead of using declamation and anathemas, he sought quiet conference with the men who had propounded these doctrines; and in each case succeeded in persuading them that they had been in error. If later controversies had been dealt with in the same spirit, what a different Christendom and a different world would now be meeting our eyes!

grievously in his own person. In that persecution of Decius in which his old fellow student and supporter Alexander died in prison, he too was cast into prison, and had to undergo a succession of tortures. Decius' reign was a short one; and on his death Origen was released from prison, shattered by the treatment which he had received, and two years later he died at Tyre, being not far from 70 years of age.[1] Though he does not bear the conventional title of saint, no saintlier man is to be found in the long line of ancient fathers of the church.

He was deeply and reverently occupied in meditation on all things in heaven and earth of which the human mind can take any cognizance; but the Bible was the center of all his thoughts and of all his studies.[2] He wrote commentaries or preached homilies, taken down by rapid writers, on a large proportion of books of both Testaments. What is lost was far more than what is preserved; but we still have much, large portions of the commentaries on St. Matthew and St. John, that on the Romans in a too free Latin condensed translation, some homilies on Jeremiah, many Greek fragments on various books, and many Latin translations of homilies, chiefly on the Old Testament. A biblical work of another kind was what is called Origen's "Hexapla," an arrangement of the books of the Old Testament in (for the most part) six parallel columns, each containing a distinct text, the Hebrew, the same in Greek letters, the Septuagint, and three other Greek translations. Numerous detached readings copied from it have been preserved, but hardly more. By this combination of texts Origen hoped to throw light on the meaning of many passages in which a Greek reader would be either bewildered or misled if he had only the Septuagint before him.

---

[1] His tomb in the Cathedral of Tyre is several times in the early Middle Ages noticed as then still visible, and the inscription of it still later; and a tradition of his place of burial is still said to be current in the neighborhood.

[2] One of the best known sentences of Butler's analogy, occurring in the introduction, is to this effect: "Hence, namely from analogical reasoning, Origen has with singular sagacity observed, that he who believes the scripture to have proceeded from him who is the Author of nature, may well expect to find the same sort of difficulties in it, as are found in the constitution of nature." These few words are characteristic of the subjects of Origen's writings.

Besides the "Exhortation to Martyrdom" mentioned before, we possess a very interesting little treatise of Origen's on prayer. Very little unhappily remains of his letters, of which a collection was made some time after his death. But we fortunately possess in one shape or other what were probably his two greatest works, the systematic doctrinal treatise on "First Principles," written before his departure from Alexandria, preserved for the most part only in a too free Latin version; and the eight books against Celsus in the original Greek, written near the end of his life. In connection with Origen's writings it is worth while to mention the "Philocalia," a small collection of extracts from them chiefly bearing on the interpretation of scripture, made late in the fourth century by Basil and Gregory of Nazianza.[1] As an easy specimen of the book on "First Principles," which chiefly consists of somewhat difficult speculative meditations, we may take a passage on the thirst for divine knowledge implanted in the heart of man, and, however little he may know in this life, intended to render him capable of even higher levels of knowledge in the stages of the future life.

> Therefore, as in those crafts which are accomplished by hand, we can perceive by our understanding the reason which determines what a thing is to be, how it is to be made and for what purposes, while the actual work is accomplished by the service of the hands; so in the works of God which are wrought by his own hand, we must understand that the reason and designs of the things which we see made by him, remain unseen. And just as, when our eye has seen things made by the craftsman, the mind, on observing something made with special skill, is forthwith anxious to enquire in what fashion or manner or for what purposes the thing has been made; so much more and in an incomparably higher degree the mind is anxious with an unspeakable longing to recognize the reason of the things which we behold made by God. This longing, this ardent desire, has we believe without doubt been implanted in us by God: and, just as the eye naturally requires light and object of vision, and our body by

---

[1] It was from this source that Butler made his quotation, and the little book deserves to be better known.

nature demands food and drink, so our intellect is possessed with a fit and natural desire for knowing the truth
of God and discovering the causes of things. Now this
desire we have received from God not in order that it
should never be satisfied or be capable of satisfaction:
otherwise vainly will the love of truth appear to have
been implanted in our intellect by God the Creator, if it is
made never capable of satisfying its longing. Wherefore
even in this life those who have laboriously given their
attention to godly and religious meditations, even though
they obtain but a small amount from the great and infinite treasures of the divine wisdom, yet just because they
keep their minds and attention turned towards these
subjects and outstrip themselves in this desire, receive
much profit from the very fact that they are directing
their minds to the search and love discovering truth and
making them more ready to receive future instruction:
just as, when a man wishes to paint a portrait, if a pencil
sketch in bare outline first marks out the plan of the
coming picture, and prepares marks on which the features may be laid, the rough outline doubtless is found
more ready to receive the true colors; so may a mere
sketch, a rough outline by the pencil of our Lord Jesus
Christ, be traced on the tablets of our heart. And perhaps it is for this reason that it is said, "For to everyone
that has shall it be given, and it shall be added to him."
Whence it is certain that to those who possess in this life
a sort of rough outline of truth and knowledge shall be
added in the future the beauty of the perfect picture.
Such, I imagine, was the desire indicated by him who
said "But I am constrained in two ways, having a desire
to depart and be with Christ, for it is far better"; knowing
that when he had returned to Christ, he would recognize
more clearly the reasons of all things which are done on
earth."[1]

The books against Celsus contain at once the best and the
most comprehensive defence of the Christian faith which has
come down to us from the days of the fathers. They defend it

[1] Origen, First Principles 2.4, page 236 (2.11.4-5).

not against popular prejudice and malice only, as the early
Apologists had done, but against the careful and powerful
indictment laid by an earnest though scoffing heathen philosopher who was also apparently an accomplished Roman lawyer,
writing in the name of the highest philosophy of the time, and
passionately devoted to the welfare of the Roman Empire. A
long time had passed between the writing of Celsus' "True
Account," as he called his literary onslaught on the Christians
and their faith, and its coming into Origen's hands. He had no
real knowledge about the author, but he evidently felt that if
he could answer him successfully, he would practically have
effectually upheld the cause of the gospel at all points. If he
sometimes fails to understand on what this or that smart saying of Celsus' really rested, he never shows the unfairness of
the mere partisan. The candor and patience of his treatise are
among its brightest qualities. The whole treatise amply repays
reading and rereading: one passage however must now suffice.[1]

> Observe here too Celsus' want of reverence when he
> most unphilosophically brings in a comic poet, whose
> object is to raise a laugh, and compares our God the
> Creator of the universe with the god in his play who
> on awaking despatches Hermes. We have said above
> that, when God sent Jesus to the human race, it was
> not as though he had just awoken from a long sleep,
> but Jesus, though he has only now for worthy reasons
> fulfilled the divine plan of his incarnation, has at all
> times been doing good to the human race. For no
> noble deed among men has ever been done without the
> divine Word visiting the souls of those who even for a
> brief space were able to receive such operations of the
> divine Word. No, even the appearance of Jesus in one
> corner of the world (as it seems) has been brought

---

[1] It is the reply to Celsus' scoff about the lateness of the incarnation
and its limitation to an obscure corner of the world, a scoff in form, but
covering a serious question. As regards the time, Celsus compared it to
the comic poet's representation of Zeus as waking out of sleep and sud-
denly sending Hermes to men. As regards the place, he asked why God
did not breathe souls into many bodies, and send them all over the
earth.

about for a worthy reason: since it was necessary that
he of whom the prophets spoke should appear among
those who had learned one God, who read his prophets and recognized Christ preached in them, and that
he should appear at a time when the Word was about
to be diffused from one corner to the whole world.

Wherefore also there was no need that many bodies
should be made everywhere, and many spirits like to
that of Jesus, in order that the whole world of men
might be illumined by the Word of God. For it sufficed
that the one Word rising like the sun of righteousness
from Judea should send forth his speedy rays into the
soul of them that were willing to receive him. And if
anyone does wish to see many bodies filled with a
divine Spirit, ministering like him the one Christ to the
salvation of men in every place, let him take note of
those who in all places do honestly and with an upright
life teach the word of Jesus, who are themselves too
called "Christ" ("anointed ones") in the passage "Touch
not my anointed ones and do my prophets no harm."
For even as we have heard that antichrist comes and
nevertheless have learned that there are many anti-
christs in the world, even so, when we recognize that
Christ has come, we observe that owing to him many
Christs have been born in the world, to wit all those
that like him have loved righteousness and hated
iniquity: and for this reason God, the God of Christ,
anointed them too with the oil of gladness. But he
however, having loved righteousness and hated iniquity to a higher degree than those who are his partners, has also received the firstfruits of the anointing,
and, if we may so term it, has received the entire
unction of the oil of gladness: while they that were his
partners partook also in his unction each according to
his capacity.

Wherefore, since Christ is the head of the church, so
that Christ and his church are one body, the ointment
has descended from the head to the beard (the symbol
of the full grown man Aaron), and this ointment in its
descent reached to the skirts of his clothing. This is my

answer to Celsus' impious speech when he says that "God ought to have breathed his Spirit into many bodies in like manner and to have sent them forth throughout the world." So then while the comic poet to raise a laugh has represented Zeus as asleep and as waking up and sending Hermes to the Greeks, let the Word which knows that the nature of God is sleepless teach us that God with regard to seasons orders the affairs of the world as reason demands. But it is not to be wondered at, if, seeing that the judgments of God are sublime and hard to interpret, uninstructed souls do err, and Celsus among them. There is then nothing absurd in the fact that to the Jews, with whom were the prophets, the Son of God was sent; so that beginning with them in bodily form he might arise in power and spirit upon a world of souls desiring to be no longer bereft of God."[1]

At Origen's death in the year 253 we are still nearly half as century from the end of the first three centuries, and nearly three-quarters of a century from the Council of Nicaea. If time permitted, it would not be difficult to give some account of fathers belonging to this interval who are quite worthy of being known. At the same time it is true that we have only fragments, sometimes hardly that, of the men who seem as if they had been best worth knowing.[2] The most attractive group is formed by the disciples of Origen, not only the two already spoken of, but Heraclas, and Pierius, and Dionysius of Alexandria of whom we can obtain a tolerably vivid and very pleasant image from the fragments of his letters preserved by Eusebius, showing how a great bishop trained by Origen would deal with the difficult questions raised by persecution without and false doctrine within. Then would come Pamphilus, the loving collector of memorials of Origen and zealous champion of his good name against the detractors who were beginning to assail it; himself a martyr in the terrible last persecution at the beginning of the

---

[1] Origen, Against Celsus 6.78 and following.

[2] Moreover, with the exception of the almost forgotten Lucianus of Antioch, they seem to have been less original and important fathers than nearly all those who have come before us this term.

fourth century. And Pamphilus in turn leads to his younger friend Eusebius the historian, who lived and wrote in the fourth century, and yet might in some ways be called the last of the Ante-Nicene fathers.

But we must be content with this very hurried glance at that most important but most obscure time between the death of Origen and Cyprian and the Council of Nicaea. A better break than at the death of Origen we could hardly desire. Not to speak of the men of later days, looking only at those other fathers who have come before us this term, we cannot help recognizing that they had often work given them to do which he could not do; and that they were enabled to see some truths which he could not see. But he is for us practically the last and most characteristic of the early fathers, properly so called, the fathers who lived while Christian thought could still be free, and while Christian faith still embraced the whole world. From all these early fathers taken together, you will, I trust, have gained the feeling, if you had it not already, that Christian pastors and teachers in this nineteenth century can ill afford to neglect the thoughts and aspirations of those earliest Christian ages, though, like the thoughts and aspirations of all intervening times, they must remain a dead letter to us till they are interpreted by the thoughts and aspirations of our own time as shone upon by the light of the Spirit who is the teacher of Christ's disciples in every succeeding age.

THE JEWISH ENVIRONMENT OF EARLY CHRISTIANITY

WRITTEN BY

G. H. BOX

Lecturer in Rabbinical Hebrew, King's College, London; Canon of St. Albans

EDITED BY

BRENT WALTERS

Curator, Ante-Nicene Archive
Dean, College of Early Christian Studies

London: Hodder and Stoughton

1916

San Jose: The Ante-Nicene Archive
Bibliographics Incorporated

1993

CONTENTS

Rabbinic and Non-Rabbinic Theology

Perhaps the most pressing problem of New Testament science at the present time, and one that is slowly, but surely ripening for solution, lies in the task of reconstructing the Jewish background and environment of the gospels and other New Testament books. The problem is one that appeals—or ought to appeal—with peculiar insistence to the rising generation of New Testament scholars; and to them the task of attempting to solve it will probably fall. It is true that much labor, energy, and even genius have been expended upon this department of work in the past.[1] The older Christian Talmudists to whom reference has just been made have handed down to us a vast mass of material; but it is unsifted material. Furthermore, new material has been discovered, of considerable importance, within comparatively recent years. In consequence the aspect of the old problems has been completely transformed. Investigation, pursued in the new scientific spirit, and applying the exacting standards of modern scientific inquiry, has, with the help of the new material, put an entirely new complexion upon the old facts.

The main features and factors of the problem as a whole, and as it now stands, may be summed up briefly as follows: (1) The external conditions of the Greco-Roman world generally during the New Testament period have had much light shed upon them by modern investigation and research. In particular new discoveries of documents—papyri—have illuminated the domestic and everyday conditions of the life of the period in a most wonderful way. All this has a more direct bearing upon the Jewish communities outside Palestine than upon Judea and Galilee. But it must not be forgotten that Palestine itself had been exposed for a considerable period to Hellenizing influence;

---

[1] The names of Lightfoot (the elder), Schoettgen, Spencer, Selden, Franz Delitzsch and Edersheim are sufficient to remind us of the debt of obligation we are under to former generations of students, who devoted their lives to the accumulation of the rich treasure of material that has been handed down to us; while Schürer's great work, in spite of a certain lack of sympathy with the idiosyncrasies of Rabbinical Judaism, will probably long remain the classical depository of the available data that concern the externals of Jewish life in the period immediately adjacent to the time of our Lord.

it possessed numerous Greco-Roman cities; and the Jewish provinces of Palestine, which were more or less closely incorporated in the vast Greco-Roman empire, were subjected in numberless ways to the subtle influence of non-Jewish civilization and culture. A potent stream of influence, too, was always flowing in upon Palestine from the communities of the Jewish Dispersion which were necessarily more deeply permeated by the spirit of Greek culture. In our estimate of Judaism, and the forces by which it was moved, we must never lose sight of the commanding importance of the larger Judaism of the countries of the Dispersion.

(2) Then within the last thirty years much energy has been devoted to the study and investigation of the apocryphal and pseudepigraphical literature of Judaism, and from this direction a fresh and vital impetus has been given to the study of Jewish religious thought, especially in connection with the rise of Christianity and the problems of Christian origins.[1] Among the new questions raised by it are some very interesting problems in psychology. But the most important new fact that has been elucidated is the traditional character of a considerable amount of the eschatological material, which carries back its origin to a period far anterior to its full literary expression. This consideration throws a flood of light upon many perplexing passages in the prophetic literature, and invests the study of the purely apocalyptic literature with enhanced interest and importance. It must constantly be remembered that while the apocalyptic books as literary productions belong to a comparatively late date, and doubtless contain much that in substance is of late origin, they yet reproduce, to a greater or less extent, material that their authors quarried from the mine of popular tradition. Indeed the authors of these works seem, as a rule, to have attached far more importance to what they derived in this way

---

[1] We in England cannot be sufficiently grateful to Dr. Charles for the splendid series of editions of various apocalyptic books that he has given us, and for his studies in eschatology and apocalyptic generally. Indeed the study of eschatology may be said to have entered on an entirely new phase, thanks largely to the epoch-making work of Gunkel, and recently of his pupil Gressmann. See especially Gunkel's Schöpfung und Chaos (1895) and Gressmann's Der Ursprung der Israelitisch-jüdischen Eschatologie (1905).

than to what was original to themselves; and so they habitually—in all good faith, it would seem—attached to their productions, which embodied parts of this ancient material, the
names of great heroic and saintly figures of the past, such as
Enoch, Baruch, Moses, Abraham, and even Adam.

The authority of such names seems, in some way, to have
been deduced from tradition, though the possibility of a symbolical or figurative meaning must sometimes be allowed for. The
importance of the apocalyptic literature in forming a just and
adequate view of pre-Talmudic Judaism cannot be over-esti-
mated. It represents vivid phases in the development of popular
religion, and sets before us the hopes and fears, the aspirations,
longings, and regrets, of deeply religious souls, who were often
perplexed by the problem of the providential government of
the world, but were always ready with the venture of faith to
believe in the imminence of a divine "parousia," in the speedy
establishment of the Kingdom of God. Apocalyptic language,
as is well known, colors much of the New Testament writings,
and it is clear that the early Jewish Christians were largely
drawn from the circles of the apocalyptists. The apocalyptic
literature is of special importance for the study of the development of Messianic doctrine.

But the apocryphal literature of Judaism is not made up
entirely, or always even predominantly, of eschatological material. Many of the apocryphal books, such as, for example, Wisdom, Tobit, Ecclesiasticus, are non-eschatological in character.
But they are of the greatest value for the elucidation of Jewish
religious thought and custom, and one supreme advantage that
attaches to them is that many can be certainly dated within the
critical period 200 BC-AD 100. They thus form an invaluable
criterion for determining what is early, and distinguishing such
elements from later developments. This is sometimes of considerable importance in dealing with the data afforded by the
Rabbinical documents. The oldest Rabbinical literature, though
it contains much early material, was not compiled in its present
form till the end of the second or beginning of the third century AD. This fact often makes it precarious to draw definite
conclusions as to the prevalence of a particular practice, or the
expression of a particular religious belief, within the first Christian century. But if the conclusion can be corroborated from an

earlier apocryphal book—as is often the case—doubt disappears, and certainty, or comparative certainty, is attained.[1]

(3) This suggests a third preliminary observation, namely, to emphasize the importance of some knowledge of Rabbinic theology and modes of thought for the study of early Judaism. I mean by early Judaism the Judaism that underlies the New Testament, and its antecedents. It may sound somewhat superfluous to stress the importance of such study in such a connection, but it is none the less necessary. Perhaps some may be inclined to ask in surprise "Have not elaborate 'Lives of Christ' been written which are full of illustrations drawn from Jewish literature and custom? Have not collections of Rabbinic parallels to the gospels and other New Testament books been made?" This is true enough, and some of these works are of great and enduring value in particular ways. "But"—if I may borrow some words I have used elsewhere[2]—"a collection of Jewish illustrations formed with the express object of pointing a particular theme is not a presentment of the Jewish religion. It still remains true that in order that such illustrations should be seen in their true bearings, and rightly appreciated, they must be viewed against a background where Judaism is realized as a

---

[1] Sometimes, indeed, the Rabbinical data, if taken alone, would prove to be positively misleading. A good instance of this occurs in connection with the doctrine of the seven heavens. In the tractate *Hagiga* of the Babylonian Talmud (12b) the formulation of this doctrine is expressly associated with the name of the Amora Resh Lakish who lived in the third century AD. But the doctrine must have been current long before, for it is found in the Testaments of the Twelve Patriarchs (*Levi* 2.7 f.), and in the Slavonic Enoch; while almost certainly allusions to it occur in 2 Corinthians 12:2-4 and Ephesians 6:12. The belief was, therefore, current in the first Christian century. In this connection it may be added that two other criteria exist which can often be used in a similar way to distinguish early elements in the Rabbinical literature, namely, the works of Josephus and Philo. The exact study of these, especially of Philo's treatises, has not yet secured the attention it deserves in this country. An important task that still awaits fulfillment is to determine Philo's exact relation to Rabbinic theology. The results of careful investigation are sure to prove illuminating and valuable. A good beginning was made by Ritter in Philo und die Halacha (Leipzig, 1879).

[2] The Religion and Worship of the Synagogue, Preface (pages vii and following in 2nd edition).

living whole"—"as a vital organism with a soul and genius of its own."[1]

---

[1] The difficulties attending such a study, it must be confessed, have until quite recently been almost insuperable to the average student. The only textbook available was a German one—Weber's pioneering work in Jewish theology (Jüdische Theologie; 2nd edition revised by Franz Delitzsch and G. Schnedermann (Leipzig, 1897). But now English students are more fortunate. Of the books which have appeared within the last few years and deal with the subject or parts of it, by far the most important is Dr. Schechter's masterly volume on Rabbinic theology— Some Aspects of Rabbinic Theology. This is a book which ought to be read and studied far and wide by all who are interested in theological questions. It will give the reader a real insight into the religious thought of the men who reconstructed from its foundations the edifice of Judaism, and determined the direction of its development down to modern days. While Schechter does not profess to give a comprehensive survey of the whole of Jewish theology, his work is yet comprehensive enough. He disengages the principles—the essential thought that is so often wrapped up in strange and, to us, bizarre methods of expression, and sets it forth in a delightfully clear and attractive guise. The study of Schechter's book ought, in a real sense, to orientate the minds of non-Jewish students to Rabbinical modes of thought, and help them to understand the genius of Rabbinism as they have never understood it before. At the same time the student must be put on his guard against supposing that Schechter's book conclusively settles any of the problems with which the study of Christian origins is directly concerned. It provides invaluable material for the student. But it does not attempt to trace the processes of theological development—it is rather a study in the genius of Rabbinic religion, than its history; nor does it deal with any but strictly Rabbinical sources and material (with some very slight exceptions). Thus the apocryphal and pseudepigraphical literature is dismissed, almost contemptuously, as being outside the pale of genuine Judaism. Referring to this literature Schechter says:

> However strange it may seem, the fact remains that while these writings left a lasting impress on Christianity, they contributed—with the exception, perhaps, of the Book of Ecclesiasticus—little or nothing towards the formation of Rabbinic thought. The Rabbis were either wholly ignorant of their existence, or stigmatized them as fabulous, or "external" (a milder expression in some cases for heretical), and thus allowed them to exert no permanent influence upon Judaism" (Aspects, 5).

This is true of Judaism, perhaps, from the middle of the second century AD, when it became self-centered, and a disastrous antipathy grew up

The great cleavage between Judaism and the outside world, and the reconstruction of the religion and community on a purely Hebrew basis—a process which was begun soon after AD 70—was only consummated in the middle of the second century (after AD 135). Too often the Jew who has been Rabbinically trained cannot enter with any real sympathy or insight into the wider conditions that environed the Judaism of the earlier period. To him all that is not specifically Rabbinic appears to be un-Jewish, or alien to the genius of Judaism.[1]

---

and was fostered between it and the outside world. But it is certainly not true of the Judaism that flourished in the first Christian century down to AD 70 and even later. Rabbinical Judaism, it must be remembered, "is but one offshoot from a larger stem. It sprang from a larger and richer Judaism which, to a greater extent than is sometimes supposed, held within itself the forces that afterwards diverged as Rabbinism and Christianity" (The Religion and Worship of the Synagogue, page x). I wish to emphasize this point strongly, as it is one of supreme importance. What afterwards emerged as Rabbinical Judaism, and gathered and concentrated into itself the forces of Jewry, was only one among other elements in the Judaism of the first century AD. This wider and earlier Judaism—which Mr. J. H. A. Hart has aptly termed "Catholic Judaism"—is perhaps, well represented in the writings of Philo. This earlier Judaism had not yet banned the Greek language, nor the allegorical method of interpreting scripture. It tolerated Greek translations of the Bible and a more or less Greek liturgy in the colonies of the Dispersion. It embraced within itself a great central body of moderate conservatives, together with an extreme right and an extreme left wing. Nor must it be forgotten that the Christian movement itself was during the first stage of its career within the Jewish body—it was regarded as a Jewish sect—while in the second stage of its career it entered into the fruits of the great Jewish missionary propaganda of the Dispersion.

[1] This seems to be the point of view naturally assumed by Schechter. He limits himself rigidly to what is specifically Rabbinic. But all Jewish scholars, happily, do not impose such restrictions upon themselves. It is a pleasure to call attention to the splendid series of articles by Kohler in the Jewish Encyclopedia ("Eschatology," "Essenes," "Merkabah," "New Testament," "Didaskalia"), where full account is taken of sources and data outside the Rabbinic literature. Kohler has represented the results of his studies in a valuable volume on the theology of Judaism (Grundriss einer systematischen Theologie des Judentums auf geschichtlicher Grundlage, Leipzig, 1910), which is unfortunately not available in English. Dr. Büchler also, principal of the Jews' College in London, takes account of non-Rabbinical data in his elaborate and learned discussions

ARCHAEOLOGY AND RABBINIC JUDAISM

I have already pointed out how indispensable some knowledge of Rabbinic theology and modes of thought is to the student of early (pre-Talmudic) Judaism. But the Rabbinical literature is valuable in other ways for the study of the earlier period. When the material is handled critically it will be found to yield much that is of importance archaeologically for the reconstruction of Jewish life and society in Palestine during the century that preceded the destruction of the temple.[1] There is, moreover, a human side to the Rabbinical literature which is not only interesting in itself, but also enshrines much that is precious of old popular life and custom. And in such matters as diction and phraseology, the mode by which ideas are expressed, the

---

of some of the problems of early Judaism (Die Priester und der Cultus im letzten Jahrzehnt des Jersusalemischen Tempels (Wien, 1895); Das Synedrion in Jerusalem (Wien, 1902); Der galiläische 'Am ha-'Ares des zweiten Jahrhunderts (Wien, 1906); The Economic Conditions of Judea after the Destruction of the Second Temple (1912), and The Political and Social Leaders of the Jewish Community of Sepphoris in the Second and Third Centuries (the two last published by the Jews' College, London). His work is specially important for questions connected with the Second Temple. But, perhaps, the most significant name in this connection is that of the Jewish scholar Moritz Friedländer. In 1905 Friedländer published a volume on The Religious Movements within Judaism in the Time of Jesus (Die religiösen Bewegungen innerhalb des Judentams im Zeitalter Jesu, Berlin, 1905), which for freshness, originality, and stimulating power it would be hard to match. The great merit of the book is that it sets forth in a most striking way the complex forces that were working within Judaism during the age of Jesus. The author divides his work into two parts. Part one, which is devoted to Palestinian Judaism, discusses the apocalyptic movement, religious movements among the "people of the land" ('Am ha-'Ares); the Essenes; the Minim (Jewish heretics); part two, which is devoted to Hellenistic Judaism, has chapters dealing with Jewish Hellenism—its teaching; life in the spirit of Jewish Hellenism (the Therapeutae), the Sibylline Wisdom, Jesus, the message of Paul. Though his work is open to correction in detail it is, as a whole, on sound lines. The book is extraordinarily suggestive, and ought to be studied by all serious students. Unfortunately it can only be read in German, not having as yet appeared in English.

[1] A vast mass of material has been collected and presented critically in S. Krauss's Talmudische Archäologie, 3 volumes (Leipzig, 1910-1912).

form in which Jewish oriental conceptions conventionally clothe themselves, this literature affords a vast field of illustration of the highest value.[1]

A good instance of the archaeological value of the Rabbinical evidence is the information afforded by this literature respecting the customs and peculiarities of the population of Galilee.[2] This population was, as is well known, of a mixed character, consisting of Jews and pagans. We are told that people living there sometimes bore two names, one for use in Galilee, the other in Judaea.[3] The Jewish population is represented as warm, generous, and impulsive, of simple manners and earnest piety. Though, on the whole, there was far less rigorism than in Judea, the Galileans were, in some respects, stricter in their piety. Thus, while it was customary in Judea to carry on servile work on the eve of the Passover till noon, in Galilee all such work was suspended the entire day.[4] In Galilee, also, marriage customs were of a more decorous character.[5] The Galileans are also said to have excelled in Haggada, that is, the homiletic element (illustrative stories, parables, and so on) in the interpretation and illustration of scripture.[6] The Galileans were not expert in the subtle dialectic that was cultivated in the legal schools of Judea.[7]

---

[1] How important it may prove to be for the New Testament scholar has been brilliantly shown in the first part of Dalman's Die Worte Jesu, which is now happily available in English under the title The Words of Jesus.

[2] See chapter 4 of Neubauer's La Géographie du Talmud.

[3] Tosefta Gittin 6.

[4] T. B. Pesahim 53a.

[5] Tosefta Kethuboth 1.

[6] Indeed, according to Geiger, the Galilean Rabbi Jose (early second century) ought to be regarded as the creator of Haggada.

[7] Only three Galilean rabbis are mentioned by name in the Mishna, R. Jose, his son R. Eliezer, and R. Hanina. In the Talmud (T.B. Megilla 24b, Erubin 53b) the Galilean pronunciation of the gutterals is ridiculed (compared, Matthew 26:73, "Your speech betrays you"). Josephus (Life 17) describes the population of the province, hard-working and brave as they were, as "by nature disposed to changes, and delighting in seditions"; and this is confirmed by the Rabbinic literature, which, apparently, represents Galilee as in a perpetual state of war; the Galilean "sicarii" were especially dreaded (Tosefta Gittin 2; compare Acts 5:37).

JUDAISM AND EARLY CHRISTIANITY

How are we to reconstruct the Jewish environment of the gospels? Our answer to this question must depend largely upon the view we take of the relation between the apocalyptic and Rabbinic types of thought during the first three quarters of the first century. It is not sufficient, as some scholars have assumed, to construe the Judaism of this period purely in terms of apocalyptic, and to ignore everything specifically Rabbinic in the process. Nor is the reverse procedure, which would ignore everything specifically apocalyptic as "un-Jewish," any more justifiable. I have ventured to remind Jewish scholars[1] that Rabbinical Judaism, that is, the type of Judaism which became dominant in the second half of the second century, and was represented in the earlier period by the party of the Pharisees, has a background. It worked on pre-existing material, which it partly rejected, partly assimilated and transformed. It is all-important for the understanding of Rabbinical Judaism itself to reconstruct, as far as we can, the larger content included in the Judaism that preceded it. Herein lies the importance of the large pre-Christian apocryphal and pseudepigraphical literature of Judaism.

This literature—which was extensive and popular in character, and in many cases, apparently, goes back to Semitic (Hebrew or Aramaic) originals—embodies an essential element of the larger Judaism of the first century, but the whole of it was ultimately rejected by Rabbinical Judaism.[2] As I have remarked elsewhere:

> What the attitude of the earlier (first century) rabbis was to apocalyptic it is difficult to determine. In any case hostility was not so marked as it became later, though the natural tendency of Rabbinic thought would at all times have been to subordinate the apocalyptic to the legalistic element. It is probably true to say that the use of apocalyptic books in Essene and Christian

---

[1] In a paper on "The Apocalyptic Movement, and Rabbinic Judaism" read at the Jews' College, London, March, 1914.

[2] See for a full discussion the writer's Ezra Apocalypse, chapter 4 of the general introduction (pages lviii. ff.).

circles—in the latter for controversial purposes against the synagogue, especially after AD 70—was largely responsible for the decided anti-apocalyptic bias of the later rabbis. But the alienation between synagogue and church was not complete till after AD 135,[1] and the existence of such books as 4 Ezra and the Apocalypse of Baruch shows that apocalyptic had not yet been finally eliminated from orthodox Judaism at the time when these books were put forth (c. AD 120). It is important to remember, in this connection, that at the end of the first century AD (and possibly later) the rabbis were much occupied with the question of the canon of scripture, and it has been suggested that in certain circles (apocalyptic and Essene), the apocalyptic books were put on a level not merely with the oral tradition, but with the canonical scriptures. In delimiting the canon precisely, at the end of the first century AD, the rabbis may have been influenced by a desire to safeguard the older collection of scripture from the possible rivalry of apocalyptic books.[2]

I cannot here discuss at any length what is a most complicated problem. But I may venture, perhaps, to state summarily the conclusions which seem to me to follow from a close study of the data. In the earlier period, then, we must picture the mass of the people as permeated with apocalyptic hopes.

These hopes and longings pervaded popular piety like a golden haze. The people were loyal to the Law, as a whole, but they longed intensely for the coming of the kingdom of God, for a real divine intervention. We must not conceive of the apocalyptic hope as expressed in a uniform and consistent body of doctrine. On the contrary it assumed divergent forms, some of which were mutually antagonistic. The political apocalypses—like the eagle vision in 4 Ezra[3]—breathe a spirit of fierce hostility to the oppressive world-power of Rome. On the other hand, there were smaller circles, of a quietist character, who were

---

[1] AD 135 marks the date of the suppression of the Bar Kokba revolt.
[2] "The Apocalyptic Movement, and Rabbinic Judaism," page 59.
[3] 2 Esdras 10:60-12:35.

awaiting the advent of a Messiah who should effect the moral and spiritual redemption of his people; who should reign as a spiritual prince in the hearts of a regenerate people, and so fulfill the old promises made to the house of David; and one who should extend his spiritual dominion to the ends of the earth. These hopes were based and nourished upon Old Testament prophecy, and were cherished within a limited circle to be found both among the learned—especially among the disciples of Hillel—and also among the people. . . . The fulfillment of these hopes in the person and career of Jesus of Nazareth may be said to be the theme of the New Testament generally. The earlier chapters of the Acts reveal to us the presence in Jerusalem and Judea of an active Hebrew-Christian church which was working—and not without considerable prospects of success—for the winning over of the Jewish people, as a whole, to acceptance of the Christian Messiah.

On the other side was the party of the Pharisees. Here, again, we must beware of making the mistake of assuming that all Pharisees were alike. There were doubtless apocalyptic Pharisees as well as Pharisaic apocalyptists. Nor were all Pharisees by any means formalists and hypocrites. As a party they were animated by a high ideal—they were intensely zealous for the Law, and expended themselves in extending its power and influence over the people generally. They tended to lay all the emphasis on the observance of the Law, and some members of the party seem to have believed that the best and only legitimate way to hasten the kingdom of God was by extending the exact and scrupulous observance of the Law. The Pharisaic schools, which more and more dominated the ideals of the party, were of an academic character, and tended to develop a scholastic theology. They were zealous in the study of the old sacred Hebrew language, and after a time succeeded in displacing, to some extent, the use of the popular Aramaic dialect in connection with the temple. Ultimately they were able to ban the use of the Greek language in Palestine, and, under stress of controversy, finally eliminated from orthodox Judaism the large pre-Christian and some later apocalyptic literature.[1]

---

[1] I have said they eliminated this literature, and this is strictly true. But the popular religious instinct behind it could not be altogether sup-

In thus cutting off the early apocalyptic and apocryphal Jewish literature, the Pharisees put a new complexion upon Judaism. It marked, to some extent, a breach with the past. And this fact is of cardinal importance for the New Testament student. In studying the Jewish background of the New Testament books, and especially of the gospels, we are often conscious of being in touch with an older Jewish tradition than that represented dominantly in the Rabbinical literature.[1] In fact it seems probable that some early Christian literature outside the New Testament may depend upon lost Jewish sources of an earlier type.[2]

JUDAISM OUTSIDE PALESTINE

So far we have confined our attention mainly to the Judaism of Palestine. But we must not pass over in silence the significance of Judaism in its wider connotation as an element of decisive importance in the environment of early Christianity. The Judaism that flourished outside Palestine during the first two centuries of our era exercised in many ways an enormously important

---

pressed. The purely apocalyptic element, however, was relegated to the background, and the whole emphasis was laid on the observance of the Law. Curiously enough, however, apocalyptic hopes, though relegated to the background, came to literary expression again at a later period in a new Hebrew literature which did not find much acceptance in orthodox Rabbinical circles, but has partially survived.

[1] This fact has been fully recognized by some of the best non-Christian Jewish scholars. Thus, to cite an example, Dr. Israel Abrahams, in an interesting note on John 7:38-39, published in the Expository Times a few years ago (Volume 23, page 180, April, 1912), says, "The fourth gospel shows throughout this context a peculiarly exact familiarity with Jewish traditions."

[2] A good, though disputed, example is the Didaché. Dr. K. Kohler has also pointed out the immense importance of the first six books of the Apostolic Constitutions for early Rabbinical Judaism as well as for early Christianity. He claims as the basis of the work a Jewish original, which has often been only slightly modified in its present Christian form. "The work," he says, "is of very great value to the student of Jewish and church history, as it contains a large amount of Haggadic and Halakic material, derived from unknown Jewish sources, and casts a flood of light upon Talmudic and New Testament literature." It is specially important, he thinks, for the reconstruction of parts of the temple-liturgy" (Article "Didascalia" Jewish Encyclopedia, volume 4, page 588).

influence upon the development of Christianity, both in its outward forms and fortunes, and also in its inner life and thought.[1]
Concentrated mostly in the cities of the Greco-Roman world
these Jewish communities no longer, as in Palestine, made
agriculture their almost exclusive occupation, but were largely
engaged in commerce. In Alexandria they were especially connected with the mechanical trades; and in the vast synagogue
there the congregation was grouped according to trades. In
Rome, strange to say, the Jewish population, mostly of slave
origin, lived in wretched quarters and followed the humblest
callings. But this was by no means the case with all Jews living
in Italy and Greece. The texts and inscriptions refer to weavers,
tent makers, dealers in purple, butchers, tavern keepers, sing-
ers, comedians, jewelers, physicians, and also poets and men of
letters, as well as preachers, lawyers and theologians. In Egypt,
under the Ptolemies, from the ranks of the Jews came forth soldiers, farmers of the revenue, and civil functionaries. Later,
however, Hadrian could only find among them astrologers,
soothsayers, and charlatans.[2]

Theoretically the intercourse of Jews with pagans was
confined to commercial relations merely, and even these were
greatly trammeled by the laws of purity. The Jews lived, as a
rule, in separate quarters grouped around their synagogues.
The pious Jew could neither dine at the table of a pagan, nor
receive him at his own table. He was not permitted to frequent the theaters, the circuses, the gymnasia, nor even to read
a secular book "unless it be at twilight." Mixed marriages were
prohibited under severe penalties. These rules, however, were
not always by any means rigidly adhered to. The Diaspora Jews
were profoundly affected by their environment in many ways.
The influence of Greek culture told heavily upon them—as
the Judeo-Alexandrine literature eloquently attests. They used
Greek even in their religious services; they read the Bible in
Greek; they adopted Greek names and, to some extent, Greek
organization in their communal institutions. Above all, they

---

[1] See the elaborate article "Diaspora" (by Theodore Reinach) in Jewish
Encyclopedia, volume 4.

[2] It is a curious fact that scarcely ever before the Middle Ages are the
Jews referred to as money lenders, bankers, or usurers.

were animated by an intense missionary zeal to win over the pagan population to the higher monotheistic religion, of which they were the chosen representatives.

That this Jewish propaganda was highly successful there cannot be a shadow of doubt. The statements of Josephus, Philo, and even Seneca, "who represent the whole world as rushing towards Jewish observances," are, no doubt, in some degree exaggerated. At the same time it is indisputable that proselytes were found in considerable numbers in every country of the Dispersion. We are told by Josephus that in his time a large portion of the Greek population in Antioch judaized.[1] Later, as we know, they became Christians. According to the same authority also "almost all the women" in Damascus observed the Jewish customs. St. Paul met with proselytes in Pisidian Antioch, in Thyatira, Thessalonica, and Athens. In Asia Minor numerous indications suggest that Jewish proselytes were numerous. In Rome the success of the propaganda is vouched for by Horace, Persius, and Juvenal. We cannot account for the enormous growth of the Jewish population in Egypt, Cyprus and Cyrene without assuming a large adhesion of gentile proselytes.

The question of the admission of proselytes stirred Judaism to its depths. It threatened, in fact, to separate Hellenistic from Palestinian Judaism, though there were divisions in both camps on the subject. The former was willing to admit gentiles after having undergone the rite of baptism; while the latter insisted upon circumcision.[2] The liberal propaganda of the Jewish Dispersion prepared the way for the coming of a broad universalistic religion, freed from the trammels of race connection.[3]

---

[1] Jewish War, 7.3.3.

[2] The story of the conversion of Queen Helena of Adiabene illustrates the controversy (see Josephus, Antiquities, 20.2.11-5). The controversy still went on—at any rate the issues were discussed—at the end of the first and beginning of the second century in Palestine, R. Joshua asserting that the baptismal rite rendered a person a full proselyte, while R. Eliezer b. Hyrkanus made circumcision an indispensable condition, and declared the baptismal rite to be of no consequence (T. B. *Yehamoth*, 46a). A similar controversy was carried on earlier between Shammaites and Hillelites. After the Roman wars the more rigorous view became prevalent everywhere.

[3] The harvest was reaped by the Christian missionaries, headed by

The Judaism of the Dispersion was subjected to Greek influence down to AD 70 (and even later), in numberless ways, and reacted in turn upon the Judaism of Palestine, especially, so long as the temple stood, by means of the steady stream of pilgrims that flowed to Jerusalem. It is important to remember this in estimating Palestinian Judaism, as it existed in the time of Christ and the apostles.

JEWISH BACKGROUND TO THE NEW TESTAMENT

Let me in conclusion try to illustrate by one or two examples how the Jewish background of parts of the New Testament can be illuminated. In the Ezra Apocalypse, which is accessible to all in our Apocrypha as 2 Esdras, we have a Jewish book which in the main belongs to the latter part of the first century AD, and is therefore partly contemporary with our New Testament. It is earlier than the present form of any part of the Rabbinical literature, and is therefore the greatest possible value for estimating the character of the earlier type of Judaism. When we examine this book what do we find? It is full of parallels with the Pauline thought and theology. As Schweitzer has said:

> It is nothing less than astounding that the close affinities [of the Pauline theology] with the Apocalypse of Ezra should so long have escaped recognition. In this work there are elaborate discussions of the problems of sin, the fall, election, faith and works, the wrath, long-suffering, and mercy of God, the prerogative of Israel, the significance of the Law, the temporal and eternal Jerusalem, the prospect of dying or surviving to the Parousia, the tribulation of the times of the end, and the last judgment.[1]

That some of the questions debated in the Ezra Apocalypse were discussed in Rabbinical circles, and that great variety of opinion prevailed on such points in these circles, is attested by

---

St. Paul. As Moritz Friedlander has said: "If Jesus was the Christ, then the religion of the Jewish Diaspora was Christendom" (Das Judenthum in der vorchristlichen griechischen Welt, 1897, page 19).

[1] Paul and his Interpreters, page 51.

the Rabbinical literature itself. One passage in the Talmud is highly significant in this connection. It runs as follows:

> Two years and a half the school of Shammai and the school of Hillel disputed among themselves. One school declared it would have been better that man had not been created as he was, while the other declared it was better that man had been created as he was than that he should not have been created at all. Finally, they came to the conclusion that it would have been better if man had not been created, but since that had taken place, a man should always examine his actions; according to another version, a man should always consider the deeds he is about to perform.[1]

On this passage Professor Schechter remarks:

> This is all the tradition (or the compiler) chose to give us about this lengthy dispute; but we do not hear a single word as to the causes which led to it, or the reasons advanced by the litigant parties for their various opinions. Were they metaphysical, or empirical, or simply based, as is so often the case, on different conceptions of the passages in the scripture germane to the dispute? We feel the more cause for regret when we recollect that the members of these schools were the contemporaries of the apostles; when Jerusalem, as it seems, was boiling over with theology, and its marketplaces and synagogues were preparing metaphysics and theosophies to employ the mind of posterity for thousands of years. What did the rabbis think of all these aspirations and inspirations, or did they remain quite untouched by the influences of their surroundings? Is it not possible that a complete account of such a controversy as I have just mentioned, which probably formed neither an isolated nor an unprecedented event, would have furnished us with just the information of which now we are so sorely in need?[2]

---

[1] T. B. *Erubin* 13b.
[2] Aspects, pages 8f.

Now in the dialogue, which is given at length in the first eight chapters of the Ezra Apocalypse,[1] between the seer and the angel, the Shammaite position that it would have been better if man had never been created is definitely stated and maintained;[2] and not only so, but this is one of the fundamental positions of this section of the apocalypse throughout, and is constantly restated and sustained by argument. We have, therefore, in these chapters a statement of some, at any rate, of the arguments adduced in support of the Shammaite position, and the silence of the Rabbinical literature on this point is partially made good in the Ezra Apocalypse. Its value for the history of the development of Rabbinic theology in some of its earlier and more obscure phases, as well as for providing the Jewish background of much of the Pauline thought, could hardly be better demonstrated.

Our next illustration may be taken from the ancient liturgy of the synagogue. I would like to be allowed to point out that in this direction lies a most fruitful line of study, which has by no means yet been adequately explored. To form anything like a just estimate of Jewish piety we must study its devotional literature, and especially its beautiful prayers. The ancient elements in these go back to the pre-Christian period. Liturgical diction would naturally influence popular religious language, and, to some extent, mold religious conceptions. I believe that this influence can be traced in the New Testament literature. One of the oldest and most popular forms of devotion still preserved in the synagogue liturgy is the Kaddish prayer. It is still recited in the old popular Aramaic dialect of Palestine. In its principal clauses it affords striking parallels to parts of the Lord's Prayer. The clauses:

> Hallowed be your name,
> Your kingdom come,

are closely paralleled in the Jewish form:

---

[1] 2 Esdras 3-10.

[2] Compare 2 Esdras 4:12: It would have been better that we had never been created than having come [into the world] to live in sins and suffer, and not to know why we suffer.

Magnified and sanctified be His great name in the world which He has created according to His will. May He establish His kingdom during your life and during your days, and during the life of all the house of Israel, even speedily and at a near time, and say Amen.[1]

Now this is based upon such scriptural passages as Ezekiel 36:23, and 38:23, which form an excellent commentary on the Prayer,

I will sanctify my great name which has been profaned among the nations, which you have profaned in the midst of them; and the nations shall know that I am the Lord, says the Lord God, when I shall be sanctified in you before their eyes. . . . And I will magnify myself and sanctify myself, and I will make myself known in the eyes of many nations; and they shall know that I am the Lord.

These verses belong to the great eschatological section of Ezekiel (chapters 36-38), the influence of which on the prayer is very apparent. Thus the prayer may be regarded as a compendious expression of eschatological doctrine. The underlying ideas are essentially eschatological, full of vivid life, and are by no means abstract expressions of colorless processes. It is significant that this has remained the most persistent and popular expression of Jewish piety.

The refrain of the angels in the angelic annunciation to the shepherds at Bethlehem, forming the "Gloria in Excelsis,"

Glory to God in the highest,
And on earth, peace to men of his good pleasure[2]

seems also to be an echo of the last clause of the same popular Jewish prayer:

May He who makes peace in the heavenly heights,
may He make peace for us and all Israel.

---

[1] Compare Singer's handy edition of the Synagogue-Prayers in Hebrew and English (The Authorized Daily Prayer Book), page 37 (published by Eyre and Spottiswoode).

[2] Luke 2:14.

And in an earlier clause,

> May there be abundant peace from heaven,
> and life for us and all Israel.

In Luke 19:38 another echo of this language occurs:

> Peace in heaven
> And glory in the highest.

The idea underlying this is that in the blessed Messianic time the peace that prevails in heaven shall descend to earth.

Much might be said about the Midrash and the large numbers of parables preserved in the midrashic literature, some of them remarkably parallel to parables in the gospels.[1] The extensive midrashic literature, largely in the form of homiletic commentary on scripture, embodies much that is exceedingly valuable for the illustration of the New Testament. It would not be difficult, for instance, to derive from this literature a good deal of illustrative material which would form a remarkably suggestive Jewish background for the fourth gospel. The Johannine gospel is indeed Jewish, through and through, and it is much to be desired that a commentary on it, written from this point of view could be produced.

Enough has been said, I hope, to show the supreme importance of the study of contemporary Judaism for the elucidation of the New Testament and some other early Christian literature. What is needed is a band of younger scholars who will devote their energies to this line of study in the interests of New Testament science. Sometimes our younger men, who start Hebrew, feel that it is hardly worth their while to pursue Hebrew studies seriously, because they imagine that the goal of such studies is specialism in the Old Testament pure and simple. They feel, perhaps, and very naturally, that their main interests lie in the New Testament. I would venture to put in a plea for the view that a course of Hebrew study, starting with the Old

---

[1] A most useful collection, with critical remarks and discussions, has been provided by P. Fiebig in his Altjüdische Gleichnisse und die Gleichnisse Jesu (1904) and Die Gleich nisreden Jesu im Lichte der rabbinischen Gleichnisse des neutestamentlichen Zeitalters (1912).

Testament, but continued into the threshold of the early Rabbinical literature, and accompanied by the study of Judaism
generally, is one of the best kinds of preparation for approaching the New Testament literature. With such an equipment the
scholar will be able to handle the problems that confront him
with a surer touch; he will approach them with a clearer vision
and a keener sense of reality; and above all they will appear to
him instinct with vivid life. No greater service, I venture to
think, could be rendered either to religion or theology than such
a deepening and vivifying of human interest in the imperishable records of the beginnings of our faith.

APPENDIX

The Didachè, or "Teaching of the Twelve Apostles"

Since its discovery numerous translations of the Didachè have been published in various languages. The first complete English translation of the document appeared on March 20, 1884, and was the work of Roswell D. Hitchcock and Francis Brown, two professors from Union Theological Seminary, New York. Their edition sold out in hours. It was entitled, ΔΙΔΑΧΗ ΤΩΝ ΔΩΔΕΚΑ ΑΠΟΣΤΟΛΩΝ Teaching in the Twelve Apostles. The following introduction and translation are reproduced from this edition.

In 1875 Philotheos Bryennios, then metropolitan of Serrae (now Serres), in ancient Macedonia, published the two epistles of Clement of Rome, from a manuscript discovered by him in the library of the Most Holy Sepulchre in Fanar of Constantinople. The last six chapters (60-65) of the first epistle, and the last eight sections (13-20) of the so-called second epistle, had never been published before. The date of the manuscript is AD 1056. As described by the finder, "it is an octavo volume, written on parchment, in cursive characters, and consists of 120 leaves." First comes Chrysostom's Synopsis of the Books of the Old and New Testament; then the Epistle of Barnabas; then the two Epistles of Clement; then the Teaching of the Twelve Apostles; then the Epistle of Mary of Cassobelae to Ignatius; followed by twelve Epistles of Ignatius (the current seven, besides one to the Virgin Mary, and four others).

The Teaching of the Twelve Apostles, Διδαχὴ τῶν δώδεκα 'Αποστόλων, occupies leaves 76-80 of the manuscript. It now seems strange to us that the document thus announced attracted so little attention. This same Bryennios, now metropolitan of Nicomedia, in Asia Minor, has again surprised the literary world by publishing, with an abundance of learned illustration, this long-lost document. It is printed in Constantinople, and the date of publication is 1883. The genuineness of the document can hardly be doubted. It is cited by Clement of Alexandria in his first Stroma; by Eusebius, who speaks of it as τῶν 'Αποστόλων αἱ λεγόμεναι διδάχαι (Eusebius, History 3.25); and by Athanasius in his Thirty-ninth Festal Epistle. Bickell and Gebhardt had recently argued that there must have been some such document underlying both the seventh book of the Apostolic Constitutions and the Apostolic Epitome. In 1882 Krawutzky undertook, from these sources, to recover and reconstruct the embedded earlier and simpler document; and with a success of the most pronounced brilliant character, as now tested by the work just published.

This document belongs undoubtedly to the second century; possibly as far back as AD 120, hardly later than AD 160. The whole tone of it is archaic. It contradicts nothing belonging to that age; corroborates some things which may henceforth be more strongly emphasized; and adds some things for which we may well be very profoundly grateful. The present editors are happy to be able to put the Teaching of the Twelve Apostles so promptly before the American public. The text has been carefully edited. The translation will be found to be studiously literal. A few notes have been added, which, it is hoped, may be of service both to students and to general readers.

Teaching of the Lord, Through the Twelve Apostles, to the Nations

1. Two ways there are, one of life and one of death, but there is a great difference between the two ways. The way of life, then, is this: First, love the God who made you; secondly, your neighbor as yourself; and all things whatsoever you would not have befall you, you, too, do not to another. Now of these words the teaching is this: Bless them that curse you, and pray for your enemies, and fast for them that persecute you: for what thank have you if you love them that love you? Do not the nations also the same? But love them that hate you and you shall have no enemy. Abstain from the fleshly and worldly lusts. If anyone give you a blow on the right cheek, turn to him the other also, and you shall be perfect; if anyone compel you to go one mile, go with him two; if anyone take your cloak, give him your tunic also; if anyone take from you what is yours, ask it not back; for indeed you cannot. To everyone that asks you give, and ask not back; for to all the Father desires to give of his own gracious gifts. Blessed is he that gives according to the commandment; for he is guiltless; woe to him that takes; for if, indeed, one takes who has need, he shall be guiltless; but he who has no need shall give account, why he took, and for what purpose, and coming under arrest shall be examined concerning what he did, and shall not go out thence until he pay the last farthing. But it has been also said concerning this matter: Let your alms sweat in your hands, until you know to whom you should give.

2. Now a second commandment of the teaching is: Do not kill, do not commit adultery, do not corrupt boys, do not commit fornication, do not steal, do not practise magic, do not use sorcery, do not slay a child by abortion, nor what is begotten shall you destroy. Do not lust after the things of your neighbor, do not forswear yourself, do not bear false witness, do not revile, do not bear malice. Do not be double-minded nor double-tongued; for a snare of death is the double tongue. Your speech shall not be false, nor empty, but filled with doing. Do not be covetous, nor rapacious, nor a hypocrite, nor malicious, nor arrogant. Do not take evil counsel against your neighbor. Hate no man, but some you shall reprove, and for some you shall pray, and some you shall love above your life.

3. My child, flee from every evil thing, and from everything like it. Be not inclined to anger, for anger leads to murder; nor jealous, nor contentious, nor passionate; for of all these murders are begotten. My child, become not lustful; for lust leads to fornication; nor foul-mouthed, nor lofty-eyed; for of all these things adulteries are begotten. My child, become not an omen watcher; since it leads into idolatry; nor an enchanter, nor an astrologer, nor a purifier, nor be willing to look upon these things; for of all these things idolatry is begotten. My child, become not a liar; since lying leads to theft; nor avaricious, nor vain-glorious; for of all these things thefts are begotten. My child, become not a murmurer; since it leads to blasphemy; nor presumptuous, nor evil-minded; for of all these things blasphemies are begotten. But be meek, since the meek shall inherit the earth. Become long-suffering and pitiful and guileless and gentle and good, and tremble continually at the words which you have heard. Do not exalt yourself, nor permit over-boldness to your soul. Your soul shall not cleave to the high, but with the righteous and lowly you shall dwell. The things that befall you accept as well-wrought, knowing that without God nothing occurs.

4. My child, him that speaks to you the word of God remember night and day, and honor him as the Lord; for where that which pertains to the Lord is spoken there the Lord is. And seek out daily the faces of the saints, that you may be refreshed by

their words. Do not desire division, but make peace between those who contend; judge justly, do not respect persons in convicting for transgressions. Do not hesitate whether it shall be or not. Become not one who for taking stretches out the hands, but for giving draws them in; if you have anything, by your hands give a ransom for your sins. Do not hesitate to give, nor when giving shall you murmur, for you shall know who is the good dispenser of the recompense. Do not turn away the needy, but share all things with your brother, and do not say they are your own; for if you are partners in that which is imperishable, how much more in the perishable things? Do not take off your hand from your son and from your daughter, but from youth teach them the fear of God. Do not lay commands in your bitterness upon your slave or handmaid, who hope in the same God, lest they perchance shall not fear the God who is over you both; for he comes not to call men according to the appearance, but to those whom the Spirit has made ready. And you, slaves, be subject to your lords, as to God's image, in modesty and fear. Hate every hypocrisy, and whatever is not pleasing to the Lord. You shall by no means forsake the Lord's commandments, but guard what you have received, neither adding to it nor taking from it. In the church you shall confess your transgressions, and shall not come forward for your prayer with an evil conscience. This is the way of life.

5. Now the way of death is this: first of all it is evil, and full of curse; murders, adulteries, lusts, fornications, thefts, idolatries, magic arts, sorceries, robberies, false testimonies, hypocrisies, duplicity, craft, arrogance, vice, presumptuousness, greed, foul speech, jealousy, over-boldness, loftiness, pretence; persecutors of the good, hating truth, loving falsehood, knowing not the reward of righteousness, not cleaving to that which is good nor to righteous judgment, on the watch not for good but for evil; far from whom are meekness and patience, loving vanities, pursuing revenge, not pitying a poor man, not laboring for the distressed, not knowing him that made them, murderers of children, destroyers of the image of God, turning away the needy, oppressing the afflicted, advocates of the rich, lawless judges of the poor, universal sinners: may you be delivered, children, from all these.

6. See that no one lead you astray from this way of the teaching, because apart from God does he teach you. For if you are able to bear the whole yoke of the Lord, you shall be perfect; but if you are not able, what you are able, that do. And concerning food, what you are able, bear; but of that offered to idols, beware exceedingly; for it is a worship of dead gods.

7. Now concerning baptism, thus baptize: having first uttered all these things, baptize into the name of the Father, and of the Son, and of the Holy Spirit, in living water. But if you have not running water, baptize in other water; and if you cannot in cold, then in warm. But if you have neither, pour water upon the head thrice, into the name of the Father and Son and Holy Spirit. But before the baptism let the baptizer and the baptized fast, and whatever other can; but the baptized you shall command to fast for one or two days before.

8. But let not your fastings be appointed in common with the hypocrites; for they fast on the second day of the week and on the fifth; but fast during the fourth, and the preparation day. Nor pray like the hypocrites, but as the Lord commanded in his gospel, thus pray: Our Father who are in heaven, hallowed by your name, your kingdom come, your will be done, as in heaven, so on earth; our daily bread give us today, and forgive us our debt as we also forgive our debtors, and bring us not into temptation, but deliver us from the evil one; for yours is the power and the glory forever. Three times in the day pray thus.

9. Now concerning the Eucharist, thus give thanks; first concerning the cup: We thank you, our Father, for the holy vine of David your servant, which you have made known to us through Jesus your servant; to you be the glory forever. And concerning the broken bread: We thank you, our Father, for the life and knowledge which you have made known to us through Jesus your servant; to you be the glory forever. Just as this broken bread was scattered over the hills and having been gathered became one, so let your church be gathered together from the ends of the earth into your kingdom; for yours is the glory and the power through Jesus Christ forever. But let no one eat or drink of your Eucharist, except those baptized into the Lord's name; for in regard to this the Lord has said: Give not that which is holy to the dogs.

10. Now after you are filled thus give thank: We thank you, holy Father, for your holy name, which you have caused to dwell in our hearts, and for the knowledge and faith and immortality which you have made known to us through Jesus your servant; to you be the glory forever. You, Master Almighty, did create all things for your name's sake; both food and drink you did give to men for enjoyment, in order that they might give thanks to you; but to us you have graciously given spiritual food and drink and eternal life through your servant. Before all things, we thank you that you are powerful; to you be the glory forever. Remember, Lord, your church, to deliver it from every evil and to make it perfect in your love, and gather it from the four winds, it, the sanctified, into your kingdom, which you have prepared for it; for yours is the power and the glory forever. Let grace come and let this world pass away. Hosanna to the son of David! Whoever is holy, let him come; whoever is not, let him repent. Maranatha. Amen. But permit the prophets to give thanks as much as they will.

11. Now whoever comes and teaches you all these things, before spoken, receive him; but if the teacher himself turn aside and teach another teaching, so as to overthrow this, do not hear him; but if he teach so as to promote righteousness and knowledge of the Lord, receive him as the Lord. But in regard to the apostles and prophets, according to the ordinance of the gospel, so do. And every apostle who comes to you, let him be received as the Lord; but he shall not remain more than one day; if, however, there be need, then the next day; but if he remain three days, he is a false prophet. But when the apostle departs, let him take nothing except bread enough till he lodge again; but if he ask money, he is a false prophet. And every prophet who speaks in the spirit, you shall not try nor judge; for every sin shall be forgiven, but this sin shall not be forgiven. But not everyone that speaks in the spirit is a prophet, but only if he have the ways of the Lord. So from their ways shall the false prophet and the prophet be known. And no prophet who orders a meal, in the spirit, eats of it, unless indeed he is a false

prophet; and every prophet who teaches the truth, if he do not that which he teaches, is a false prophet. But every prophet, proved, true, acting with a view to the mystery of the church on earth, but not teaching others to do all that he himself does, shall not be judged among you; for with God he has his judgment; for so did the ancient prophets also. But whoever, in the spirit, says: Give me money, or something else, you shall not hear him; but if for others in need, he bids you give, let no one judge him.

12. But let everyone that comes in the Lord's name be received, but afterward you shall test and know him; for you shall have understanding, right and left. If he who comes is a traveller, help him as much as you can; but he shall not remain with you, unless for two or three days, if there be necessity. But if he will take up his abode among you, being an artisan, let him work and so eat; but if he have no trade, provide, according to your understanding, that no idler live with you as a Christian. But if he will not act according to this, he is one who makes gain out of Christ; beware of such.

13. But every true prophet who will settle among you is worthy of his support. Likewise a true teacher, he also is worthy, like the workman, of his support. Every first fruit, then, of the products of wine-press and threshing-floor, of oxen and of sheep, take and give to the prophets; for they are your high priests. But if you have no prophet, give it to the poor. If you make a baking of bread, take the first of it and give according to the commandment. In like manner when you open a jar of wine or oil, take the first of it and give to the prophets; and of money and clothing and every possession take the first, as seems right to you, and give according to the commandment.

14. But on the Lord's day assemble and break bread, and give thanks, after confessing your transgressions, in order that your sacrifice may be pure. But everyone that has controversy with his friend, let him not come together with you, until they be reconciled, that your sacrifice may not be profaned. For this is that which was spoken by the Lord: At every place and time, bring me a pure sacrifice; for a great king am I, says the Lord, and my name is marvellous among the nations.

15. Now appoint for yourselves bishops and deacons worthy of the Lord, men meek and not avaricious, and upright and proved; for they, too, render you the service of the prophets and teachers. Despise them not, therefore; for they are the ones who are honored of you, together with the prophets and teachers. And reprove one another, not in anger, but in peace, as you have it in the gospel; and to everyone who errs against another, let no one speak, nor let him hear anything from you, until he repent. But your prayers and your alms and all your deeds so do, as you have it in the gospel of our Lord.

16. Watch for your life's sake; let your lamps not go out, and your loins not be relaxed, but be ready; for you know not the hour in which our Lord comes. But come together often, and seek the things which befit your souls; for the whole time of your faith thus far will not profit you, if you do not become perfect in the last time. For in the last days the false prophets and the corrupters shall be multiplied, and the sheep shall be turned into wolves, and love shall be turned into hate; for when lawlessness increases they shall hate one another, and shall persecute and shall deliver up, and then shall appear the world deceiver as Son of God, and shall do signs and wonders, and the earth shall be given into his hands, and he shall commit iniquities which have never yet been done since the beginning. Then all created men shall come into the fire of trial, and many shall be made to stumble and shall perish. But they that endure in their faith shall be saved from this curse. And then shall appear the signs of the truth; first the sign of an opening in heaven, then the sign of a trumpet's sound, and thirdly, the resurrection of the dead; yet not of all, but as it has been said: The Lord will come and all this saints with him. Then shall the world see the Lord coming upon the clouds of heaven.